D1593516

Voices of the Buffalo Soldier

VOICES of the BUFFALO SOLDIER

Records, Reports, and Recollections of Military Life and Service in the West

FRANK N. SCHUBERT

UNIVERSITY OF NEW MEXICO PRESS

ALBUQUERQUE

To Irene

First Edition

LIBRARY OF CONGRESS CATALOGING-IN-PUBLICATION DATA

Voices of the Buffalo Soldier : records, reports, and recollections of military life and service in the West / [edited by] Frank N. Schubert.—1st ed.
p. cm.
Includes bibliographical references (p.) and index.
ISBN 0-8263-2309-x (cloth : alk. paper)
1. African Americans—West (U.S.)—History—19th century—Sources.
2. African American Soldiers—West (U.S.)—History—19th century—Sources.
3. African American Soldiers—West (U.S.)—Biography.
4. African Americans—West (U.S.)—Biography.
5. United States. Army—African American Troops—History—19th century—Sources.
6. Frontier and pioneer life—West (U.S.)—Sources.
7. United States. Army—Biography.
8. Indians of North America—Wars—1866–1895—Sources.
9. West (U.S.)—History—1860–1890—Sources.
10. West (U.S.)—Race relations—Sources.
I. Schubert, Frank N. \

E185.925.V65 2003
355'.089'96073078—dc21

2002012298

DESIGN: MINA YAMASHITA

Contents

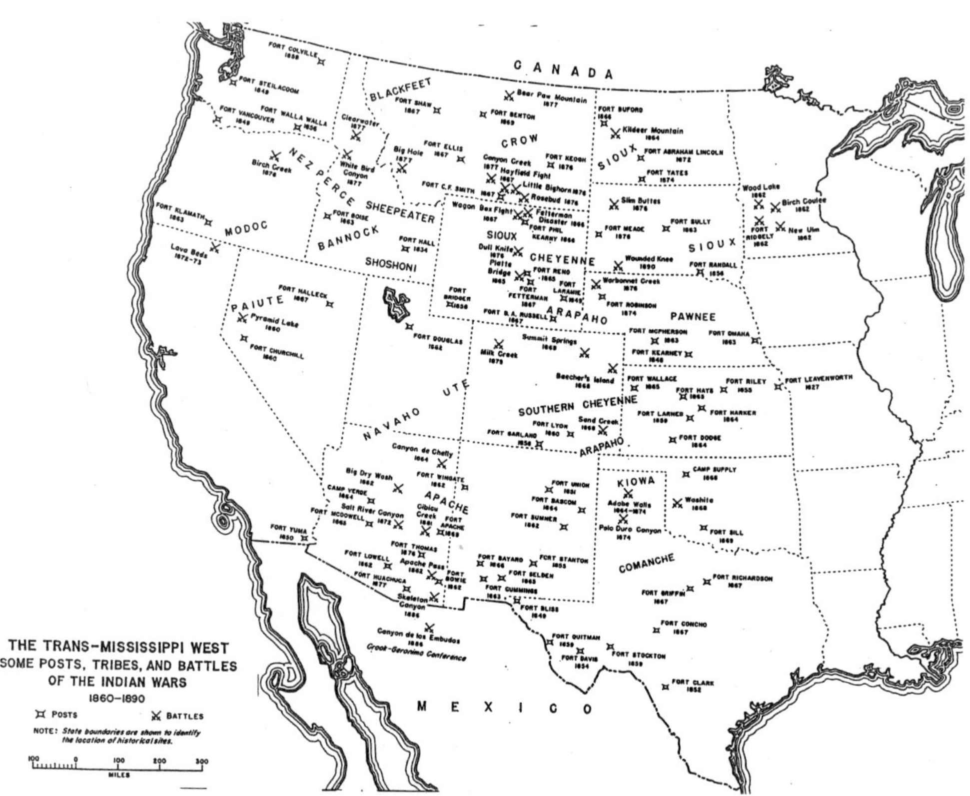

THE TRANS-MISSISSIPPI WEST
SOME POSTS, TRIBES, AND BATTLES
OF THE INDIAN WARS
1860–1890

Illustrations

MAPS

Acknowledgments

All works of history depend on the assistance of colleagues and friends, and this book is no exception. In completing *Voices of the Buffalo Soldier*, I benefited from the assistance and encouragement of many who shared documents and photographs or read and commented on the text. I would like to thank David A. Armstrong, Thomas R. Buecker, Lee N. Coffee, Roger Cunningham, Patricia and Mark Erickson, Arthur S. Hardyman, Robert F. Jefferson, Lawrence M. Kaplan, James B. Knight, James N. Leiker, Susan Lemke, Margaret Lewis, Wayne E. Motts, Thomas D. Phillips, Tony Skiscim, Eva Slezak, and James Yarrison. I also thank Durwood Ball and David Holtby at the University of New Mexico Press for their guidance and support. This project was Durwood's idea, so without him there would have been no book.

At the Pentagon library, the gracious and helpful reference department librarians were universally helpful. Whether my queries concerned my work as a historian in the Office of the Chairman of the Joint Chiefs of Staff or my research on Buffalo Soldiers, they always went the extra mile for me. I have been privileged to work with Kathleen Heincer, Yolanda Miller, Barbara Risser, Debbie L. Reed, and Lily Waters.

Three people contributed most significantly to this book. William A. Dobak shared his extensive research files and allowed me to use documents that he had collected. Few historians are as generous in sharing their research. In addition, longtime friend and colleague Gordon Olson and my wife and best friend Irene Schubert both helped me shape my ideas about this book. Irene also helped hunt down illusive documents and citations, and she always listened. To Willy, Gordon, and especially Irene, I am particularly grateful. Thank you all.

—Frank N. Schubert
Fairfax County, Virginia

Introduction

"Buffalo Soldiers" have become a familiar part of contemporary American culture. These African Americans who served in the Regular Army between the Civil War and World War I fought in some of the most difficult wars against western Indians. Like other soldiers of their time, they also performed a variety of duties necessary to plant and secure the Anglo American civilization that was spreading over the continent, reconnoitering little-known territory, guarding and improving roads, stringing telegraph wire, and fighting bandits. The Army that served in the West usually consisted of fewer than 25,000 men, and black units were a small portion of this force, 20 percent of the cavalry and 8 percent of the infantry, or about 11.4 percent of the entire strength, through the frontier period. African American soldiers participated in 168 or almost 13 percent of 1,296 skirmishes and battles between 1866 and 1897, playing major roles in the decisive conflicts with the tribes of the Southern Plains in the early 1870s, the savage combat with the Apache leaders Victorio and Nana during 1879–1881, and the Pine Ridge campaign of 1890–1891.[1] Eighteen black troopers received the Medal of Honor for bravery during this period.

Today images of these men are everywhere, from monumental statuary to phone cards, jigsaw puzzles, coffee mugs, and refrigerator magnets. In addition, representations adorn tee shirts and offer profitable subject matter for a growing number of painters and printmakers. The troopers are also featured in films and plays, poetry and song, and historical reenactments and are the subjects of books ranging from scholarly studies to romance novels.[2]

This collection of documents has been assembled in the hope that it will add to an understanding of who the Buffalo Soldiers were, what they did, how they lived, and what sources are available for the study of their lives. The materials cover a wide range, including official military documents, journalists' reports from black and white newspapers and magazines, and soldiers' accounts from a variety of sources. With the single exception of the personal letters of Private Charles Cook, lent generously by my longtime colleague and National Defense University special collections librarian, Susan Lemke, the documents selected are all from the public record preserved in the National Archives and other manuscript depositories and libraries that are open to the public. This is not "hidden history" in any sense.

Some of the best sources, heavily used here, are the official records of the soldiers' military service. These include reports of combat and other activities and descriptions of living conditions, occasionally by the black soldiers themselves but more frequently by their officers. Among them are the records of military courts, correspondence to and from many levels of headquarters, and personnel records.[3] Astute readers will notice that this documentation seldom touched on social relations except in cases where officialdom sensed danger from the soldiers, usually to nearby civilians, or when relations among soldiers or between soldiers and officers became tense, hostile, or abusive. Information on the personal aspects of the soldiers' lives frequently comes from pension records, which are also in the National Archives, and which contain affidavits from soldiers and their acquaintances, describing their lives, families, and service.

Pension files are one of several sources for recollections of the soldiers themselves and the officers who served with them. Periodicals—religious and secular, professional and general—contain firsthand accounts of Buffalo Soldier service and activities. These include soldier correspondents in two venues. One is the *Army and Navy Journal*, a semi-official weekly newspaper that reported on the comings and goings of military personnel and commented on issues of professional importance. The other is the black press nationwide. Numerous African American newspapers had soldier correspondents at Western posts, informing the folks back home on the activities and social life of black soldiers. No clearer evidence exists of the high status of the soldiers in the black community than the interest of civilians in reading troopers' reports of social activities in far off corners of Indian Territory and Montana. Ironically, the high regard in which black soldiers were held among African Americans, resulting as it did in the appearance of numerous reports of soldier activities in newspapers, makes it easier for the historian to come to know the black soldier than his white counterpart, to whom the general population was largely indifferent.

Other firsthand accounts appear in *Winners of the West*, the monthly organ of the National Indian War Veterans, a lobby for soldier pensions published through the 1920s and 1930s. In addition, there are interviews with former soldiers, in the Works Progress Administration (WPA) collection of the narratives of former slaves, and in one case by a prominent historian of the frontier Army, the late Don Rickey. Material also appears in the magazine *Frontier Times*, in soldier and officer letters from private collections, and even in the form of published poetry.

This book is organized into sixty chapters, arranged chronologically because it proved too difficult to fit the documents into a topical framework. Many of them deal with more than one subject, the relationship between sergeants and privates as well as combat operations, or social life along with soldiers' views of Indians. Additionally, this structure allows a look at how the available materials changed over time. The earlier documents emphasize actual operations, reflecting the high tempo of active field service in the early years, while the later selections show an Army that spent more time in garrison and less on campaign, in an environment that was more conducive to a flourishing family life.

More than half (fifty-four) of the 105 separate documents contain the first-person accounts of black soldiers, officers, and chaplains, as speakers, authors, the subjects of interviews, or sources directly quoted. Twenty-four others feature the views of white officers who served with black units. There are also some editorial voices, from the black as well as the white press, and the voices of wives and other women.

In most cases, these documents are presented as I found them. I have left them as written where I think the irregularities either add some interest or do not cause confusion. I have changed spelling and punctuation where it appeared necessary to ensure clarity and readability. In rare cases I have added a word or two in brackets, resorted to ellipses, or added footnotes.

These glimpses of the Buffalo Soldiers' relations with the world around them and of life inside their community show some of the tensions and contradictions between being soldiers and being black. As soldiers, the troopers occupied positions in the national mainstream. They were respectable, secure, powerful men who bore arms and participated, along with other Americans from a variety of backgrounds, in major chapters of the American national epic—the spread of the republic across the continent and the accompanying dispossession of the native peoples. As black men, the soldiers were sometimes reviled and discriminated against, and always vulnerable, so they carried out their roles as soldiers in particularly trying circumstances. These documents illuminate both of these sides of the soldiers' lives.

Theirs was a complex human story. As James Leiker noted in his perceptive article, "Black Soldiers at Fort Hays, Kansas, 1867–1869: A Study in Civilian and Military Violence," the soldiers were neither "villainous enforcers of white oppression or heroic subjects of injustice."[4] They were men of "conscious agency," "capable of human error," and indeed the entire range of human emotions, understandings, desires, aspirations, achievements, and failings. In their assessment of the Indians, they also shared the values of the dominant culture to a degree that modern readers might find disconcerting.[5] This collection sheds light on the troopers' comprehension of their complex situation, their reactions, accommodations, and resistance.

The social milieu in which the soldiers lived and worked did not consist exclusively of black and white men. Native Americans were significant actors, not just as tenacious and dangerous foes, but also as comrades and as members of Buffalo Soldier families. Hispanic residents of the Southwest also represented a substantial part of the world of the Buffalo Soldiers. Moreover, the soldiers' West included women and children, members of their own families and those of their officers as well as parts of the civilian community. These documents are selected to illuminate some of the interaction among all of these groups.

Here then are the voices of the Buffalo Soldier, along with those of his officers, and others who knew him and had an interest in his life and work. They speak to us of his service and his community and of opportunity and its limits. They are not just black voices; they are American voices.

Chapter One

A new kind of soldier for the post–Civil War Regular Army

During the Civil War, about 180,000 black soldiers bore arms for the Union. Although they did not have a great impact as combatants on the course of military operations,[1] they were a major presence, about 10 percent of the total, in northern forces. They fought well when they got the opportunity; performed logistical, security, and other support duty; and as a significant portion of northern men under arms underscored the overwhelming numerical superiority of Union forces. All in all their contribution was without question significant.[2]

The first post–Civil War Congress recognized this contribution in the reorganization of the Army in 1866. The Army that was embodied in this law had two noteworthy characteristics. At about 45,000, it was dramatically smaller than the huge establishment that had won the war, and for the first time it incorporated African Americans in the Regular Army. The law specifically set aside six regiments, the 9th and 10th Cavalry and the 38, 39th, 40th, and 41st Infantry, for black enlisted men.[3] Moreover, it contained no specific prohibition against black commissioned officers.

Only one other provision related directly to the service of black troops. The act authorized one chaplain per black regiment and made him responsible for the common-school education of the soldiers, many of whom had never been allowed access to schools under slavery. This departed from the practice in the rest of the Army, where the chaplain was appointed to a post, not a unit.

In 1869, the Army was further reduced to about 25,000 by cutting the forty-five infantry regiments to twenty-five. As a result of this reduction, the 38th and 41st were consolidated into the 24th, and the 39th and 40th became the 25th. Neither the provision reducing the infantry regiments nor any other portion of the law stipulated that any of the twenty-five infantry regiments had to be composed of black enlisted men.

Thirty-Ninth Congress. Sess. I. CH. 299. July 28, 1866

Be it enacted by the Senate and House of Representatives of the United States of America in Congress assembled, That the military peace establishment of the

United States shall hereafter consist of five regiments of artillery, ten regiments of cavalry, forty-five regiments of infantry, the professors and corps of cadets of the United States Military Academy, and such other forces as shall be provided for by this act, to be known as the Army of the United States.

Sec. 3. *And be it further enacted*, that to the six regiments of cavalry now in service there shall be added four regiments, two of which shall be composed of colored men, having the same organization as is now provided by law for cavalry regiments, with the addition of one veterinary surgeon to each regiment, whose compensation shall be one hundred dollars per month; but the grade of company commissary sergeant of cavalry is hereby abolished. The original vacancies in the grade of first and second lieutenant shall be filled by selection from among the officers and soldiers of volunteer cavalry and two thirds of the original vacancies in each of the grades above that of first lieutenant shall be filled by selections from among the officers of volunteer cavalry, and one third from officers of the regular army, all of whom shall have served two years in the field during the war, and have been distinguished for capacity and good conduct. . . .

Sec. 4. *And be it further enacted*, That the forty-five regiments of infantry provided for by this act shall consist of the first ten regiments of ten companies each, now in service; of twenty-seven regiments, of ten companies each, to be formed by adding two companies to each battalion of the remaining nine regiments; and of eight new regiments, of ten companies each, four regiments of which shall be composed of colored men and four regiments of ten companies each to be raised and officered as hereinafter provided for, to be called the veteran reserve corps; and all the original vacancies in the grades of first and second lieutenant shall be filled by selection from among the officers and soldiers of volunteers, and one half of the original vacancies in each of the grades above that of first lieutenant, shall be filled by selection from among the officers of volunteers, and the remainder from officers of the regular army, all of whom shall have served two years during the war, and have been distinguished for capacity and good conduct in the field. . . .

Sec. 30. . . . [O]ne chaplain may be appointed by the President, by and with the advice and consent of the Senate, for each regiment of colored troops, whose duty shall include the instruction of the enlisted men in the common English branches of education. . . .

Fortieth Congress. Sess. III. CH. CXXIV. March 3, 1869.

Be it enacted by the Senate and House of Representatives of the United States of America in Congress assembled. . . .

Sec. 2. . . . That there shall be no new commissions, no promotions, and no enlistments in any infantry regiment until the total number of infantry regiments is reduced to twenty-five; and the Secretary of War is hereby directed to consolidate the infantry regiments as rapidly as the requirements of the public service and the reduction of the number of officers will permit. . . .

Chapter Two

First skirmishes with Plains tribes

The first armed combat of black regulars did not involve the well-known 9th or 10th Cavalry. Instead small detachments of the 38th Infantry, guarding surveying parties or stations along railroad and wagon routes, engaged war parties, probably Cheyenne, in the summer of 1867. As these orders and reports concerning four skirmishes show, a number of these encounters took place with no white officer present. Black noncommissioned officers provided the leadership, among them Sergeants S. Davis and John Reid, and Corporals Alfred Bradden and David Turner.

Corporal Turner led the troops in the first such encounter. Turner was barely twenty-one but still an experienced soldier, with Civil War service in the 15th U.S. Colored Infantry. Born in Richmond, Indiana, he claimed Detroit, Michigan, as his permanent residence when he enlisted at Sandusky, Ohio, in May 1867. He had clearly traveled around the Midwest. The enlistment register identified him as a laborer, 5' 9" inches tall, with dark eyes, black hair, and a yellow complexion. He signed his oath of enlistment with an "X." The actions in which these sergeants and corporals commanded men in combat are described here.

Corporal David Turner:[1]

Hd Qrs. Fort Harker, KS,
June 25th, 1867

Special Orders
No. 113,

II. . . . In compliance with Special Field Orders, No. 46, dated Hd Qrs Dist. of the Upper Arks, June 24, 1867, (2) two Non Commissioned Officers and (10) ten men of Company "K" 38th U.S. Infantry, are hereby detailed to proceed to Wilson's Creek, Ks, as guard to the surveying party at that place, the detachment will be furnished with (6) six days rations and fifty rounds of ammunition to each man. They will be under the direction of Mr. Riley, Engineer, and will remain at Wilson's Creek until the morning of the 29th inst. when they will return to Fort Harker.

The Quartermasters Dept will furnish the necessary transportation. . . .
Extract from Muster Roll, K/38TH Infantry:

A detachment of Co. K under the command of Corporal David Turner was attacked at Wilson's Creek near Fort Harker on the 26th of June 1867 by Indians. The Indians were repulsed with a loss of five killed.

Sergeant S. Davis:[2]

Head Quars Post
New Fort Hays, Ks.
July 30, 1867

Bvt Brig Genl Chauncy Williams
Ast Adj Genl Dpt Mo
Fort Leavenworth Ks
General

I enclose for the information of the Comg General a copy of a note from Sergt Davis 38th Inf (of this day) who is stationed on the U.P.R.R.&D near thirty miles west of this Post. The R.R. people speak very highly of the conduct of the men. No stock was lost.

I am General
Your obedient svnt
Henry C. Corbin
Capt 38 Inf
Cmg Post

Capt.

July 30th 1867

We had a very large fight last night and night before and it was [lucky] that we had a box of ammunition [with] us. None of the boys got killed. We killed 10 Indian Ponies that we found here this morning. We don't know whether we killed the riders or not. The sentinels like to got shot when they halted there but happened to lay down and they shot over and the balls went through the tents.

S. Davis
Sergt 38th U.S. Inf

Corporal Alfred Bradden:[3]

Hdqrs Post near Ft Hays Ks
Aug 2/67

Lieut. T. B. Weir
A.A.A. Genl Dist Uppr Ark
Lieut

I send you a statement for the information of the Comdg Genl made by Corpl Alfred Bradden "C" Co, 38th Infty, who has just returned from Fort Wallace. He says, "that on Monday July 21st while himself & 10 men acting as escort to wagon train enroute to Ft Wallace were marching along, when about 1 mile east from Monument Station they were attacked by about 25 Indians, at the same time there were about 300 Indians on the Bluffs some two miles distant who did not fire or in any way interfere with them. The small party fired but two or three shots and being answered by a volley from the guard & teamsters wheeled about and joined the large party on the Bluffs. Nothing further was seen of them."

I remain Lieut
Your Obed Servt
Henry C. Corbin
Capt 38th U.S. Inf.

Sergeant John Reid:[4]

Hd Qrs Post New Ft Hays
Aug 6/67

Lieut T. B. WeirÃ
A.A.A. Genl Dist of the Upr Ark
Lieut

I enclose for the information of the Comdg General a Copy of a Statement made by Sergt John Reid "C" Co 38th Infty.

I am Lieut
Very Respectfully
Your Obedt Servt
Henry C. Corbin
Capt 38th U.S. Infty
Comdg Post

"The Battle of Prairie Dog Creek," by Ralph Heinz, depicts soldiers of the 10th U.S. Cavalry and 18th Kansas Volunteer Cavalry operating together in August 1867 (Courtesy National Guard Bureau)

Sergt John Reid "C" Co 38th U.S. Infty with 10 men escorting train with Rations to Monument Station states that on his way returning and while camped at White Rock Station Aug 3/67 about 12 o'clock at night states they were attacked by a party of Indians (supposed to be Cheyennes) about 400 in number, who attempted to stampede the mules. The Indians all had torch lights and tried to throw them among the wagons so as to burn them but did not succeed. They kept up a fire for about an hour and a half, but did not succeed in doing any damage, he finds it impossible to say whether he killed any or not, they departed about 2 o'clock A.M. and nothing further was seen of them.

Chapter Three

The 10th Cavalry in the Summer of 1867: First Battles and First Casualty

In the summer of 1867, Kansas was a major battleground, with frequent fighting between the Army and the Cheyennes. The 10th Cavalry's first involvement came early in August, when the F Troop under Captain George A. Armes was attacked while responding to a report of an Indian raid along the railroad right-of-way. Later in the month, the 10th, again with Armes in command, became involved in a larger fight, with the black regulars fighting side by side with white Kansas volunteers on Beaver Creek in the Republican River Valley.

Armes's reports, filed at the National Archives in Record Group 393, were also published in his memoir.[1] In his book, Armes cleaned up the prose, punctuation, and syntax somewhat, and in one letter changed "sons of bitches" to "sons of guns." The versions reproduced here are based on the original handwritten reports.

Captain Henry C. Corbin, 38th Infantry, who commanded Fort Hays, forwarded Armes's report of the second fight to Department Headquarters. Corbin's endorsement contained the intriguing observation that "All think that many of our own race were with the enemy from the fact that our forces were repeatedly challenged in plain English." Corbin also emphasized that "the warriors are described as being highly painted. They acted altogether on the offensive and from their superior numbers and fine condition of their stock compelled our forces to act on the defensive." According to Armes, the Cheyenne war chief Roman Nose, the Kiowa Satanta, and Charlie Bent, a son of fur trade entrepreneur William Bent and a Cheyenne woman, were among the warriors. Corbin praised Armes, his men, and the 18th Kansas for conduct that was ". . . highly creditable, not only to themselves but to the service to which they belong."

Sergeant William Christy, who came off of a Pennsylvania farm to join the regiment, was shot dead in the fight of August 2. He became the first 10th cavalryman to be killed in action. Christy Avenue at Fort Huachuca, Arizona, bears his name.

The fight of August 2:

New Fort Hays, Kans.
August 3, 1867

Capt. H. C. Corbin
Thirty-eighth Infantry,
Commanding Post

Captain—I have the honor to submit the following report:

In compliance with instructions received from you I left this camp at 3 o'clock, the afternoon of the 1st inst., with forty-four mounted men, and proceeded as far as Campbell's Camp, thirteen miles down the railroad, where I saw seven of his men, who had just been killed by the Indians, and learned that they had gone up the north branch of Big Creek, which I followed eighteen miles, but could not find the trail, as the night was dark.

I returned to Campbell's, on the opposite side, and dispatched six men to the post for an additional support of thirty men and one piece of artillery. I intended to start at daybreak north for the Saline, where the Indians were supposed to have gone.

I waited four hours, and no men came, so I started out at daybreak, the 2d inst., with thirty-four mounted men, leaving four sick. I reached the Saline (fifteen miles) at 8 o'clock this morning, which I followed up twelve miles, where I was met and attacked by about seventy-five Indians.

I dismounted my command, threw out some flankers to save my horses, and gave orders to advance on up the creek for the purpose of recapturing the stolen stock, but in ten minutes I was surrounded, and fires were built all around the command on the tops of the bluffs.

I kept my flankers well out, and advanced until I saw what was supposed to be a herd of buffalo, but close investigation discovered them to be Indians coming to the support of those around me. I gave the command, "To the left, march!" and started for the post. In half an hour I was entirely surrounded. A few Indians at a time would occasionally dash through the command.

Sergeant Christy was shot through the head and killed while getting his men in place.

My first sergeant, Thornton, Corporals Spriggs and Posy had their horses shot from under them. Three more horses were wounded, but I managed to get them into camp.

The Indians followed about fifteen miles, during which time at least 2000 shots were fired at us, with very little effect.

The only reason I can give for their being such poor marksmen is that they had not become accustomed to the use of our new firearms. The most of them seemed to be armed with the improved Spencer carbine, others with rifles and revolvers.

Very few arrows were shot at the command.

I was wounded in the hip by a rifle ball. When this was generally known the men became nearly uncontrollable; some fired all their ammunition away at random, and rushed to me with the report that they were out. Being unable to walk or stand up, I was put on my horse, and then ordered every man back to his place on the flank and rear who was without ammunition, so as to give the Indians the impression that we were well supplied and not alarmed.

With the assistance of Lieutenant Bodamer and my two guides (Mr. Becker and Mr. Brink) we succeeded in keeping the men in their places by sending them back without ammunition as fast as they came in; others took warning and did not waste their supply, and finally became cool.

No man was allowed to ride except the sick, who led the horses; in that way the command was saved.

Sixty-four miles were marched from the time of leaving Campbell's Camp until my return to this post last night.

Total number of miles marched since 3, the afternoon of the 1st inst., 113, without rations or forage. It is my opinion, as well as of those who were with me, that we were surrounded by at least 350 to 400 Indians, of whom six were killed and several wounded while making dashes through the command, but were soon picked up, tied to their horses, and hurried to the rear, thus preventing the capture of them or their horses or ponies.

Two white men or half-breeds were with the Indians, who took an active part, but were very careful not to dash through the command. They were mounted on the finest and most active horses I ever saw. It is my opinion that a large number of Indians are encamped between the Saline and the Solomon, where any amount of stolen stock could be recaptured, provided a sufficient force could go after them.

It would not be safe to send a less number than 200 or 300 well-armed and equipped men, as the country which they would operate in is so broken up, full of gullies, cañons and hills, that it would take a large force to drive them out.

It is the greatest wonder in the world that my command and myself escaped being massacred, as we had to retreat fifteen miles through a hilly country, full of cañons, rocks and gullies, fighting our way foot by foot, the Indians dodging from one gully and rock to others and firing on us at every chance.

Great credit is due Lieutenant Bodamer, Mr. Becker and Mr. Brink for the coolness and daring they displayed on several occasions when the Indians dashed upon us. If it had not been for their coolness and efficient aid not one of the command would have returned.

I would recommend that a strong force be dispatched to that section to drive them out as soon as possible, as they have formed the opinion that they can whip any force sent against them.

I am Captain
Very respectfully,
Your obedient servant,
Geo. A. Armes
Capt. Commanding Co. F, Tenth U.S. Cavalry

The fight of August 21:

New Fort Hays, Kansas
August 24, 1867

Capt. H. C. Corbin
38th U.S. Infantry
Comdg Post, New Fort Hays, Kas

Sir:

I have the honor to report that in obedience to S.O. No. 71, dated Headquarters, New Fort Hays, Kansas, August 12, 1867, I assumed command of Companies "B" and "C," 1st Batt. 18th Kansas Cavalry under command of Capt E. A. Barker, 18th Kas Cav'y, and "F" Co, 10th U.S. Cavalry; marched to the Saline River, and followed the course of the stream west until I met Major Moore, Commanding Co's "A" and "D" 18th Ka's. Vol. Cav'y, coming down. About 4 o'clock on the 14th we decided to march to the Solomon. Major Moore went to the north-west and I to the north-east; we were to meet each other on the Solomon.

I followed the Solomon forty 40 miles, examining all its tributaries thoroughly, failing to find Maj. Moore. I took a southwest course intending to come by Monument Station and scout down the Smoky, but on the 17th finding a very large trail running north-west, I followed it. After coming to the Saline, I halted my command, forty-five miles from Fort Hays. I rode with three men as an escort into Fort Hays, and ordered up four wagons with forage and one with rations, and took twenty-two dismounted Cavalry for guard to train. Rejoined my Command on the eve of the 18th, and on the 19th started on the trail, when I started to Beaver Creek, seventy miles. I then halted to wait for Captain Jennis and several scouts whom I had sent out to look for Indian signs. Reached Beaver Creek 9 A.M. on the 21st. While eating breakfast one of my videttes was attacked by one Indian. Supposing more to be very near, I at once pushed on, leaving my wagons in charge of Lieutenant Price and sixty-five men of the 18th Kansas, with orders to come on as fast as possible to the Republican and then to await further orders. Fearing that he would follow directly after me, I sent Sergeant Carpenter 18th Ka's. & Sergt. Johnson, "F" Co. 10th Cavalry, back with twenty men and instructions to follow Beaver Creek down eight miles before they crossed. Before he had proceeded three miles, he met Capt. Jennis, 18th Ka's. Cav'y, and scouts, whom I had sent out that morning. Captain Jennis assumed command of the party, twenty-nine 29 men. Seeing the Indians circling around, he decided to attempt overtaking me but failed, as he was attacked by too many Indians. Enclosed is his report. During my forward movement I was attacked about 3 P.M., by between two and three hundred Indians. I sent Capt. Barker to the left with half of the command to make a charge on the largest portion. Before he had proceeded a hundred yards, I discovered reinforcements of Indians coming from the north-west, and found it necessary to fence my animals in the nearest ravine, and throw my men to the right, left, front, and rear, which was done just in time to save my stock, by repelling a charge of the Indians made just as I had dismounted. The Indians fought me from 3 to 9 o'clock P.M. "Satanta" in full uniform on a beautiful grey horse, sounded the charge with his bugle at least a dozen times, whooping and yelling, and endeavoring to get his men to charge into the ravine, but only getting them near enough to have at least twenty of his saddles emptied at a volley or a dozen or so ponies killed and wounded. During the fight eight of my men were severely wounded. Under the cover of darkness I attempted to find the rest of the command. Reaching Beaver Creek at 4 o'clock on the 22nd, and seeing no signs of the wagons, I halted till sunrise to rest my exhausted men, then followed the creek up two 2 miles and found Lieut. Price and Lieut. Thomas 18th Ka's. Vols., with the wagons encamped in a ravine, all safe, but entirely surrounded by Indians, in groups of fifty or more, evidently trying to either starve them out; to seize an opportunity to charge, or to run off the stock.

I soon learned that Capt. Jennis was nearby in a helpless condition. I immediately sent out a sufficient force and brought him and his wounded into camp. The Indians continued charging and fighting until 4 o'clock P.M., when I mounted twenty 20 men, which was all I could raise, and charged on the Indians, driving them across the creek but found it policy to get back to camp as soon as possible, as about three or four hundred commenced circling around, endeavoring to cut me off from camp. It is my honest opinion that not less than fifty Indians were killed, and a hundred and fifty wounded. Seventy cavalry is as many as I had to oppose at least eight hundred Indians. Lieut. Price had sixty five men with the wagon train. Captain Jennis had twenty nine. Total strength of the command: one hundred and sixty four men, which were divided into three separate detachments, attacked by various odds of Indians. About 4 o'clock P.M. on the 22nd several Indians came towards us, from among a hundred or so, waving a white flag. I sent out my guides with a white handkerchief tied to a stick, with instructions to receive the messenger and ascertain what he wished, and if necessary for me to see him to let me know. The Indian came near enough to recognize the scout and call him by name, cursed him, and fired his pistols at him; at the same time several Indians darted out from among those behind, carrying a red flag, singing out in plain English "Come here, come here, you sons of bitches, we want to fight, we don't want to fight the niggers, we want to fight you white sons of bitches, & etc." The guides report that they recognized "Satanta," "Roman Nose," "Charlie Bent" and other prominent chiefs. In my opinion Satanta considers himself to be "in command of the District."

While returning for rations on the night of the 18th, I met Major Elliott, Com'd'g. Detachment 7th U.S. Cavalry, who agreed to start on the morn of the 19th for the Republican, and co-operate with me. On no other conditions would I have returned so far with so small a command. Supposing him and Maj. Moore 18th Ka's. to be in my vicinity gave me confidence to push forward, and had they co-operated with me, we might have re-captured twelve or fifteen hundred head of stolen stock. It is my opinion that large numbers of Indians may be found on the tributaries of the north fork of the Republican, and from appearances they intend soon to move north of the Platte. While returning to this post I met Major Elliott, with six companies of cavalry, going northwest toward the region of our recent operations, and if a force could be sent from the Platte to meet him on the Republican, at least two thousand head of stock could be captured. I would recommend that if pursuit of Indians is to be continued on the plains, a temporary post of supplies be established near the north and south fork of the Republican.

It gives me pleasure to recommend to the favorable notice of the Com'd'g Gen'l the following Officers, Guides and enlisted men who, by their cool determination and examples of courage and perseverance under dangers the most trying, contributed so greatly to the salvation of the Command.

Capt. E. A. Barker, "B" Co 18th Ka's. Cav'y
Capt. G. B. Jennis, "C" Co 18th Ka's. Cav'y
2nd Lieut. Reynolds, 18th Ka's. Cav'y
1st Lieut. Price, 18th Ka's. Cav'y
1st Lieut. Thomas. 18th Ka's. Cav'y
2nd Lieut. John A. Bodamer, 10th U.S. Cavalry
A.A. Surg. Richard Westenburg, USA
Mr. P. A. Becker, Scout, whom I recommended for a commission in another report.
Mr. A. I. Priley, Scout
1st Sergt. Francis M. Stahl, Co, "B" 18th Ka's. Cavalry
Sergeant Springer, "C" Co. 18th Ka's. Cavalry
Sergeant Geo. A. Campbell "C: Co 18th Ka's. Cavalry
Sergeant C. A. Crummel, "F" Co 10th Cavalry
Corporal Butler, "F" Co., 10th Cavalry
Corporal James Tarvell, "C" Co., 18th Ka's. Cavalry
Private E. I. Werley, "C" Co., 18th Ka's. Cavalry
Private James Gordon, "B" Co., 18th Ka's. Cavalry

The whole command acted nobly and I have set a fine example for other volunteers from Kansas to follow. I reached Fort Hays at 5 o'clock P.M. today, bringing all my wounded. Two died on they way, whom I buried.

The following is a list of the wounded:

Sergt. Thomas Lannigan "B" Co 18th Kansas
Private Thomas Anderson "B" Co 18th Kansas died
Private William Hickey "B" Co 18th Kansas
Private T. Forrester "B" Co 18th Kansas
Private Joseph Gordon "B" Co 18th Kansas
Pvt Hayes "B" Co 18th Kansas
Capt. G. B. Jennis "C" Co 18th Kansas

Black soldier and white officer (From George A. Armes, *Ups and Downs of an Army Officer* [Washington, DC, 1900], 468.)

Sergt G. A. Carpenter "C" Co 18th Kansas
Corpl Jas Tarvell, "C" Co 18th Ka's.
Pvt. Wm. Sutherland, "C" Co 18th Ka's
Sergt. G. A. Springer, "C" Co 18th Ka's
Sergt. G. A. Campbell, "C" Co 18th Ka's
1st Sergt. Jacob Thornton, "F" Co 10th Cavalry
Sergt. Wm Johnson, "F" Co 10th Cavalry
Corpl. Thomas Shepherd, "F" Co 10th Cavalry
Pvt. T. Crosby, "F" Co 10th Cavalry
Pvt. J. Anderson, "F" Co 10th Cavalry
Pvt. Chas. Gartrill, "F" Co 10th Cavalry
Pvt. Isaac Marshall, "F" Co 10th Cavalry
Pvt. James Brown, "F" Co 10th Cavalry
Pvt. John W. Robinson, "F" Co 10th Cavalry
Pvt. Chas Murray, "F" Co 10th Cavalry
Scout A. I. Priley
Pvt. T. D. Masterson "C" Co 18th Ka's.
Pvt. Wm. Turner, "F" Co, 10th Cavalry

Eleven men are missing from the Command.

I have the honor to be, Capt.,
Very respectfully your obt. servt.
Geo. A. Armes
Capt 10th US Cav'y, Bvt. Maj. USA

Chapter Four

Sergeant Shelvin Shropshire's observations on service in Kansas

Frederic Remington wrote several articles that focused on the black regulars and their activities. Generally, Remington was impressed with their soldierly qualities, and his writings are full of praise and respect for them. He and a few of the other observers whose comments are included in this volume, sometimes resorted to "dialect," an effort to emulate or caricature the speech of rural Southern black people, in recording the comments of the soldiers. This literary usage became popular in the works of Thomas Nelson Page and Joel Chandler Harris and is frequently associated with efforts to promote a post–Civil War mythology of happy, contented slaves in the pre-War South.[1]

Robert Ewell Greene, author of a number of books on black soldiers, has expressed strong irritation at what he considers to have been Remington's indulgence of stereotypes through such usage.[2] However, Remington and the others quoted herein who used this patois do not appear to have meant any disrespect. Moreover, at this remove it is hard to determine how much of the "dialect" belonged to the voice of the soldier-informer and how much should be attributed to the recorder-narrator.

In "Vagabonding With the Tenth Horse" (*Cosmopolitan*, February 1897), Remington reported a conversation with one of the regiment's veteran noncommissioned officers, First Sergeant Shelvin Shropshire of H Troop. Shropshire served a total of thirty-three years, from the Civil War with the 15th U.S. Colored Infantry (the same regiment in which Corporal David Turner of the 38th Infantry had served) to the Spanish-American War with the 10th Cavalry. Remington wrote down Shropshire's recollections of the fighting in Kansas, but the sergeant also had significant observations about the relations between privates and sergeants.[3]

Frederic Remington, "Vagabonding With the Tenth Horse."

Some of the old sergeants have been taught their battle tactics in a school where the fellows who were not quick at learning are dead. I have forgotten a great many miles of road as I talked to old Sergeant Shropshire. His experiences were grave and gay and infinitely varied.

"We used to have a fight every day down on the Washita, Mr. Remington," said he, "and them Indians used to attack accordin' to your ideas. A feller on the flanks nevah knew what minute he was goin' to have a horse-race back to the command, with anywhar from ten to five hundred Indians a close second.

"Ah, Mr. Remington, we used to have soldiers in them days. Now you take them young fellers ahead thar—lots of 'em 'il nevah make soldiers in God's world. Now you see that black feller just turnin' his head; well, he's a 'cruit, and he thinks I been abusin' him for a long time. Other day he comes to me and says he don't want no more trouble; says I can get along with him from now on. Says I to that 'cruit, 'Blame yer eyes, I don't have to get along wid you; you have to get along wid me. Understand?'"

Chapter Five

The battle at Beecher Island, September 1878

The bloody fight between a group of fifty white frontiersmen led by Lieutenant Colonel George Forsyth and a large party of Cheyenne warriors took place at an island in the Arickaree Fork of the Republican River in Colorado near the eastern border with Kansas. The most important outcome of this fierce battle was the death of the charismatic Northern Cheyenne war chief Roman Nose. The fighting ended when H Troop of the 10th Cavalry rode to the rescue, forcing the Cheyennes to withdraw.

According to George Bird Grinnell, the Cheyennes did not consider the battle to be particularly noteworthy: "It was a hard fight, but one of the everyday happenings of the time."[1] The men of the 10th, on the other hand, considered it a major episode in their history. Lieutenant John Bigelow, who joined the regiment as a young lieutenant fresh from the Military Academy in 1877, kept the memory of the episode alive with two paragraphs devoted to the fight in an 1892 essay on the regiment's history.

Reuben Waller, who served ten years as a soldier in the regiment and who rode with Captain Louis H. Carpenter to the aid of the besieged scouts, always remained very proud of his service and participation in the rescue. In the 1920s, he wrote a number of letters to *Winners of the West*, the monthly organ of the National Indian War Veterans, an organization that lobbied for better pensions on behalf of Indian war veterans. These letters concerned his life in the Army. In one he mentioned that soldiers and Indians alike had scalped enemy dead, but his correspondence emphasized mainly the rescue at Beecher Island, named after Lieutenant Frederick H. Beecher, who died in the battle.[2] Waller devoted considerable space to the Tenth's part in the fight in his reminiscence of his life.

Most writers agree that the Indians at Beecher Island vastly outnumbered Forsyth and his men. However, the agreement ends there. Bigelow claimed the Cheyennes numbered 700; Waller said 2,000. Such discrepancies occurred frequently in accounts of Plains battles. Soldiers and white civilians were usually unable and in all likelihood too distracted to make accurate counts or even agree on their guesses. Their enemy, on the other hand, appeared indifferent to such matters, so books such as George Grinnell's *The Fighting Cheyennes* do not include counts despite extensive interviews with Indian participants, and their descendents and acquaintances.

From John Bigelow, "Tenth Regiment of Cavalry"[3]

... On the 17th of this month [September 1868] Lieut. Colonel G. A. Forsyth, A. D. C. to General Sheridan, with a party of white scouts, was attacked and "corralled" by a force of about 700 Indians on an island in the Republican River. Two of Forsyth's scouts stole through the Indian lines and brought word of the perilous situation of the command to Fort Wallace. Parties were soon on the way to its relief. First and last the following troopers were started towards it from different points: Captain Bankhead with about 100 men of the 5th Infantry, Captain Carpenter with Troop H and Captain Graham with Troop I, of the 10th Cavalry, and two troops of the 2nd Cavalry under Major Brisbin.

Captain Carpenter's troop was the first of these commands to arrive upon the scene. It found Forsyth and his men out of rations, living on horse-flesh without salt or pepper. All of the officers had been killed or wounded. Every horse and mule, too, had been killed. Forsyth, who had been twice wounded, was lying in a square hole scooped out in the sand, within a few feet of a line of dead horses which half encircled the hole and impregnated the air with a terrible stench. Captain Carpenter immediately pitched a number of tents in a suitable place near by, had the wounded men carried to them, and the rest removed to a more salubrious air. Twenty-six hours later Captain Bankhead arrived bringing with him the troops of the 2nd Cavalry...

From Reuben Waller, "History of a Slave Written by Himself at the Age of 89"[4]

I was born January 5th, 1840, and the first sensation of my life was the falling stars in 1849. All the slaves and their masters got together and began a mighty fixing for the judgment day. Of course our masters had a greater cause for fixing up things, than we poor slaves did, but we followed their advice.

Well, the next was the '56 Border Ruffian War, and the comet in 1860 just before the Civil war. Well, we all got scared at the comet as its tail reached from West to East. It did look frightful. As we think of it now we believed it was a token of the great Civil war and the completing of our freedom, 400,000 [sic] of us.

Well, I come now to the War of the Rebellion. My master was a general in the Rebel army, and he took me along as his body servant and I was with him all through the war, was with him in 29 battles.

We were with Gen. Forest at the shameful massacre at Fort Pillow of 600 colored troops. And in several battles after that I saw our rebel soldiers reap what they had sown at Fort Pillow.

On one occasion my master's regiment was whipped by Gen. Bank's [sic] black soldiers and they captured several hundred of our soldiers and they slaughtered most all of them, crying "remember Fort Pillow."

I told my master that the black men done our men like we did them at Fort Pillow, and I asked him why it was that way, as they had slaughtered his son and several boys who were raised with me, and his son that was raised at my mother's breast with me, all was slaughtered as a result of the Fort Pillow massacre. Being a slave and ignorant, I could not understand it and master did not enlighten me on the subject, and I never really understood it till I saw Master Robert E. Lee hand his sword to General Grant at Appomattox Court House.

Well, while being with Stonewall Jackson's cavalry, I engendered a great liking for the cavalry soldiers, and on July 16th 1867, I went to Fort Leavenworth, Kansas, and Colonel L. H. Carpenter was raising the 10th U.S. Cavalry, and I enlisted on the 16th day of July, 1867, for the Indian wars that was then raging in Kansas and Colorado.

Well, we plunged right into the fights—Beaver Creek, Sand Creek, Cheyenne Wells, and many others. One great sensation was the rescue at Beecher Island, on the Arickare Creek, in Colorado, September, 1868. The Indians had surrounded General Forsyth and 50 brave men, and had killed and wounded 20 men, and had compelled the rest to live on dead horse flesh for nine days on a small island. Colonel L. H. Carpenter, with his Company H, 10th U.S. cavalry, was at Cheyenne Wells, Colo., 100 miles from Beecher Island. Jack Stillwell brought us word of the fix that Beecher was in and we entered the race for the island, and in 26 hours Colonel Carpenter and myself, as his hostler, rode into the rifle pits. And what a sight we saw—30 wounded and dead men right in the middle of 50 dead horses, that had lain in the hot sun for ten days.

And these men had eaten the putrid flesh of those dead horses for eight days. The men were in a dying condition when Carpenter and myself dismounted and began to rescue them.

By this time all the soldiers were all in the pits and we began to feed the men from our haversacks. If the doctor had not arrived in time we would have killed them by feeding them to death. The men were eating all we gave them, and it was plenty. Sure, we never gave a thought that it would hurt them. You can imagine a man in starvation, and plenty suddenly set before him. He can't think of the results until too late. That is the condition that Company H, 10th Cavalry, fixed for the Beecher Island men. We were not aiming to hurt the boys. It was all done through eagerness and excitement.

God bless the Beecher Island men. They were a noble set of men.

Now, I shall explain the fight as told to me by the men at the time I rescued them. There were 2,000 Indians under the great Chief Roman Nose. They were preparing to raid Kansas and Colorado, and there were no soldiers within 200 miles and all Roman Nose had to oppose him and his 2,000 braves was Major Forsyth and 50 scouts. all dead shots and armed with the famous Spencer 7-shot carbines, a very deadly weapon. The Indians surrounded Beecher, Forsyth and 50 men on this island, which was not protected by anything but a sandbar.

The men dug rifle pits in the sand with their spoons and pocket knives. Well, the Indians shot their 50 horses in about 45 minutes. Every horse was dead and the men made breastworks of the dead horses till they could dig rifle pits in the sand, but before that was done, five men were killed and several wounded, and by this time they had dug deep pits in the sand, and had good rifle pits with high banks of sand. You know a bullet can't have good luck going through 10 inches of sand. After Roman Nose had killed all the horses, he was sure he had the 50 men at his mercy and so he fixed up for a grand charge that he thought would be fatal to the white men, but he had better not have made the charge. It was the greatest mistake that Roman Nose ever made.

I had several rounds with him and he was always careful about mistakes when he met regular soldiers, he was too smart for us. We most always had "heap too many" (buffalo soldiers) and I suppose he thought 50 whites "heap little," but also his fatal mistake.

Well, now to the fight as explained to me by the rescued men. After the horses were all killed, the rest of us by this time were well concealed in the sand pits. The grand charge formed. Here they come, 100 yards away, 200 in number, 300 in ambush, opens 45 Spencer brand new carbines. Roman Nose and his grand charge is wiped off the face of the earth. Only 35 brave scouts did this job so you see by the brave stand made by the Forsyth and Beecher scouts, hundreds of lives of settlers of Kansas and Colorado were saved from massacre and destruction, by the brave stand of 50 brave men.

Let me say here that I had many fights with the Indians for ten years after the Beecher fight, and I never saw anything to equal it. I say it was the greatest fight that ever was fought by any soldiers of the regular army at any time, not excepting the Custer fight or the massacre at Fort Phil Kearney, and I say further that in all the fights we had with the Indians, I mean the regular army, we never killed as many Indians. I saw Lone Wolf, who was in the Beecher fight, and he told us that they lost 400 killed and fatally wounded in the Beecher fight. Well, after the fight and rescue we stayed on the island three days. We buried the five men who were killed. Lieutenant Beecher, Dr. Mooers, Louis Farley and others, with military honors. We used the funeral flag of Company H to bury the dead, which flag I now have in my possession.

At present I have in my possession a scalping knife and a horseshoeing knife that I picked up on the battlefield.

We arrived at Fort Wallace and the scouts were disbanded, and were reorganized under the leadership of Lieutenant Pappoon and rendered military service under the leadership of Lieutenant Pappoon.

Well, after we had been at Fort Wallace about two weeks, and the scouts had gotten rested a lot of soldiers took French leave one night and went to Pond Creek, three miles west of Wallace. Well, when we got there we met the Beecher scouts, as they had been paid off. They sure treated us black soldiers right for what we had done for them.

Of course we lost all respect for prohibition, and of course all got on a very wet drunk. The scouts would have us drink, and we did not resent their courtesy, and everyone in town was on a drunk, and we had everything going our way. But, listen! BANG! BANG! BANG! rang out the shots from a sod house saloon. We rushed in to see what the trouble was and found Sharp Grover lying on the floor with one shot through the brain and one through the heart. Killed by one of the boys who was in the Beecher fight with him. I know the man's name who fired the shots, but I will leave it a blank. He (Sharp Grover) came to his death from a pistol shot, in the hands of one named ———.

It will be remembered that in April or May, 1868, five miles southwest of Fort Wallace that one William Comstock had a ranch and was one of the greatest scouts on the plains. He had charge over all the scouts. In the U.S. service, whenever the Army wanted a scout we just called on Comstock and he would furnish the man we wanted.

He had under him at his ranch twelve good scouts. He had sent them all out but Sharp Grover, and Sharp one morning came galloping in to the Fort with the tale that the Indians had attacked him and Comstock and had killed Comstock. I myself was in the party that charged out to the Comstock ranch to find him shot through the back and through the head. Sharp went back with us.

We examined the battlefield. It was a sandy field and it had been tracked, it looked like, by many ponies, in the way the Indians attack. But when we got through we compared the pony tracks to the pony that Sharp had ridden to the fort with the report. All the tracks absolutely compared corresponded with the tracks made by Sharp's pony.

You see, it was this way. Mr. Comstock was brutally murdered, and Sharp marked the battlefield by riding over it to show that the Indians had attacked him. Well, one of the solders said, "Sharp, this looks most damn suspicious, and you had better come across."

We arrested him and took him back to the fort. But he convinced Colonel Bankhead and got out of it. But the man who killed Sharp knew all about how Comstock was killed. Comstock is buried in the old cemetery at Fort Wallace. Sharp is also buried there.

I was at the old cemetery in September, 1928, and saw the grave of Comstock, but I could not find just where Sharp was buried, but I know he was buried there for I helped bury him.

Well, we wintered at Fort Wallace and in the spring of 1869 we took our last farewell of Fort Wallace and we never returned there any more.

We went on a long Indian campaign, almost two years in the cavalry saddle. In the winter of 1870 we go to Camp Supply and build winter quarters for men and horses. Here we had six thousand Indians on our hands to feed. We had to herd cattle for their beef. Well, we had some exciting time getting acquainted with the Indians. They were on a treaty, you know, and just as we were getting acquainted, every devil of them broke and went on the war path. We lost several men.

There was a stage station about 30 miles from the fort, taken care of by eight white soldiers. They knew the Indians were at peace at the fort and the Indians were at the station every day to trade with the soldiers. But the soldiers didn't know that they had "broken for the war path," and the Indians slaughtered them at one stroke.

Now came some hard times for us worn out soldiers. We had a hard campaign all winter, but in the spring of 1870 we rounded them up at Fort Sill, Indian Territory. We had the same gang that we had at Fort Supply. We got them good and fat and they broke again and raided a family by the name of John Friend, scalped Mrs. Friend, brutally outraged several young girls and killed several others.

Well, we were on their trail. We followed them down through Mexico and back through Colorado and Kansas and rounded them up at Fort Sill. Old Chief Santank [Satank] and Santa [Satanta], Lone Wolf and Big Tree, were the chiefs that were at the head of all this.

Well, you see they had out-generaled the soldiers and got to Fort Sill five days ahead of us. When we arrived they were all in camp playing "good Indians." We had two prisoners and some ponies we got from them and they could not deny their guilt. General Sherman had come through Texas and saw and knew all they had done, and was waiting at Fort Sill until we brought them in, so the next day we reported and produced the prisoners and ponies. General Sherman had boots and saddles sounded, mounted seven companies of cavalry, and surrounded the Indian camp. He demanded that they bring out Satank, Lone Wolf and Big Tree. And they refused to comply, and Sherman gave the command, "Ready, Aim." He gave them five minutes before the word "Fire." Well, they came across very quick. Well, it sure saved an awful slaughter for there were 2,000 Indians in the camp. Every man, woman and child in the camp was ready to fight, and if they had not complied with Sherman's request that would have been one of the greatest massacres in the history of Indian wars. Well, we arrested the chiefs, to send to Texas, and the Second white cavalry came after them, and when they started back to Texas with them, the Indians broke, but the troops were in the saddle when they broke.

Well, two mighty dark hours. I hate to talk of it. The Second cavalry had to kill Satank before they left the fort. He concealed a knife under his blanket and attacked his guard and died "game."

Well, I was discharged from the army honorably after ten years, and came to Eldorado, Kansas, and have made my home here ever since.

Well, after a period of 60 years, there is printed in St. Joseph, Mo., a small paper called *Winners of the West*, printed in the interest of the Indian War Veterans, and after 60 years, and in this little paper, I wrote a letter describing the Beecher Island fight of Sept., 1868, not knowing that there was a survivor of that yet alive. After a few days there was a big automobile rolled up to my door, and who should it be but J. J. Peate, of Beverly, Kansas, one of the survivors who was there with me at the rescue. And all honor to J. J. Peate. Peate and myself want to be at the monument this September, 1929, if we can. As far as we know there are only three living who were at the rescue, J. J. Peate, Thomas Murphy and Ruben [sic] Waller, who were with Colonel Carpenter at the rescue. One word more about Sharp Grover. He was Beecher's chief scout and should have been the one to go for relief, but he failed to volunteer to do anything to help.

Reuben Waller (Courtesy Kansas State Historical Society)

Major Forsyth, in his writeup of that fight, named one man in his scouts who proved to be a coward, in the person of a man named Lane. He must have made a mistake in the name. I don't know why it was not "Grover." It is all over now, only the rising generation ought to have the truth in history.

I visited in June, 1929, I think, as far as I know, the only survivor of the Beecher fight, Thomas Murphy, at Corbin, Kansas. He was in the fight. Well, as my memory fails me in remembering so many things of the past I conclude by saying I have told the facts as near as I could remember them.

I remain, Yours truly,

Ruben Waller

Late Co. H, 10th U.S.Cavalry.

Eldorado, Kansas, July 23, 1929

Chapter Six

The 9th Cavalry in Texas: mutiny at San Pedro Springs, Texas, April 1867

The first blood spilled by members of the 9th Cavalry belonged to its own. An incident triggered by the brutality of Lieutenant Edward Heyl resulted in the deaths of Sergeant Harrison Bradford and Lieutenant Seth Griffin.[1] Heyl had ordered several of his men suspended from tree limbs by their wrists for their failure to respond quickly enough to his orders. While Heyl was in a saloon, one of the three freed himself. The officer returned and beat the soldier with the flat of his saber. Sergeant Bradford protested, and the shooting that ultimately led to the deaths of Bradford and Lieutenant Griffin soon started. The incident at San Pedro Springs, just outside of San Antonio, is usually called a "mutiny," but is more accurately seen as a protest against barbaric leadership, in a tradition already established by black soldiers in the Civil War.[2]

Black troops were not well received in post–Civil War Texas, where the unreconstructed South met the untamed West. It would probably have been hard to find a black soldier who would have disagreed with General Philip Sheridan's assertion that "If I owned hell and Texas I would rent out Texas and live in hell."[3] Relations between the soldiers and white Texans sometimes became extremely hostile and even violent, but the local newspaper report of the San Pedro Springs incident was remarkably restrained.[4]

MUTINY.—About noon yesterday, our city was thrown into great excitement by rumors that the United States colored troops stationed at the San Pedro Springs, had mutinied and killed several of their officers, and also that the war having been escalated into Africa, many of the Negroes were killed. There had been hurrying to and fro among the military stationed in the city and they were soon off at a double-quick. The rumors continued growing in number and varying in details until there was no way of getting at the truth without going to the seat of war, and we went. We found one officer—Lieutenant Griffin we understood the same to be lying mortally wounded, his head split wide open with a sabre; another wounded in the hand; while the Negro Sergeant who had struck the blow with the sabre was lying dead on the spot where he fell. From citizens living in the vicinity, we learned that this Sergeant had protested before the officer of the day, Lieut. Griffin, against the tying up by the thumbs of some of his company, and that the officer had ordered him to his quarters, which order he refused to obey, threatening to report to Gen. Merritt. Whether the officer then attempted to shoot or not, we could not learn, but immediately the Sergeant drew his sabre and cut; another officer then shot the Sergeant through the head, while the latter officer was wounded in the hand by still another soldier; in the meantime the whole camp was alive and numbers of bullets went whistling through the air. The dash and boldness of the senior officer present is said and believed to have done much towards quieting down the mutiny, which at one time indicated an indiscriminate massacre of the officers in camp. Gen. Merritt was very energetic in examining into the causes and ascertaining who were the instigators.

Chapter Seven

William Cathay/Cathay Williams: A woman in the 38th Infantry

On November 15, 1866, Cathay Williams enlisted as William Cathay for the 38th Infantry at St. Louis, Missouri. At 5'9" the recruit was quite tall, had a black complexion, black eyes and hair, and claimed to be a cook by trade. Depending on whether one accepts the statement of age he gave at the time of enlistment or the one she provided at the time of her pension application in 1891, he was either twenty-four or fifteen. In August 1868, his company commander noted that since May 1867 Williams "has been . . . feeble both physically and mentally and much of the time quite unfit for duty." He was discharged for disability two months later, on October 14, 1868, the military physician noting that Private Cathay was "continually on sick report without benefit," and that he was "unable to do military duty and [was] unfit for any service involving the least exposure." According to the doctor, the condition dated from before his enlistment.[1]

William Cathay never amounted to much as a soldier. He failed even to complete his three-year term of enlistment. Clearly, however, the interest in his service comes from the fact that he later turned out to be a woman.[2] After remaining in the west for more than a decade and working as a cook and laundress in various locations in New Mexico and Colorado, she applied for a pension as Cathay Williams. At the time of her 1891 application for a pension, which is reproduced below, a board of three physicians examined her and characterized her as "a large stout woman in good general health." They noted that she walked with a crutch, the result of the amputation of a number of her toes, that her hearing was adequate, and that no other disability existed. The government rejected her claim that her infirmities were related to her service and denied her application for a pension.[3]

There are no photographs or other contemporary visual images of Cathay Williams. Such a lack has never deterred artists from painting historical figures, and there is a modern portrait, called "Female Buffalo Soldier," by William Jennings. Jennings claims that Williams "was conscripted" as a cook and a laundress in the Union Army "at the beginning of the Civil War." He contends that he did the painting "to highlight and honor the triumphs, trials, and tribulations of women in the military and on the frontier, and to serve as a beacon and benchmark for future generations."[4] This is a big burden for one undocumented representation to carry.

State of Colorado
County of Las Animas

In the matter of the claim of Cathay Williams No. 1032593:

I Cathay Williams of lawful age and being first duly sworn according to law upon oath say:

That I am the person Cathay Williams who made application No. 1032593 for pension:

That in the month of October 1868 at the city of St. Louis in the state of Missouri affiant then being in the regular military service of the United States contracted small-pox on account of which affiant was placed in the hospital for treatment; that a very short time thereafter affiant was discharged from the hospital and was sent with her company unit Co. A 38th Regt U.S.I. to Fort Bayard New Mexico; that at the time of her discharge from the hospital affiant had not recovered from all of the effects of said disease and still suffered from the effects of said illness during the trip from St. Louis to New Mexico and in crossing the Rio Grande river in New Mexico affiant was compelled to swim said river and by reason of said exposure and hardship and by reason of effects of the small-pox from which affiant had barely recovered, affiant became very ill and among other things resulted in the deafness as claimed by affiant in her application for pension on file, by which she claims the right to pension;

And affiant further states that on account of said last mentioned illness she was then finally discharged at Fort Bayard New Mexico from service.

Cathay Williams *alias*
William Cathay

Witness
James Martin

State of Colorado
County of Las Animas
Subscribed & sworn to before me this 14th day of July 1891.

William Littlefield
Notary Public

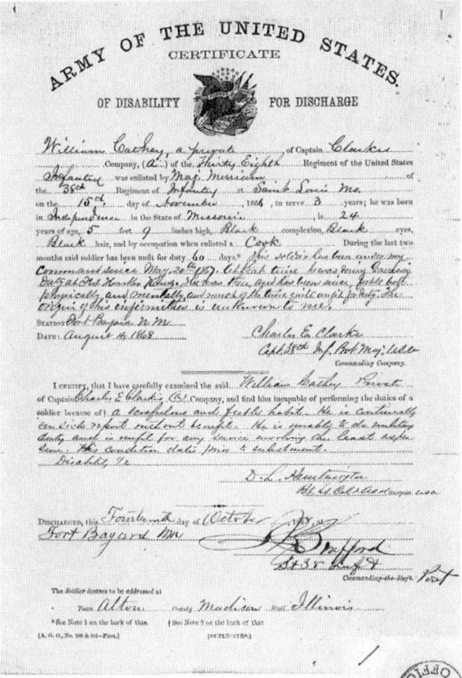

William Cathay's discharge and Cathay Williams's Pension Declaration (Courtesy National Archives and Records Service)

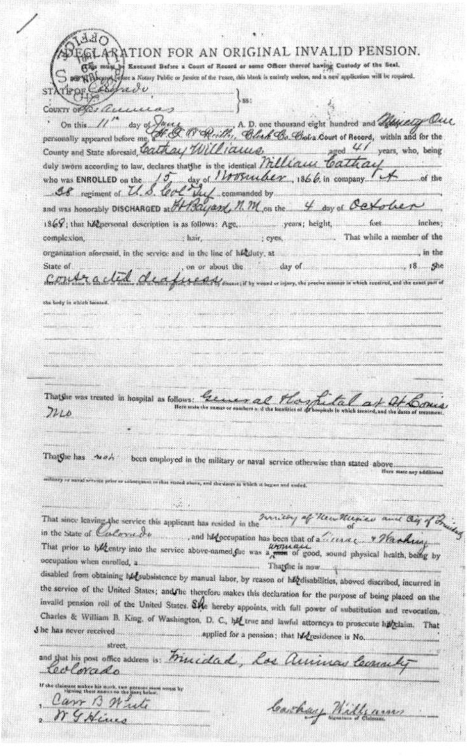

Chapter Eight

Sergeant Emanuel Stance and the Medal of Honor

Emanuel Stance, one of the original members of the 9th Cavalry, was the first of eighteen Buffalo Soldiers to receive the Medal of Honor for bravery in the West.1 This correspondence, from National Archives microfilm M-929, reel 2, shows Stance's leadership and his troop commander's approbation. It also contains Stance's response to receipt of the medal.

Fort McKavett, Texas,
May 26, 1870
Lieutenant B. M. Custer
Post Adjutant

Lieutenant:

I have the honor to make the following report of a scout after Indians made in compliance with Special Orders No. 73, extract 2, Headquarters Post of Fort McKavett, Texas, May 19, 70. I left camp on the 20th of May taking the Kickapoo road. When some fourteen (14) miles out I discovered a party of Indians making across the hills having a herd of horses with them. I charged them and after slight skirmishing they abandoned the herd and took to the mountains. Having secured the horses—9 in number—I resumed my march to Kickapoo Springs and camped for the night. The following morning, I decided to return to the Post with my captured stock, as they would embarrass further operations, as my command was small numbering ten all told.

I accordingly started about 6 o'clock A.M., when about two miles from Kickapoo, I discovered a party of Indians about 20 in number, making for a couple of Government teams, which were about three miles in advance of me. They evidently meant to capture the stock as there was only a small guard with the teams. I immediately attacked them by charging them. They tried hard to make a stand to get their herd of horses off, but I set the Spencers to talking and whistling about their ears so lively that they broke in confusion and fled to the hills, leaving us their herd of five horses. Resuming the march towards Camp, they skirmished along my left flank to the eight mile water hole, evidently being determined to take the stock. I turned my little command loose on them at this place, and after a few volleys they left me to continue my march in peace. I reached camp at 2 P.M. of the 21st with 15 head of horses captured from the Indians.

The casualties of this scout was one horse slightly wounded.

I have the honor to be,

Very respectfully

Your Obt. Servant

Emanuel Stance

Sergeant, Co. "F," 9 Cavalry

Special Order 73, directing Sergeant Emanuel Stance to lead a scouting party from Fort McKavett, May 1870 (Courtesy National Archives and Records Service)

Endorsement

Headquarters Fort McKavett, Texas,

June 1, 1870

Respectfully forwarded to HdQrs Sub Dist. of the Pecos. The gallantry displayed by the Sergeant and his party as well as good judgment used on both occasions, deserves much praise. As this is the fourth and fifth encounter that Sergt. Stance has had with Indians within the past two years, in all of which occasions he has been mentioned for good behavior by his immediate Commanding Officer it is a pleasure to commend him to higher authority.

Henry Carroll,

Captain 9 Cavalry

Commanding Post

Fort McKavett, Texas

July 24, 1870

To the

Adjutant General

United States Army

Washington, D.C.

General:

I have the honor to acknowledge the receipt of a communication of July 9, 1870, from the Adjutant General's Office, inclosing my Medal of Honor. I will cherish the gift as a thing of priceless value and endeavor by my future conduct to merit the high honor conferred upon me.

I have the honor to be,

very respectfully,

Your obedient Servant

Emanuel Stance

Sergeant F Co, 9th Cavy

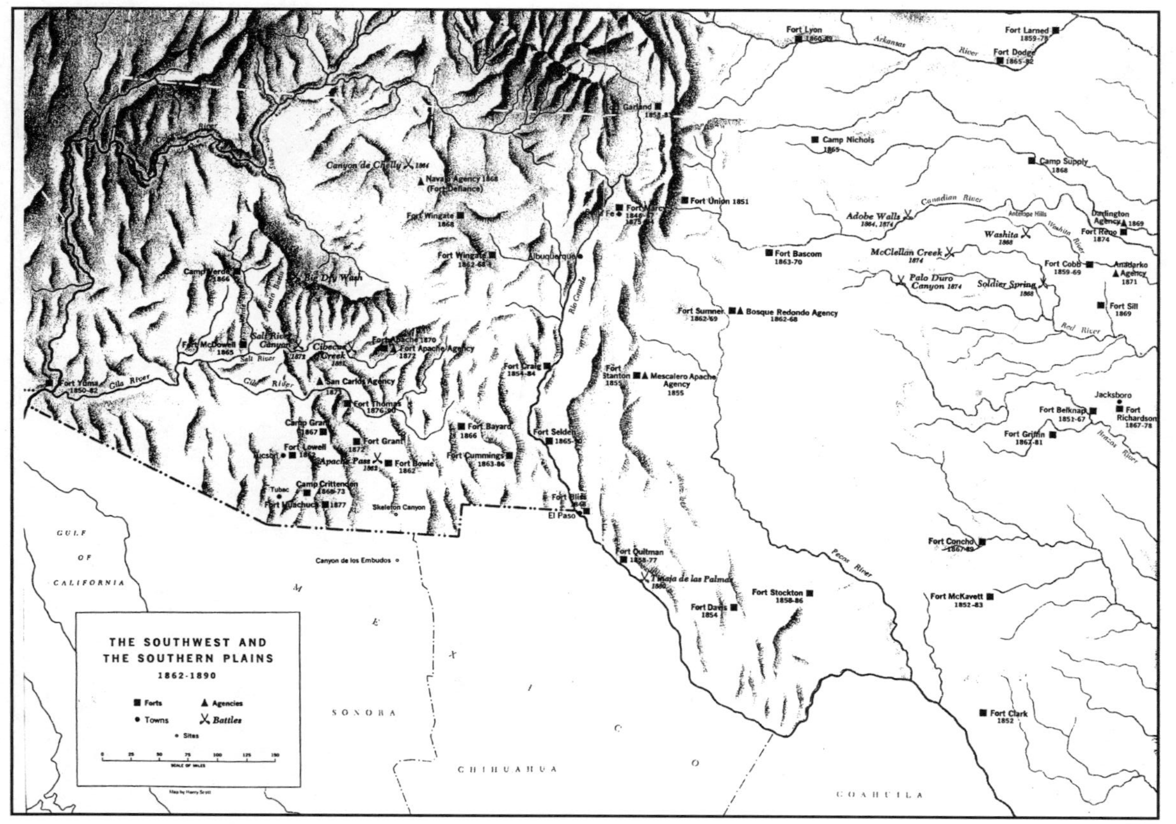
THE SOUTHWEST AND
THE SOUTHERN PLAINS
1862-1890
Forts
Towns
Agencies
Battles
Sites
SCALE OF MILES
Map by Harry Scott
Fort Lyon
Arkansas River
Fort Larned 1859-78
Fort Dodge 1865-82
Camp Nichols 1865
Camp Supply 1868
Fort Union 1851
Canadian River
Adobe Walls 1864, 1874
Antelope Hills
Darlington Agency 1869
Fort Reno 1874
Washita 1868
Washita River
Fort Bascom 1863-70
McClellan Creek 1874
Fort Cobb 1859-69
Anadarko Agency 1871
Palo Duro Canyon 1874
Soldier Spring 1868
Fort Sill 1869
Red River
Fort Sumner 1862-69
Bosque Redondo Agency 1862-68
Albuquerque
Rio Grande
Canyon de Chelly 1864
Navajo Agency 1868 (Fort Defiance)
Fort Wingate 1868
Fort Wingate 1862-68
Camp Verde 1866
Big Dry Wash
Fort McDowell 1865
Salt River Canyon 1872
Salt River
Cibecue Creek
Fort Apache 1870
Fort Apache Agency 1872
Fort Craig 1854-84
Fort Stanton 1855
Mescalero Apache Agency 1855
San Carlos Agency
Fort Yuma 1850-82
Gila River
Fort Thomas 1876-90
Camp Grant 1867
Fort Bayard 1866
Fort Selden 1865
Fort Grant 1872
Fort Lowell
Tucson
Apache Pass
Fort Bowie 1862
Fort Cummings 1863-86
Tubac
Camp Crittenden 1868-73
Fort Huachuca 1877
Skeleton Canyon
El Paso
Jacksboro
Fort Richardson 1867-78
Fort Belknap 1851-67
Fort Griffin 1867-81
Brazos River
Fort Concho 1867-89
Pecos River
Fort Quitman 1858-77
Tinaja de las Palmas
Fort Stockton 1858-86
Fort Davis 1854
Fort McKavett 1852-83
Fort Clark 1852
GULF OF CALIFORNIA
Canyon de los Embudos
M E X I C O
SONORA
CHIHUAHUA
COAHUILA

Chapter Nine

Recollections of active service in Texas, by Sergeant Jacob Wilks, 9th Cavalry

Jacob Wilks, Harrison Bradford, and Emanuel Stance all enlisted in northern Louisiana in October 1866. Stance and Wilks both served as sergeants in Captain Henry Carroll's F Troop during the hard early years in western Texas. At twenty-six, Wilks was several years older than Stance. He had been born a slave in Kentucky, and fled across the Ohio River with his parents as a child. During the Civil War, he served in the 116th U.S. Colored Infantry, and was present at Appomatox Court House, Virginia, on the day of General Robert E. Lee's surrender. Stance was by far the more volatile of the two. Less than a year after receiving the Medal of Honor for bravery in 1870, he was reduced to private, so he was a member of a detachment of eight that left Fort McKavett, Texas, on a scout under Wilks's command. Wilks was also no saint. Shortly after that assignment, he too was reduced to private as a result of the fourth of his five court-martial convictions in nine months, this time for an unauthorized absence and drunkenness. Both men won their stripes back, and Wilks remained in the Army until 1876, received his discharge at Fort Selden, New Mexico, and settled near Fort McKavett. He died in 1922, the oldest black citizen of San Angelo, Texas.[1]

"A Negro Trooper of the Ninth Cavalry"[2]

The reminiscences of soldier life on the border, as given below, were related to John Warren Hunter, at San Angelo, Texas, in 1914, by a negro—a plain old time darkey, whose politeness and respectful bearing toward his superiors commanded the respect and confidence of the white people of San Angelo, among whom he had resided many years. Only a negro, but he had a military record the which any man might be proud, a record substantiated by valuable documents in his possession and by honorable scars that he bore upon his war-battered anatomy.

Jacob Wilks was born a slave, in Kentucky, about thirty miles south of the Ohio river. While yet in infancy, his father and mother gathered their two children in their arms and fled under cover of darkness to the Ohio river, where they found concealment in the jungle until they could attract the attention of a group of fishermen on the north bank of the river. These fishermen, so it chanced, were connected with the "Underground Railroad," of which we have so often heard mention, and of which Mrs. Harriett Beecher Stowe had much to say in "Uncle Tom's Cabin," and being on the alert for runaway negroes, these fishermen soon caught the signal, and during the night, the second out from old Mastah Wilks' plantation, the refugees were taken across the river and landed in the free state of Ohio. A Mrs. Waddell stood ready to receive them and on her farm they were given food, shelter and employment. A year or so later the parents died and their last request was that their benefactress take charge of Jake, and care for him until old enough to take care of himself. Jake grew to manhood in the Waddell family and when the war came on he was among the first to join the army. He enlisted in the 116th regiment colored infantry at Camp Nelson, Ky., and served three years and nine months during which time his regiment saw hard service under Grant in his Virginia campaigns. Wilks had been promoted to a sergeancy during this time and was present at Lee's surrender at Appomattox, after which his regiment was sent to New Orleans and disbanded. The Ninth Cavalry, colored, was being organized and immediately after receiving his discharge from the infantry he enlisted in the Ninth, which was ordered to Texas via Galveston. When the regiment reached San Antonio, the companies were detached and sent to various posts along the border, mainly Forts Concho, McKavett, Stockton, Clark, Davis, Quitman, and Fort Bliss at El Paso. Sergeant Wilks' company was stationed on diverse occasions at posts in New Mexico and Arizona, where they saw hard service while campaigning against Indians.

"In 1873," said Sergeant Wilks, "I was sent with a detail of twelve men of my company to carry the mail to Fort Bliss. Each man carried a mail sack strapped to the cantle of his saddle, and we were armed with seven-shooting Springfield rifles. At Eagle Springs we were attacked by about 100 Apaches. The fight lasted several hours, during which the Indians made repeated charges. We were on an open plain without any protection whatever, but we dismounted, held our horses by the halter-reins, kept close together and withheld our fire until the Indians charged up within close range. Our rapid fire from long range guns wrought such havoc that in the evening they drew off, after killing one of our men. During the fight they made six charges and it was after a repulse of one of these charges that our man Johnson was killed. Contrary to orders, he mounted, dashed away calling us to follow him and charged right in among the Indians and was killed. When the Indians drew off they went in a direction that convinced me that they we going to ambush us in Buss Canyon, through which our route lay and several miles ahead. I decided to thwart their scheme and with the body of Johnson strapped on the horse, we left the road and struck out through the mountains for the Rio Grande below Fort Quitman. Five or six miles out where we had the fight we came to a small valley of loose sandy soil where with our butcher knives and tin cups we scooped out a rude grave and buried our comrade. When we reached the Rio Grande we came up with a mule train belonging to Adams and in charge of a Mr. Naile, which was heavily laden with army supplies and stores for Fort Bliss. We told him that the Indians were near and that we had been fighting them all the day before and for him to corral his wagons at once. He did as directed and had scarcely finished preparations when the Indians appeared in large numbers and a furious attack followed. They were driven off and crossed into Mexico and after they were gone Mr. Naile said to me: 'Sergeant, you just saved my train.'

"It was while I was stationed at Fort McKavett in 1874 that orders came for six companies of the Ninth Cavalry to march to Fort Concho, where we were joined by several companies of infantry and a large supply train. General McKenzie was in command and the object of the expeditions was the destruction of several Indian villages far out on the Staked Plains. We went by way of Fort Griffin where other forces joined us and after long and weary marches we came upon the main village, situated in Tule Canyon. The Indians discovered us long before we reached this canyon and employed every strategy to draw us away from the locality of the village, but General McKenzie was not so easily deceived but kept his column moving toward the canyon. The battle that ensued has been so often described that it is needless that I should go into detail here. We destroyed everything in their village. They had many guns, mostly citizens' rifles, and a good supply of ammunition besides bows, arrows, quivers, lances, etc. These, we destroyed. We found a vast amount of buffalo robes, of which each man made choice of the best—the rest were destroyed. Their tents were made of poles over which hides were stretched and these were all burned. We also captured a vast store of dried turkeys and buffalo meat; also a considerable amount of peculiar food made in the form of a paste from mesquite beans and other ingredients and put up in the maw of deer and buffalo. In this fight the squaws fought like demons and many of them were killed who otherwise would have been spared. We captured 112 prisoners, mostly women, children, old "bucks" and three or four of the younger warriors. These were brought to Fort Concho

Jacob Wilks, with his wife Elizabeth at Fort McKavett, Texas, and later with his daughters Maggie and Mamie Sue, in San Angelo, Texas, about 1901 (Courtesy Margaret Lewis)

Ptebloka by Marty Grant Two Bulls ©

As this cartoon from the *Lakota Times* in the early 1990s shows, Native Americans today do not necessarily agree on the positive connotation of the term "Buffalo Soldier"

and held six or eight months and finally taken to the Fort Sill reservation. While on the march to Fort Concho, three of the younger "bucks" committed suicide by batting out their brains, preferring a violent death to captivity.

"You ask me to tell you about the fight at White Sand Mountain. We were stationed at Fort Davis when scouts reported a large body of Mescalero Apaches passing out towards Mexico. Lieutenant Bullis with a part of two companies immediately took the trail. We followed them four days over a fearfully rough country and while passing their camping places, every sign showed that they had held a big war dance. Late one evening the scout came in and stated that just across the mountains in our front, the Indians had encamped for the night.

This scout was ordered to return and watch the camp and report about midnight. Meantime our pack animals and extra stock were driven into the head of a narrow canyon, while a detail set to work to build a wall at the entrance in order that the stock might be secure. At about the hour of midnight our scout and trailer came in and reported to Lieutenant Bullis. He said the Indians were holding a big war dance and that they seemed to have no apprehension of impending danger. He also described the position of their horse-herd and the approaches to their camp, which was in a small valley with very little timber growth. We were ordered to mount and instructed to move with the utmost silence. The guide led us by a very circuitous route and at dawn we rode out of the valley, where the enemy lay in camp. The Indian in charge of the horse-herd was the first to discover us, and give the alarm, but too late. We charged pell mell into the encampment, killing old and young and but few escaped. Several prisoners were taken, among whom, was an old chief—the most ancient-looking individual I ever saw. He might have been feigning extreme decrepitude, but he gave us the impression that he was utterly helpless. He was too old and venerable in appearance for us to kill; we did not care to be encumbered with him as a prisoner, so we placed a ham of venison and an olla of water near him and left him alone to fare the best he could. We gathered up the spoils, such as we wanted to carry away, destroyed the rest, and with the large herd of captured horses, we started on our return to Fort Davis. Among the prisoners taken was a beautiful Apache girl whose age we took to be about 17 years. She proved to be a most vicious, intractable prisoner and sought every occasion to inflict injury on her captors. She was mounted astride behind one of our troopers who was continually exposed to her sly means of insult and torture. As was the custom, each cavalryman carried a six-shooter in a scabbard or holster the flap of which was buttoned down. Several times this girl was foiled in the act of reaching forward and trying to seize the trooper's pistol and would have succeeded except for the difficulty in releasing the flap from the button. The men reasoned and agreed among themselves that it were better to kill this prisoner than to take the risk of having one or more of their number killed by her, and the morning following this agreement, she made another attempt to get possession of the trooper's pistol and was promptly shot, and nothing was said about it, although it was expected that the offender would have to face court martial.

"I have often been asked about Bullis' Seminole scouts, and the general impression went abroad to the effect that these scouts were Seminole Indians, but this was a mistaken idea. Bullis' scouts were all negroes from Mexico. A number of them were ex-slaves who before and during the war had run off from their masters in Texas and got into Mexico, while the most of them were sons of negro parents who had been adopted into the tribe of Seminole Indians in Florida and went with a branch of that tribe into Mexico when driven from Florida. Many of these were part Indian. They all spoke Spanish; only a few of them, the Texas ex-slaves, spoke any English, and they were conceded to be the best body of scouts, trailers and Indian fighters ever engaged in the Government service along the border. Their efficiency was due wholly to the skill and military genius of Lieutenant Bullis."

Chapter Ten

The earliest known documented use of the name "Buffalo Soldiers"

Although black regulars from the period of the frontier wars are now almost universally known as Buffalo Soldiers, the origins, significance, and prevalence of the phrase are not clear. There is general agreement that the Indians, either the Comanche or Cheyenne, first called the troopers "Buffalo Soldiers," sometime around 1870. Some historians, including William Leckie in his pathbreaking book *The Buffalo Soldiers*, claimed that because the buffalo was so important to these tribes the term was probably meant as a sign of respect and that the soldiers so comprehended it.[1] Since publication of Leckie's book, other writers have followed his lead in this regard.[2] However, since there is no contemporaneous evidence that the soldiers themselves actually used or even referred to this title, any claims concerning their views of the usage remain unproved suppositions.

The earliest known uses date from the early 1870s. Frances Roe, the wife of an Army officer, used the phrase in letters from Camp Supply in Indian Territory that were dated in 1872 but were not published until 1909. The magazine *The Nation* published an article by an unnamed correspondent that contained the term in 1873. Through a reprint in the *Army and Navy Journal*, the article reached a wide military audience and, because it was complimentary of the black troopers, caused quite a stir among white soldiers. From that point into the 1890s, other, usually derogatory nicknames for black troops appeared regularly enough, but few examples of the usage "Buffalo Soldiers" are known.[3] Then, it began to appear with some regularity in articles in the *Army and Navy Journal*, in the writings of Frederic Remington, and elsewhere.[4] Self-referential use by the soldiers themselves—in pension affidavits, black newspapers, or other venues—is virtually unknown. The only instance seems to be the 1929 reminiscence by Reuben Waller reproduced in chapter 5 here.

Frances Roe, whose mention of Buffalo Soldiers dates from 1872, was the wife of Lieutenant Fayette Washington "Faye" Roe of the 3d Infantry. She and her husband served with elements of the 10th Cavalry in Indian Territory during 1872–1873. Her observations on the black soldiers, published almost forty years later, are followed by the *Nation* article and the reaction to its republication by the *Army and Navy Journal.*

Frances M. A. Roe, *Army Letters from an Officer's Wife*[5]

Camp Supply, IT, May 1872: There is one advantage in being with colored troops—one can always have good servants. Mrs. [Captain] Vincent has an excellent colored soldier cook, and the butler was thoroughly trained as such before he enlisted. It did look so funny, however, to see such a black man in a blue uniform.

Camp Supply, IT, June 1872: The officers say that the negroes make good soldiers and fight like fiends. They certainly manage to stick on their horses like monkeys. The Indians call them "Buffalo Soldiers" because their wooly heads are so much like the matted cushion that is between the horns of the buffalo.

Camp Supply, IT, October 1872: Faye says that the colored troops were real soldiers that night [when Camp Supply was attacked by Indians], alert and plucky. I can readily believe that some of them can be alert, and possibly good soldiers, and that they can be good thieves too, for last Saturday night they stole from us the commissary stores we had expected to last us one week—everything, in fact, except coffee, sugar, and such things that we keep in the kitchen, where it is dry.

Camp Supply, IT, February 1873: Many changes have been made during the few weeks General Bourke[6] has been here, the most important having been the separating of the white troops from the colored when on guard duty. The officers and men of the colored cavalry have not liked this, naturally, but it was outrageous to put white and black in the same little guard room, and colored sergeants over white corporals and privates. It was good cause for desertion.

"The Comanches and the Peace Policy"[7]

Fort Sill, Indian Territory, October 5, 1873

Since I have by way of holiday accompanied Gov. Davis, at his request, to the great Indian council to be held with the Comanches and Kioways at this post, I have somewhat of interest to write you. This is the best arranged and most complete military post I have yet seen. The barracks, officers' quarters, and quartermaster's buildings are built of limestone around a square parade-ground of near ten acres area. Hard by are a fine hospital and guard-house. All are kept in fine order by a garrison of (just now) five companies of colored cavalry of the Tenth Regiment, and two companies (colored) and one (white) of infantry. The colored troops (called by the Comanches the "Buffalo Soldiers," because like the buffalo, they are woolly), are in excellent drill and condition. The Indians at first treated them with utter contempt, and when they chanced to kill one would not take his scalp. After a while, when they had had a taste of their fighting qualities, they began to respect them, and to show their respect by scalping a few that they have managed to kill. These "Buffalo Soldiers" are active, intelligent, and resolute men; are perfectly willing to fight the Indians, whenever they may be called upon to do so, and appear to me to be rather superior to the average of white men recruited in time of peace. Their officers explain this by saying that the best colored young men can be recruited in time of peace, while, under the same condition, only indifferent or inferior whites can in general be induced to enlist.

Two miles and a half from this post are the famous Medicine Bluffs, some 280 feet high, perpendicular on the side next the creek, and said to be of basalt. The Governor, Gen. Davidson, who is the commander of this post, with others, myself included, rode out to see them this afternoon, and passed through the Comanche camp, not far off on the other side. We were well armed, of course, and had a squad of "Buffalo Soldiers" along. . . .

Responses.[8]

Fort Sill, I. T.—In the *Journal* of November 8 we copied an article from the *Nation* for the sake of the description it gave of this post. It contained also, unfortunately for us, a comparison between the "Buffalo soldiers" and the white soldiers, which seems to have unnecessarily disturbed some of the latter. We do not publish their letters, for we think we can find better use for our space. . . .

Chapter Eleven

Two old soldiers recall their youth and service in the 25th Infantry, 1870–1880

William Branch was born in southern Virginia and enlisted at Baltimore, Maryland. He outlived two wives and divorced two others. Branch served ten years in the frontier Army and participated in the campaigns against the Comanches, Kiowas, and Cheyennes in 1874–1875. He later joined the Abraham Lincoln Lodge of the National Indian War Veterans in San Antonio and wrote several letters about his military service to *Winners of the West*.[1]

When Branch was in his eighties, he lived with William Watkins, a former comrade in the 25th Infantry, who had also been born a slave on a tobacco plantation in Virginia. They joined the Army at about the same time, but Watkins's service turned out differently. His enlistment was cut short, he claimed, because of a dispute with a noncommissioned officer that led to his dismissal from the service. Both men agreed that the Cheyennes were the tallest Indians they had ever faced, and over the years these Indians grew in their minds until they were seven-foot giants. Branch and Watkins were among many Buffalo Soldiers who stayed in the West after leaving the Army. They were also among a large number who lived together, sharing their meager resources and providing each other mutual support.[2]

Their recollections are two of only a few among the slave narratives recorded by Works Progress Administration employees during the Great Depression of the 1930s to contain any substantial commentary on military service.[3] Some additional accounts mentioned in passing military service, in either in the frontier army or in Cuba and the Philippines. Both of these narratives start with the interviewer's notes.

William Branch's story:[4]

> William Branch, born 1850, 322 Utah St., San Antonio, Texas. Eyesight is so poor someone must lead him to the store or to church. William kneels at his bedside each evening and says his prayers. In this ceremony he spends a half hour or more chanting one Negro spiritual after another.

Yahsur, I was a slave. I was bo'n May 13, 1850, on the place of Lawyer Woodson in Lunenburg County, Virginia. It was 'bout 75 miles southwest of Richmond. They was two big plantations, one on one side the road, yother the yother. My marster owned 75 slaves. He raised tobacco and cotton. I wukked tobacco sometime, sometime cotton. Dere wasn't no whippin' or switchin'. We had to wuk hard. Marster Woodson was a rich man. He live in a great big house, a lumber house painted white. And it had a great big garden.

De slaves lives in a long string of log houses. Dey had dirt floors and shingle roofs. Marster Woodson's house was shingle roof too. We had home cured bacon and veg'tables, dried co'n, string beans and dey give us hoe cakes baked in hot ashes. Dere always was lots of fresh milk.

How'd us slaves git de clothes? We carded the cotton, den de women spin it on a spinnin'wheel. After dat day sew de gahment togeddah on a sewin' machine. Yahsur, we's got sewin' machine, wid a big wheel and a handle. One woman tu'n de handle and de yuther woman do de sewin'.

Dat's how we git de clothes for de 75 slaves. Marster's clothes? We makes dem for de whole fam'ly. De missis send de pattern and de slaves makes de clothes. Over nigh Richmond a fren' of Marster Woodson has 300 slaves. Dey makes all de clothes for dem.

I was with Marster twel de Yankees come down to Virginia in 1861. De sergeant of de Yankees takes me up on his hoss and I goes to Washington wid de Yankees. I got to stay dere 'cause I'd run away from my marster.

I stay at de house of Marse Frank Cayler. He's an ole time driver. I was his houseboy. I stay dere twel de year 1870, den I goes to Baltimore and jines de United States Army. We's sent to Texas 'count of the Indians bein' so bad. Dey put us on a boat at Baltimore and we landed at Galveston.

Den we marches from Galveston to Fort Duncan. It was up, up, de whole time. We ties our bedclothes and rolls dem in a bundle wid a strap. We walks wid our guns and bedclothes on our backs, and de wagons wid de rations follows us. Dey is pulled by mules. We goes 15 miles ev'ry day. We got no tents, night come, we unrolls de blankets and sleeps under de trees, sometime under de brush.

For rations we got canned beans, milk and hardtack. De hard tacks is 3 or 4 in a box, we wets 'em in water and cooks 'em in a skillet. We gits meat purty often. When we camps for de night de captain say, "You'all kin go huntin'." Before we git to de mountains dere's deer and rabbits and dey ain't no fences. Often in de dark we sees a big animal and we shoots. When we bring 'im to camp, de captain say, "Iffen de cow got iron burns de rancher gwinter shoot hisself a nigger scout." But de cow ain't got no iron, it's—what's de name of de cow what ain't feel de iron? Mavrick, yahsuh. We eats lots of dem Mavricks. We's goin' long de river bottom, and before we comes to Fort Duncan, we sees de cactus and muskeet. Dere ain't much cattle, but one colored scout shoots hisself a bear. Den we eats high. Fort Duncan were made of slab lumber and de roof was gravel and grass.

Den we's ordered to Fort Davis and we's in de mountains now. Climb, climb all day, and de Indians give us a fit ev'ry day. We kills some Indians, dey kills a few soldiers. We was at Fort Clark for a while. At Fort Davis I jines de colored Indian Scouts. I was in Capt. George Andrews's Co. K.

We's told de northern Cheyennes is on a rampus and we's goin' to Fort Sill in Indian Territory. Before we gits to Fort Concho (San Angelo) de Comanches and de Apaches give us a fit. We fitten' 'em all de time and when we gits away from de Comanches and Apaches we fitten de Cheyennes. Dey's seven feet tall. Dey couldn't come through that door.

When we gits to Fort Sill, Gen. Davidson say de Cheyennes is off de reservation, and he say, "You boys is got to git dem back. Iffen you kill 'em, dey can't git back to de reservation." Den we goes scoutin' for de Cheyennes and dey is scoutin' for us. Dey gits us first, on de Wichita River was 500 of 'em, and we got 75 colored Indian Scouts. Den Red Foot, de Chief of de Cheyennes, he come to see Capt. Lawson and say he want rations for his Indians. De captain say he cain't give no rations to Indians off de reservation. Red Foot say he don't care 'bout no reservation and he say he take what we got. Capt. Lawson 'low we gotter git reinforcements. We got a guide in de scout troop, he call hisself Jack Kilmartin. De Captain say, "Jack, I'se in trouble, how kin I git a dispatch to Gen. Davidson?" Jack say, "I kin git it through." And Jack, he crawl on his belly and through de brush and he lead a pony, and when he gits clear he rides de pony bareback twel he git to Fort Sill. Den Gen. Davidson, he soun' de gin'ral alarm and he send two companies of cavalry to reinforce us. But de Cheyennes give 'em a fit all de way, dey's gotter cut dere way through de Cheyennes.

And Col. Shafter comes up, and goes out in de hills in his shirt sleeves jus' like you's a sittin' dere. Dey's snow on de groun' and de wind's cole, but de colonel don't care, and he say, "Whut's dis order Gen. Davidson give? Don' kill de Cheyennes? You kill 'em all from de cradle to de Cross."

And den we starts de attack. De Cheyennes got Winchesters and rifles and repeaters from de government. Yahsur, de government give 'em de guns dey used to shoot us. We got de ole fashion muzzle loaders. You puts one ball in de muzzle and shove de powder down wid de ramrod. Den we went in and fit 'em, and 'twer like fightin' a wasp's nest. Dey kills a lot of our boys and we nearly wipes 'em out. Den we disarms de Cheyennes we capture, and turns dere guns in to de regiment.

I come to San Antonio after I'se mustered out and goes to work for de Bell Jewelry Company and stays dere twel I cain't work no more. Did I like the army? Yahsuh, I'd ruthuh be in de army den a plantation slave.

William Watkins's story:[5]

> William Watkins, born 1850, to Julia and Hudson Watkins. All were slaves on the Watkins plantation where William was born, on the edge of Charlotte County, Virginia. William is tall, heavy set, and does not look his age. He lives with William Branch, who came from an adjoining county in Virginia. Both men served in the same campaigns in the United States Army.

My name is William Watkins. De name comes frum de name of Terbaccer Watkins, who owned de Watkins Terbaccer Plantation. He got a factory in Richmond and de plantation in Charlotte County in Virginia, 'bout 50 mile east of Richmond. Marse Watkins got a big frame house and 400 acres and 100 acres is terbaccer. Yassuh, dey's other crops—barley, oats, and den dey's stock—hogs, cows, hosses, and mules.

We lives in log cabins wid plank floors and we made de beds ourself. Dey feeds us good and we gits milk and bread and lotsa pork. Marse Watkins got lotsa hogs.

Yassuh, we's got a church. De slaves built it in de woods. We never got no wages but sometimes he give us four bits or six bits. What we do wid it? We buys candy. Sometimes we run de rabbits or goes fishing. De Marster gives us lil' patches of groun'. He's good but de overseer's rough. He whips all de slaves.

Dey's a patrol what watches for slaves dat runs away, but we don't have no patrol on our plantation. We has dances Sat'day nights. Sundays we didn't wuk much.

Dey's ghosts dere—we seed 'em. Dey's white people wid a sheet on 'em to scare de slaves offen de plantation. We wears charms to keep us well. Dere's asafoetida in a bag and we wear's it roun' de neck. It cure most ev'ryting. When we gits real sick, dey sends medicine frum de big house.

Ev'ry year de slave traders come and de Marster sells some slaves down river to New Orleans. Who dey sell? Jes' no count slaves. Dey walks all de way. De traders dey rides in ox-carts. We never wuk much Sundays, only to milk de cows. Jes' dat. Yessuh, I was married on de plantation. De preacher say de words and we's married.

Den de war come and de Yankees come down thick as leaves. Dey burns de big house and de slave houses and ev'rything. Dey turns us loose. We ain't got no home or nuthin' to eat, 'cause dey tells us we's free.

We's gotta leave de plantation. De Marster's gone, de crops is gone, de stock's gone. We goes to anudder place and works on shares. De first time we sees de Ku Klux is right after de war. Dey whips de slaves what leaves the plantations, dey don' wan' dem to be free.

'Bout 1870 I goes to Ohio and enlists in de army at Jefferson Barracks and right off dey sends us to Texas to fight Indians. I goes to San Antonio and dey puts us on guard at de Alamo to fight off de Indians. Den I goes to Fort Davis. I'm in de cullud Indian Scouts, Co. K, and dey's a banker name of Miller in de Chihuahua jail. One night de kuhnel takes us from Fort Davis, and we marches all night wid guns and 150 rounds of ammunition in belts, and rations for 30 days. We marches all night long twel we gits to Del Norte, Texas (Presidio) and we crosses de river and takes Mr. Miller out of jail.

While we's at Fort Davis a wagon train comes through de canyon and de Apaches rolls big rocks down on de white people and kills 26 of dem. Dey scalps all dey kills and we go out and fit de Apaches. De lieutenant is killed in de fight. Yassuh, we fit Apaches all de time and when we goes to Fort Concho dey gives us a fit all 'long de road. Den we fitten de Cheyennes and dey is wust of all. Dey's great big Indians 'bout seven feet tall and at de battle of de Wichita in de Indian Territory a Cheyenne shoots an arrer through my wrist. (He exhibited the scar. Same battle described in interview with Wm. Branch.)

Den after my wound heals we's sent to Fort Clark and de sergeant, Jeff Walker, got it in for me. Kuhnel Andrews is at Fort Davis and Jeff Walker trumps up some charges dat I'se mistrusted, so dey gives me a dishonnuble discharge 'cause of dat Jeff Walker. I ain't had no court martial nor no trial and I cain't get no pension 'count of de dishonnuble discharge.

And now I'se strong and well but I cain't get no wuk 'cause I'se so ole. And 'cause' Jeff Walker didn't like me, I gits a dishonnuble discharge.

Chapter Twelve

Captain J. Lee Humfreville's court-martial conviction, 1874

Convictions of officers for brutality toward their enlisted men were rare. Extremely vicious behavior, such as that of Lieutenant Edward Heyl in 1867, could go unpunished, but Captain Humfreville of the 9th Cavalry exceeded even the very elastic limits of the time in his treatment of his men during a march in Texas during the winter of 1872–1873. The court-martial order detailed in a repetitive military legalese style the actions that led to his dismissal, after thirteen years of service, including eight in the 9th Cavalry.

Twenty-five years after he was cashiered, Humfreville published his reminiscences of the frontier. He had some observations about the frontier army, but never mentioned that he had commanded black troops. A chapter called "The American Trooper as an Indian Fighter" made no mention of the 9th Cavalry. As far as he was concerned, the conflict in the West involved whites and Indians.[1]

General Court-Martial
Orders No. 23

War Department
Adjutant General's Office
Washington, April 3, 1874

I. Before a General Court Martial which convened at San Antonio, Texas, December 4, 1873, pursuant to Special Orders No. 212, dated October 27; No. 222, dated November 8; and No. 230, dated November 18, 1873, War Department, Adjutant General's office, Washington, D. C., and of which Lieutenant Colonel William R. Shafter, 24th Infantry, is President, was arraigned and tried—

Captain *J. Lee Humfreville*, 9th Cavalry.

Charge I.—"Conduct prejudicial to good order and military discipline."

Specification 1st—"In this: that he, Captain *J. Lee Humfreville*, 9th Cavalry, while on detached service per Special orders No. 136, Headquarters, Department of Texas, series of 1872, and Special Orders No. 134, Headquarters Post of

Fort Clark, Texas, series of 1872, in command of an escort, consisting of his, Captain *Humfreville's*, Company 'K,' 9th Cavalry, detailed to protect a surveying party, did, without proper authority, abandon said command, in the vicinity of Weatherford, Texas, without turning the command over properly to the officer next in rank, 2d Lieutenant D. H. Floyd, 9th Cavalry, and did remain absent for about ten days, visiting the city of Galveston, Texas, in the meanwhile. This on or about the 26th day of November, 1872, until the 6th day of December 1872, at or near the places specified above."

Specification 2d—"In this: that he, Captain *J. Lee Humfreville*, 9th Cavalry, commanding Company 'K,' 9th Cavalry, *en route* from Fort Richardson to Fort Clark, Texas, *via* Forts Griffin, Concho, and McKavett, a distance of 450 miles, accomplished in nineteen (19) marching days, did without justification, summarily and illegally punish Privates Rufus Slaughter, James Imes, Jerry Williams, Levi Comer, Henry Robinson, Jim Wade, and Farrier, now Private E. Tucker, all of 'K' Company, 9th Cavalry, by causing them to be handcuffed in pairs, and fastened in a gang two abreast, by a rope, to the rear of an army wagon, and in this manner compelling them to march and keep up with the said wagon moving at an average rate of twenty-five miles a day when the command marched, the said wagon and its team going at a trot whenever practicable; this punishment lasting, in the case of the aforesaid Slaughter, Imes, Williams, and Comer, throughout the march between the posts specified; and in the case of the aforesaid Tucker, until the 24th day of December, 1872, at or near Phantom Hill, Texas; in the case of the aforesaid Wade, until the 30th of December, 1872; and of the aforesaid Robinson, until his discharge at Fort McKavett, Texas, January 6, 1873; and, moreover, did further from the time of leaving Fort Richardson until the arrival of the command at Phantom Hill, about December 24, 1872, every day after the arrival of his wagons in camp, cause the said Privates Slaughter, Imes, Williams, Comer, Wade, Robinson, and Tucker, each to carry a log weighing twenty-five pounds, more or less, and, manacled in couples, to walk before a sentinel till 12 o'clock midnight; and did, after the last named date, cause the aforesaid Privates Slaughter, Imes, Williams, and Comer to walk a ring as stated above, with the exception of requiring each to carry a log, until the arrival of the command at Fort Clark, Texas; and did cause the aforesaid Privates Robinson and Wade to do the same until released as above stated, and did, also, as a further punishment, cause each and every one of the men named above, while undergoing treatment as above recited, to be deprived of coffee and every article of food the rest of the company received, except bread and meat. All this from the 15th of December, 1872, to the 20th January, 1873, between those dates, and at and about the places and dates specified above."

Charge II.—"Drunkenness on duty."

Specification—"In this: that Captain *J. Lee Humfreville*, 9th Cavalry, while in command of his company on the march on detached service per Special orders No. 136, Headquarters, Department of Texas, series of 1872, and Special Orders No. 134, Headquarters Post of Fort Clark, Texas, series of 1872, did become drunk. This on the road from Black Springs, or Willow Branch, Texas, to Fort Richardson, Texas, on or about the 12th day of December, 1872."

Charge III.—"Conduct unbecoming an officer and a gentleman."

Specification 1st—"In this: that he, Captain *J. Lee Humfreville*, 9th Cavalry, commanding Company 'K,' 9th Cavalry, on escort duty with a surveying party of the Texas Pacific Railroad, per Special orders No. 136, Headquarters Department of Texas, series of 1872, and Special orders No. 134, headquarters Post of Fort Clark, Texas, series of 1872, and having absented himself from his command, in the vicinity of Weatherford, Texas, remaining absent therefrom from about the 26th day of November, 1872, to the 6th day of December, 1872, (without proper authority, and without turning over his command in the proper manner,) did sign, at some time subsequent to his return, the official morning report books of his company, wherein he was recorded as present for duty with his company during the whole time of his absence, thus vouching for the correctness of the morning report in said books for each and every day of the said time, which record of his presence for the time alleged was false, and known to be so by him, the said Captain *Humfreville*. All this near Weatherford, in the State of Texas, and on or about or subsequent to the dates specified."

Specification 2d—"In this: that he, Captain *J. Lee Humfreville*, 9th Cavalry, commanding Company 'K,' 9th Cavalry, did render to the Headquarters of his regiment and the Adjutant General's office a monthly return of his company for the month of November, 1872, signed by himself, and dated 'In the field, November 30, 1872,' in which return the said Captain *Humfreville* is reported as present for duty, which return was false, within the knowledge of Captain *Humfreville*, in as much as on the 30th November, 1872, the date on which the report was required and purported to be made out, and for several days prior and subsequent thereto, the said Captain *Humfreville* was absent from his company without proper authority. This at or near Weatherford, Texas, about the date specified."

Specification 3d—"In this: that he, Captain *J. Lee Humfreville,* 9th Cavalry, commanding Company 'K.' 9th Cavalry, did, without justification, brutally maltreat Private Jerry Williams, an enlisted man of his company, by striking the said Williams over the head with a carbine, when he, the said Williams, was in a defenseless position, being held by two non-commissioned officers, and did again shortly afterward strike him over the head with a club, when the said Williams was still at his mercy, suspended from a tree. This at or near Fort Richardson, Texas, on or about the 15th day of December, 1872."

Specification 4th—"In this: that he, Captain *J. Lee Humfreville,* 9th Cavalry, commanding Company 'K.' 9th Cavalry, did brutally cause private Malachi G. Pope, Company 'K,' 9th Cavalry, to be thrown into a stream of water at a time when the weather was very cold; this to the great jeopardy of the health of said Pope, who became so stiff, and whose condition otherwise, party or wholly in consequence of the above treatment, became such that it necessitated his removal to the post hospital. This at or near Fort Richardson, Texas, on or about December 15, 1872."

Specification 5th—"In this: that he, Captain *J. Lee Humfreville*, 9th Cavalry, commanding Company 'K,' 9th Cavalry, *en route* from Fort Richardson to Fort Clark, Texas, *via* Forts Griffin, Concho, and McKavett, a distance of 450 miles, accomplished in nineteen (19) marching days, did without justification, summarily and illegally punish Privates Rufus Slaughter, James Imes, Jerry Williams, Levi Comer, Henry Robinson, Jim Wade, and Farrier, now Private E. Tucker, all of 'K' Company, 9th Cavalry, by causing them to be handcuffed in pairs, and fastened in a gang two abreast, by a rope, to the rear of an army wagon, and in this manner compelling them to march and keep up with the said wagon moving at an average rate of twenty-five miles a day when the command marched, the said wagon and its team going at a trot whenever practicable; this punishment lasting, in the case of the aforesaid Slaughter, Imes, Williams, and Comer, throughout the march between the posts specified; and in the case of the aforesaid Tucker, until the 24th day of December, 1872, at or near Phantom Hill, Texas; in the case of the aforesaid Wade, until the 30th of December, 1872; and of the aforesaid Robinson until his discharge at Fort McKavett, Texas, January 6, 1873; and, moreover, did further from the time of leaving Fort Richardson until the arrival of the command at Phantom Hill, about December 24, 1872, every day after the arrival of his wagons in camp, cause the said Privates Slaughter, Imes, Williams, Comer, Wade, Robinson, and Tucker, each to carry a log weighing twenty-five pounds, more or less, and, manacled in couples, to walk before a sentinel till 12 o'clock midnight; and did, after the last named date, cause the aforesaid Privates Slaughter, Imes, Williams, and Comer to walk a ring as stated above, with the exception of requiring each to carry a log, until the arrival of the command at Fort Clark, Texas; and did cause the aforesaid Privates Robinson and Wade to do the same until released as above stated, and did, also, as a further punishment, cause each and every one of the men named above, while undergoing treatment as above recited, to be deprived of coffee and every article of food the rest of the company received, except bread and meat. All this from the 15th of December, 1872, to the 20th January, 1873, between those dates, and at and about the places and dates specified above."

Specification 6th—"In this: that he, Captain *J. Lee Humfreville*, 9th Cavalry, commanding Company 'K,' 9th Cavalry, while causing Privates Rufus Slaughter, James Imes, Jerry Williams, Levi Comer, Henry Robinson, Jim Wade, and Farrier, now Private E. Tucker, all of 'K,' Company, 9th Cavalry, to undergo the treatment specified in the 5th specification to the 3d charge, during the march from Fort Richardson to Fort Griffin, Texas, did brutally refuse to allow them to have any fire in camp for their use in warming themselves or drying their clothes; this notwithstanding their exposure to wet and cold by being forced to wade through mud and water, and the coldness and inclemency of the weather during the time, and the fact that the enlisted men named were not supplied with a change of clothing. All this to the bodily injury of, and causing suffering to, the said men at and *en route* between the posts above specified, from the 16th to the 22d December, 1872, both days inclusive."

Specification 7th—"In this: that he, Captain *J. Lee Humfreville*, 9th Cavalry, commanding Company 'K,' 9th Cavalry, while causing Privates Rufus Slaughter, James Imes, Jerry Williams, Levi Comer, Henry Robinson, Jim Wade, and Farrier, now Private E. Tucker, all of 'K,' Company, 9th Cavalry, to undergo the exhaustive treatment specified in the 5th specification, 3d charge, did refuse to allow or neglect to furnish them, the said enlisted men, the same shelter at night that the remainder of the company were provided with; this while all or some of said men were insufficiently supplied with blankets, which fact the said Captain *Humfreville* failed and neglected to ascertain or to remedy. All this to the bodily injury of, and causing suffering to, the said men on the march from Fort Richardson, Texas, to Fort McKavett, Texas, from the 15th December, 1872, to about the 1st January, 1873, the weather during a greater portion of the time being unusually cold and inclement."

Specification 8th—"In this: that he, Captain *J. Lee Humfreville*, 9th Cavalry, commanding Company 'K,' 9th Cavalry, did, without justification, brutally maltreat Private James Imes, an enlisted man of his company, by striking the said Imes several times with his fist and once with a revolver or club, the said Imes being so struck when he was in a defenseless condition, *while* he was being held and tied by the hands. This at or near Fort Richardson, Texas, on or about the 15th day of December, 1872."

To which charges and specifications the accused, Captain *J. Lee Humfreville*, 9th Cavalry, pleaded "Not Guilty."

Finding.

The court, having maturely considered the evidence adduced, finds the accused, Captain *J. Lee Humfreville*, 9th Cavalry, as follows:

Charge I.

Of the 1st *Specification*, "Guilty."

Of the 2d *Specification*, "Guilty, excepting the figures '450,' substituting therefore the word and figures 'about 402;' the words 'twenty-five,' substituting therefor the words 'twenty-one;' the words 'the said wagon and its team going at the speed of a trot whenever practicable;' the words 'this punishment lasting, in the cases of the aforesaid Slaughter, Imes, Williams, and Comer, throughout the march between the posts specified,' substituting therefor the words 'this punishment lasting, in the cases of the aforesaid Slaughter, Imes, and Williams, throughout the march between the posts specified,' the Court finding that the being compelled to march fastened behind a wagon lasted in the case of Comer until the arrival of the command at Fort McKavett on the 31st December, 1872; the words 'Fort Clark,' where they appear immediately after the words 'with the exception of requiring each to carry a log until the arrival of the command at,' substituting therefore the words 'Fort McKavett,' and of the excepted words, Not Guilty."

Of the Charge, "Guilty."

Charge II.

Of the *Specification*, "Not Guilty."

Of the Charge, "Not Guilty."

Charge III.

Of the 1st *Specification*, "Guilty."

Of the 2d *Specification*, "Guilty, excepting the words 'and the Adjutant General's office,' and of the excepted words, Not Guilty."

Of the 3d *Specification*, "Guilty, excepting the words 'without justification' and 'brutally,' and of the excepted words Not Guilty; but the Court attaches no criminality to the remainder of the specification under the circumstances then existing."

Of the 4th *Specification*, "Guilty, excepting the word 'brutally;' the words 'this to the great jeopardy of the health of said Pope, who became so stiff,' and the words 'partly or wholly in consequence of the above treatment,' and of the excepted words, Not Guilty."

Of the 5th *Specification*, "Guilty, excepting the figures '450,' substituting therefor the figures 'about 402;' the words 'twenty-five,' substituting therefore the words 'twenty-one;' the words 'the said wagon and its team going at the speed of a trot whenever practicable;' the words 'this punishment lasting, in the cases of the aforesaid Slaughter, Imes, Williams, and Comer, throughout the march between the posts specified,' substituting therefor the words 'this punishment lasting, in the cases of the aforesaid Slaughter, Imes, and Williams, throughout the march between the posts specified,' the Court finding that the being compelled to march fastened behind a wagon lasted in the case of Comer until the arrival of the command at Fort McKavett on the 31st December, 1872; the words 'Fort Clark,' where they appear immediately after the words 'with the exception of requiring each to carry a log until the arrival of the command at,' substituting therefore the words 'Fort McKavett,' and of the excepted words, Not Guilty."

Of the 6th *Specification*, "Guilty."

Of the 7th *Specification*, "Not Guilty."

Of the 8th *Specification*, "Guilty, excepting the words 'without justification, brutally,' and of the excepted words, Not Guilty; but the Court attaches no criminality to the remainder of the specification under the circumstances then existing."

Of the Charge, "Guilty."

Sentence.

And the Court does therefore sentence him, Captain *J. Lee Humfreville*, 9th Cavalry, "*To be dismissed [from] the service.*"

II. The proceedings in the foregoing case of Captain *J. Lee Humfreville*, 9th Cavalry, are approved.

All the findings are approved except the findings on the third and eighth specifications to the third charge, which, as far as they excuse the conduct of the accused, are disapproved.

The sentence is approved.

III. Captain *J. Lee Humfreville*, 9th Cavalry, ceases to be an officer of the Army from the date of this order.

IV. The General Court Martial of which Lieutenant Colonel William R. Shafter, 24th infantry, is President is hereby dissolved.

By Order of the Secretary of War:

E. D. Townsend

Chapter Thirteen

A RESOLUTION OF MOURNING

The same issue of the *Army and Navy Journal* that reported the Humfreville court-martial contained an expression of grief from members of the 9th Cavalry and 24th Infantry because of the death of Senator Charles Sumner of Massachusetts.[1] Sumner had been one of the most consistent and most ardent promoters of the abolition of slavery, and the soldiers stated their sadness and sympathy for the old Republican's family. The soldiers, stationed at remote Ringgold Barracks, near the head of navigation on the Rio Grande in Texas, paid attention to the news, were aware of its significance, organized a public meeting, and wrote and published its result. This resolution is a very early example of what later became widespread practice among the black regulars. Over the next half century, they many times acted in a similar concerted fashion, taking positions, expressing grievances, and warning hostile whites of possible retaliation.

Department Of Texas

Brigadier-Gen. C. C. Augur: Headquarters, San Antonio, Texas

. . . *Ninth Cavalry.*—At a meeting of the members of the Ninth Cavalry and Twenty-fourth Infantry of Ringgold Barracks, Texas, on March 18, 1874, the following resolutions were unanimously adopted:

"*Whereas,* It has pleased the Almighty God, the great and just Ruler of the universe, to remove from this stage of action, the advocate of our equal rights with all men, Honorable Charles Sumner, U.S. Senator, from Massachusetts, therefore be it

"*Resolved,* That while we bow in humble submission to the works of the Divine Ruler, we greatly deplore the loss of such a noble friend as was the Honorable Mr. Sumner to our race, as a reference to his history (which is a part of the history of the country for the past thirty years) will show;

"*Resolved,* That in the death of Honorable Charles Sumner, the country loses one of its most faithful servants, the republican party a hard working, untiring, and zealous member, and the colored people of the United States, a true friend, as Mr. Sumner has shown himself to be ever since his connection with the Senate;

"*Resolved,* That we deeply sympathize with the family and friends of the deceased in their sad bereavement;

"*Resolved,* That a copy of these resolutions may be forwarded to the family of the deceased, and to the *New National Era,* the *Washington Chronicle,* New York *Times*, and the *Army and Navy Journal*, for publication.

Chas. Chinn, Saddler Sergeant
Ninth Cavalry, Chairman

Joseph Rey, Sergeant Major
Ninth Cavalry, Secretary

Chapter Fourteen

Perry Hayman's recollections of service with the 10th Cavalry

The military campaigns on the Southern Plains peaked in 1874 and 1875, and the 10th Cavalry was in the middle of the action. The destruction of the buffalo, the corrosive effects of whisky, and the spread of white settlement all helped precipitate the crisis that forced a military conclusion.[1] As Private Perry Hayman of the 10th drolly observed, "the Indians were mad sure enough. . ."

Private Hayman was born near Philadelphia. He enlisted at the age of 20 and served two five-year enlistments, in the 10th Cavalry and the 25th Infantry. He was with the 10th during some of the heaviest fighting around Fort Sill, Indian Territory, in 1874, and at the Cheyenne and Arapaho Agency (later Fort Reno, Indian Territory) during the following year. This reminiscence of his service was published fifty years after the actions described.[2]

Mr. Geo. W. Webb, Pub.
Dear Comrade:

In reply to your letter concerning Indian War pensions allow me the privilege to narrate this sketch. I enlisted on the 6th day of January, 1874, in Philadelphia, and was sent to the St. Louis barracks, and in February, 1874, was assigned to the 10th Cavalry, arriving at Fort Sill, Indian Territory, on the 22nd day of February, and was assigned to Troop M under Captain Stephen T. Novele, Colonel Grierson commanding the 10th Cavalry. I was drilled from the 22nd day of February until the 8th of March. Troop M was then detailed on summer campaign, and went into camp at Camp Beaver, Texas, where we remained until about the middle of May, 1874. Prior to this time I did not use tobacco. During this time the supply train came in with the rations. Of course we had to accept that which was issued. Well, about the middle of the month the boys ran out of their supply of tobacco, but as I did not use it, I still retained mine. Some of you old timers will agree with me when I say that a man was out of luck in those days when he was shy on tobacco. To make a long story short I sold my tobacco at auction. I cut the plug in half, receiving $4.50 for one piece, and $4.00 for the other piece. This incident was the beginning of good times, as I thought, not knowing that reverse times were just around the corner, so to speak.

Now my first excitement as a soldier occurred in April, 1874, in this manner. A man and his son whose name we did not know, came into camp with a wagon load of candies, cakes, and such things that would appeal to the taste of a soldier. There were two troops of us, C and M.

A soldier by the name of Charles Holden of C Troop, thinking this peddler had whiskey, deliberately shot the son dead and mortally wounded the father in an attempt to rob them. We all heard the shots fired. Now as a matter of fact we were in a bad Indian country, and naturally our captain hearing a shot fired, at once started to investigate its origin. Finding no trace of hostile Indians, the captain at once reached the conclusion that the shot must have been fired by one of our men. On further investigation we discovered the dead and wounded men. Now the captain after propping up the father against a stump had the two troops formed in single file, and marched past the wounded man for identification. Now right here, comrades allow me to state that although I knew I was innocent, I sure was a scared recruit, thinking he might mistake me for the guilty one. As each man marched by him the injured man would shake his head in the negative until Holden confronted him. Though mortally wounded when he saw Holden he tried to get up and get to him, thereby proving beyond a doubt that Chas. Holden was the guilty one. Holden was arrested, placed in double irons, and turned over to the civil authorities at Fort Smith, Texas. I have never heard of Holden since. The injured man did not live thirty minutes longer, after he identified Holden.

Early in May the Indians attacked a ranch about six miles from Camp Beaver. The rancher had two men and this fact the Indians were aware of, and they took advantage of the situation. The rancher managed in some way to dispatch a courier to the camp for help and M Troop responded. This occurred about 11 o'clock in the forenoon. We took out after those Indians, who in meantime had sighted us, and we chased them from 11 o'clock until about the edge of dark. I want to note that the larger number of us were recruits and in the saddle for the first time. Darkness caused our commander to abandon the chase and the recruits when they dismounted were unable to stand erect. We made a dry camp that night, and the next day we started back to Camp Beaver, and it took us three days to return, while during the chase we covered the distance in about 6 or 7 hours. Several of the recruits were forced to go on sick report as a sequel to the outcome of that ride. In the latter part of May we were ordered to Fort Sill, Indian Territory, and in October ordered on a general co-operating campaign with General Miles. The troops represented were C, D, H, L, K and M. We camped at the base of Mt. Scott preparatory to being inspected by Gen. Philip Sheridan, prior to entering the campaign. First Sergeant Levi Hainer of M Troop detailed me on the greatest detail that ever befell me in my ten years of army career. He detailed me to act as mounted orderly to Gen. Phil Sheridan. Let me add that I was still a recruit. Some of you readers will remember about this period, October, 1874, when the Indians were mad sure enough, and to add to the deal Lieut. Papoon on the first day in camp committed suicide, about eight miles from Fort Sill. The next day we scouted the plains, and did so until the last of October. Now General Miles' command had driven the Indians our way, and we ran into them at Goose Creek. We captured a band of 205 and 2000 ponies. After a general roundup we started for Fort Sill. On the night of October 28th along about 8 o'clock, the whole herd of horses stampeded. Every horse got away but one, the trumpeter's horse, Charles Hazzard. We recovered the horses the next day, and they gave me a log the next day as a reward for my horse breaking his side lines, and I carried that log two hours. I am still mad over the incident yet, this happened in 1874. I ought to have an increase in pension for that. The next day we started for Fort Sill, arriving about the first week in November. The chief of the band we captured was Lone Wolf. He was sent to Atlanta, Ga. We came in off that campaign and remained until February, 1875. I had been in the army just three months when I was made a corporal.

My troop was detailed on detached service at Cheyenne Agency. We had no clothes with us except those we had on, and we stayed 72 days. The cooties had full possession of our backs, and that demanded the greater part of our attention for quite a while. Everything went all right until the 6th of April, 1875, when Chief Stone Calf's Indians came into the Cheyenne Agency with two white girls. Stone Calf's warriors had overtaken the family, and after killing the father, mother and son, made captives of the two girls. In the meantime, a courier had come in and told us that the Indians were there with the two girls. There were three troops of cavalry stationed at Cheyenne Agency at this time, D and M of the 10th, and M of the 6th, and two companies of the 11th Infantry. We received orders to saddle up and rescue the girls, in which we were successful. While we were engaged in putting the brave that led the band in irons, a squaw ran out, waved a blanket, gave the warwhoop, and 'then the fun began.' The Indians broke for cover, and by the time M Troop of the 10th got there the Indians had crossed the north fork of the Canadian River. As the first set of fours crossed the river, the Indians opened up on us, and Corp. George Berry[3] was wounded. After we

WINNERS OF THE WEST

A Campaign Paper Published in the Interests of the Veterans of All Indian Wars, Their Widows and Orphan Children

ST. JOSEPH, MISSOURI, APRIL, 1924

VICTIMS OF WAR AGAINST THE SIOUX

Colonel Norris Tells of Burial of Men Killed in Indian War

Veterinary surgeon and sutler of one of Custer's campaigns sleep in graves recently discovered near Calabar.

Declaring that he was a scout with the Custer and Stanley expedition in 1873, when a little skirmish with the Sioux Indians took place on the north side of the Yellowstone river resulting in the death of two white men, Colonel G. R. Norris of Great Falls, writes that one of the men was a veterinary surgeon, a Dr. Halsinger by name, who with his sutler, were the victims of that engagement.

This incident in the early frontier history of this section of the state is recalled by the fact that recently Patrick and James McEvoy of Calabar, reported the discovery of the graves of these two white men, but no traces of their names could be found as the markings, which were upon a lone cottonwood tree, had been completely destroyed. The McEvoys are old-time residents of that section, but were unable to ascertain the identity of the men buried there.

"As I was a scout with the Custer and Stanley expedition in 1873," writes Mr. Norris, "we had a little fight with the Sioux Indians on the north side of the Yellowstone across and in the bottom above the mouth of the Tongue river. In the fight the veterinary surgeon (Dr. Halsinger) of Custer's cavalry, and sutler were killed and the bodies buried; and mules tramped over the graves so the Indians could not find them to scalp them. These must have been the bodies found, and only two, I and my partner, Charles Reynolds, saw them killed."

For many years, it is stated, a lone cottonwood tree marked the site of the burial place of these two victims of that early engagement with the Sioux Indians who were then actively on the war-path. Their names and others were carved upon the tree, but it being destroyed all trace has been removed and nothing now marks the spot. The site is described as being about 25 miles west of Miles City, and on the north side of the Tongue river.—Hardin (Mont.) Tribune.

WINNING THE WEST

The few remaining survivors of the Indian wars are hoping for the early passage of the Bursum bill.

But few persons realize the hardships and privations endured by these soldiers during the sixties and seventies. Their services and sacrifices have rarely been appreciated, their sufferings have been lightly regarded, their valor has only occasionally received suitable reward, and their lives not valued at their true worth.

The mountains and plains of the great West know the story of their devotion to duty, and many a hero sleeps today in an unknown grave, where his only requiem is sung by the tall sycamores and cottonwoods that border some nameless stream.

In the winter of '68 Troops L and D of the 10th U. S. Cav. were stationed at Fort Arbuckle, Indian Territory. A part of their duty was to furnish details for the mails between Forts Gibson and Arbuckle. There were a number of relay stations between these two points, but each rider had to cover a distance of about thirty miles daily. This was no pleasure ride when one considers that besides fording the icy waters of the Canadian, the Washita, and Wild Horse, there was always the danger of capture by Indians.

I recall one occasion when the mail rider failed to report at Arbuckle a detachment was sent out to look for him. At the first relay post the Sergeant in charge reported that he had left on time. After scouring the prairie in all directions, the detachment returned and reported its failure to locate him. He was dropped from the rolls as a deserter. Some months later, when the waters of the Canadian had receded the body of this soldier (Filmore Roberts, a boy of 19) was found fifteen miles below the ford lodged in the willows, with the mail pouch strapped to his skeleton. He had lost his life in the performance of his duty.

During the months of August, 1877, Troops A and L, 10th U. S. Cav., under command of Capt. Nicholas Nolan, left Fort Concho, Tex., and established a supply camp on Cow Creek, from which an expedition started in pursuit of hostile Indians. The first day out, arriving at a place known as the Double X, a confluence of two streams, a fresh trail was struck leading westward. This was followed until night overtook us and a dry camp was made. The animals had no water that night and the men only what remained in their canteens. Next morning the march was resumed shortly after daybreak, and continued throughout the day without a drop of water for the animals, and the canteens were empty. Three men were abandoned on the trail during the day.

About 4 o'clock a sergeant and three men left the command and turned in a westerly direction. Four or five days later this sergeant and his men reported at Fort Concho and were placed in arrest. One of the men abandoned during the day came into camp that night, the other two strayed to the westward from the trail, and two months after their remains were found near a place known as Bitter Lake, which at times afforded water strongly impregnated with alkali. Their bodies were entirely naked; in fact, the living men of the command were nearly all naked, the heat being so intense that they threw away their clothing.

On the morning of the third day out from Cow Creek the command had been reduced to about one-half of its original number. By 10 o'clock a. m. it had dwindled to not more than the three officers and a dozen men. The commander having ordered the men to scatter and search for water, the small remnant of the command went into camp without water. About 5 o'clock that afternoon a slight rain fell upon the suffering camp, rubber blankets were spread out and a few precious drops caught. By this time nearly all of the horses were dead. All efforts were made by those who were able to arouse their dying comrades. Woolen blankets were dragged over the damp grass and wrung out for the few drops they might soak up.

The next day Capt. Lee and a detachment from the post arrived with water and supplies, the condition of the expedition having been reported by the sergeant who had returned to the post.

Some of the men of the command made their way to distant posts, some as far as New Mexico. Some were never heard of, having died of thirst or been captured by the Indians.

These incidents can be multiplied a hundred times by any cavalry troop serving in the West at that period.

GEO. W. FORD,
First Sergeant, Troop L,
10th U. S. Cav.
R. R. 1, Springfield, Illinois.

Front page of *Winners of the West*, April 1924, featuring a letter from George W. Ford, an original member of the 10th Cavalry had crossed the river Captain Novele of M Troop formed the line and gave command to dismount to fight on foot. Capt. Novele gave me the command to inform Cap. Keys of D, who was 300 yards to the right of our command, to form his troop at right angles in order to make the attack on three sides. Being dismounted, I had to carry the dispatch on foot. I had to run for it, the Indians shooting at me all the time. Having delivered the dispatch, I started on the hot foot back, and reached my troop O.K. I can venture to say truthfully that I believe there were a hundred shots fired at me in carrying that dispatch. The next was the order to charge. We charged them and dislodged them, our captain now giving the command to take cover. While under cover a rain came up that only lasted about five or ten minutes, just enough to wet the sand. While rolling around on the ground my rifle got some sand in the stock breech. I had to get a stick to clean it out, and in doing so I got in full view of the Indians. It was here that I got shot in the right side. I laid down behind a stump, and again those Indians fired a number of shots, but none of them hit me. Some came so close to me that they threw sand in my face as they hit the ground. Laying as if I was dead, the Indians gave up shooting at me, as they no doubt thought I was dead. This was between 11 and 12 o'clock in the day when the scrap started. I stayed there until dark and then I managed to crawl away from my hiding place. After dark the Indians forded the river and got away. The next morning the soldiers saddled up and took the trail. There was only one man killed, Clarke Young. I crawled out of my tent and wanted to saddle my horse but the captain made me go to the hospital. The troop followed those Indians for one month, overtook them at Medicine Lodge, and wiped them out. I was not in the Custer massacre, but was stationed at Ft. Stockton. When the news reached the fort, which was the end of the telegraph line, Private Paine and I were detailed to carry the dispatch to Ft. Davis, 75 miles distant. We covered that 75 miles from 11:45 A.M. to 4 A.M. the next day. Twelve miles of this distance was through mountain passes, and I have never seen it rain harder, and lightning and thunder more terrific than it did on that occasion. I served 10 years on the frontier, five being in cavalry and five in Infantry. I am at this writing 71 years old. I would appreciate any letter or news from any of my old comrades.

Yours in comradeship,
Perry A. Hayman
Late Troop M, 10th U.S. Inf [sic]
Late Co. B, 25th U.S. Inf.
Sharon Hill, Pa.

Chapter Fifteen

Lieutenant John Lapham Bullis's report on the heroic behavior of three Seminole-Negro scouts

John Lapham Bullis, while a lieutenant in the 24th Infantry during the mid-1870s, commanded a unit of Seminole Negro scouts. These scouts were descended from black slaves who had fled bondage and found refuge with the Seminoles in Florida, married into the tribe, and moved west when the Seminoles were forced out of Florida. Some then fled to Mexico to avoid reenslavement and only returned after the Civil War. The Army recruited them as scouts and tolerated their indifference to military uniforms, routine, and ceremony because they were superb trackers, highly skilled at reading signs, very knowledgeable of the borderlands, and tough.[1]

Lieutenant Bullis and the scouts shared hardships and mutual respect. Their bond was strong enough for three of the scouts to risk their lives to rescue him after he lost his horse in a skirmish with Comanches. Afterward, he recommended them all for the Medal of Honor, which they received. His report, published in Department of Texas orders so soldiers in the department could learn of the scouts' bravery, described the fight and contained information on the country that military and civilian travelers alike would find useful.[2]

Headquarters, Department Of Texas
San Antonio, Texas, May 12, 1875

General Orders
No. 10

The following report of a scout made by First Lieutenant J. L. Bullis, 24th Infantry, commanding scouts at Fort Clark, Texas, is published to the command:

Fort Clark, Texas
April 27, 1875

Lieutenant G. W. Smith,
9th Cavalry, Post Adjutant

Sir:

I have the honor to render the following report of a scout, made in compliance with verbal instructions received from the commanding officer of the post, the object of which was to find out if a large party of Indians were camped on the lower Pecos or Rio Grande rivers, or between them.

I would say that I left the garrison on the 16th day of the present month with but three Seminole Scouts, as I desired to leave but little or no trail and not to be seen. We accompanied Co. A, 25th Infantry, (*en route* to Fort Stockton), as far up as Beaver lake, distant one hundred miles, and during the time we kept our horses upon corn, transported with the infantry train. We left the company on the morning of the 22nd inst. And marched west toward the Pecos, on the east side. We marched this day about fifty miles and went into camp, after dark at a water hole in a rock, grass good.

The following morning (the 23rd inst.) we left camp at 4:30 o'clock and marched southwest for about twenty miles and struck the Pecos at the mouth of Howard's creek. At this place we went into camp and remained for about four hours. Then crossed to the west side of the river and marched about twelve miles west and went into camp after dark without water, but had plenty of good grass for our horses; we marched this day forty miles and went over a very rough country. The following morning (the 24th inst.) we left camp very early (3:30 o'clock) and marched west, toward the Rio Grande, for about forty miles; then marched southwest for about fifteen miles and went into camp, after dark, near the Rio Grande, without water, but had plenty of good grass for our horses; we marched this day about fifty-five miles and fortunately found plenty of water, standing in holes, for both men and horses.

The following morning (the 25th inst.) we left camp at 4 o'clock and marched south for about eighteen miles and crossed the Pecos, about a mile above its mouth, at an Indian crossing; we then marched southeast for about six miles and went into camp at a spring, in a cave (known as Paint Cave). I would here say that in traversing the country between the Pecos and the Rio Grande we did not see any fresh Indian signs, but plenty of old, nearly all of which went toward a shallow crossing of the Rio Grande, known as Eagle's Nest crossing. We left the spring at 1 o'clock P.M. and marched east for about three miles and struck a fresh trail going northwest toward Eagle's Nest crossing. The trail was quite large and came from the direction of the settlements, and was made, I judge, by seventy-five head or more, of horses. We immediately took the trail and followed it briskly for about an hour, and came upon a party of Indians, unobserved, attempting to cross the Pecos to the west side. We immediately dismounted and tied our horses, and crept, back of a bush, up to within about seventy-five yards of them (all of which were dismounted, except one squaw) and gave them a volley which we followed up lively for about three-fourths of an hour, during which time we twice took their horses from them, and killed three Indians and wounded a fourth. We were at last compelled to give way, as they were about to get around us and cut us off from our horses. I regret to say that I lost mine with saddle and bridle complete, and just saved my hair by jumping on my Sergeant's horse, back of him. The truth is, there were some twenty-five or thirty Indians in all, and mostly armed with Winchester guns, and they were too much for us. As to my men, Sergeant *John Ward*, Trumpeter *Isaac Payne*, and Private *Pompey Factor*, they are brave and trustworthy, and are each worthy of a medal, the former of which had a ball shot through his carbine sling, and the stock to his carbine shattered. Relative to the Indians, I would say that in my opinion, they were Comanches, and were from Mexico.

After the fight we marched about twelve miles and went into camp at Paint Creek, grass and water plentiful and good. We marched this day fifty-six miles.

The following morning (the 26th inst.) we left camp at sunrise and took the main road to Fort Clark, where we arrived at 3 P.M.; we marched this day forty-three miles. Total distance marched three hundred and twenty-six miles.

I remain, Sir,
Very respectfully,
Your obedient servant,
JOHN L. BULLIS
1st Lieutenant 24th Infantry,
Commanding Scout.

Words commendatory of the energy, gallantry and good judgment displayed by Lieutenant *Bullis* and the courageous and soldierly conduct of the three scouts who composed his party, are not needed. The simple narrative given by himself explains fully the difficulties and dangers of his expedition. His own conduct, as well as that of his men, is well worth imitation, and shows what an officer can do who means business.

By Command of Brigadier General Ord:
J. H. Taylor
Assistant Adjutant General.

Chapter Sixteen

Sergeant John Marshall, of the 10th Cavalry, reports on a scout from Fort Concho, Texas

Soldiering for the most part was tedious routine work, but at times tedium turned to anxiety and then dissipated in a violent, dangerous encounter with inconclusive results. Sergeant John Marshall was an original member of the 10th Cavalry, who had enlisted in A Troop when it was organized in February 1867. In May 1875, he filed this report of a scout and a skirmish with the help of Sergeant Major Joseph Parker. Marshall was unable to compose the report himself, and signed the document with his "X."[1]

Ft Concho, Texas
May 12, 1875

Post Adjutant, Fort Concho, Tx.
(Thro Commanding officer Co. A 10 Cavalry)
Sir,

I have the honor to report that in compliance with Special Orders No. 96, Hdqrs Fort Concho, Texas, I left this post in pursuit of hostile Indians reported in this vicinity.

May 4 proceeded up the N. Concho river for about twenty miles, when darkness coming on, went into camp.

The next morning resumed the march up the N. Concho river as far as Catfish Creek where we remained until three o'clock in the morning of next day in anticipation of making a long march to Battle Point. Arrived at the latter place at two o'clock A.M. and concealed ourselves in the hope of discovering Indians. About 4 o'clock in the afternoon of that day (6th) the vidette, who was posted on high ground (but concealed) reported to me that a body of eight (8) Indians were approaching. I immediately gave orders to saddle up. The Indians continued to approach our place of concealment (which was near a spring) until they were within 800 yards of my command when they halted and appeared to make preparations to dismount and either camp or water their horses; at this time and before they had dismounted a pack mule with my command began to bray, upon which the Indians ran. The men immediately commenced to fire and gave chase at about the 4th volley. One Indian threw up his arms as if he was shot, discarded the blanket tied around his waist, dismounted, and leaving everything ran to some thicket on his left and disappeared. Three of my men searched for over an hour to discover him but without success, the balance of the command continuing the chase of the remaining Indians. The chase was kept up for over seven miles, when finding that they were gaining considerably on me, owing to the fact that the sandy nature of the ground prevented rapid travel, and that the horses were nearly exhausted, I returned to the place where the three men were looking for the Indian. The whole command thoroughly searched the ground for signs of him, but without success. I picked up the pony he had left, as also the blanket he had discarded, and discovered on the latter a bullet hole in two places (as if the bullet had gone through his body) and fresh blood in and around each hole. From the manner in which the Indian who was shot wore his blanket I am certain that the bullet went through his back and stomach and that consequently he was killed. The Indians had no stock with them other than the animals they were riding. Pvt. Geo. Smith, Co. F, 10 Cav. who had the fastest horse, kept up close to the Indians firing continually at them. I especially mention his good conduct on this occasion.

Finding that further pursuit was useless, and acting upon the advice of the post guide with me, I returned to this post bringing the pony and blanket before mentioned.

Very respectfully & c. & c.
his
Signed John X Marshall
mark
Sergeant Co. A 10 Cav.

Chapter Seventeen

Destroying Indian villages

During the 1870s, the Army on the Plains seldom forced the Indians to fight set-piece battles. Illusive bands of warriors usually avoided costly direct confrontations. Native villages, on the other hand, were extremely vulnerable, especially in winter, and troops achieved some success against Plains tribes by burning their villages and destroying tribal possessions—tipis, stores of meat, buffalo robes, and implements—rather than killing the people.[1] The largest such occurrence represented the key encounter of the Red River War of 1874, when Colonel Ranald Mackenzie's expedition, guided by Seminole Negro scouts, surprised a large encampment of Comanches, Cheyennes, and Kiowas in Palo Duro Canyon on the Red River in Texas. The soldiers slaughtered about 1,400 mules and horses and torched a winter's supply of meat. Repeated often enough, this tactic deprived the Indians of protection against the elements, created widespread hunger, and ultimately forced them onto reservations.[2] This report by Captain Nicholas Nolan of the 10th Cavalry describes an expedition of his A Troop in the summer of 1875 that succeeded in finding and destroying two villages, complete with about six months of supplies, in West Texas.[3]

Camp near Maa-Cha-Ro-Way Mountain, Texas
August 1, 1875

Lieut. Col. W. R. Shafter, 24th infantry
Commanding Scouting Expedition

Sir:

I have the honor to report that on the 28th July, while Enroute from Mustang Springs to Sand Hills, and when 15 miles Southwest of former place, my guides found an Indian trail running Northwest.

When first seen, only the trail of one horse could be seen, on following trail a few miles, it became certain that the trail was made by a hunting party, as other single trails led to the one first seen. After following the trail 5 miles, I saw Indians and soon after discovered their Camp, about 10 miles Northeast of us.

I made all possible haste, but when I reached the Camp it was deserted. Found another village within 1½ miles of first one. Burned both and with them about six months supplies, seventy four (74) Lodges, cooking utensils, packsaddles & c. They took very little with them. It was 4 P.M. when I reached the villages and I had then marched 26 miles. I did not deem it prudent therefore to pursue. I moved my camp after dark, Indians fired into their old village, where I first Encamped, but did not disturb me during night. On the morning of the 29th we had such a hard rain that I could not move till one P.M. My guide thinking that the trail led N.E., I marched in that direction about 8 miles, finding no trail I encamped.

The trail must have gone to Sand Hills, or in that direction. We captured two mules and 15 head of horses. There were probably one hundred (100) warriors in the two villages. I could only have followed trail about two days and could not have accomplished much, I therefore continued the march towards Supply Camp, in order to communicate with you before you had sent out your other Companies.

To-day guides found trail of Mexicans and Indians going N.E., they are probably returning from a thieving Expedition. The Indians have been following us, watching our movements up to yesterday.

This is my reason for not having communicated with you before this.

Very respectfully
Your obdt. servant
Nicholas Nolan
Capt. 10th Cavalry
Commanding

Chapter Eighteen

Borderland operations: cattle thieves and civil authorities

In addition to the fierce borderland tribes, Colonel Edward Hatch and the 9th Cavalry had to contend with robbers on both sides of the Rio Grande and Texas civil authorities, who, according to Hatch, were at best indifferent to his plight and at worst allied with the thieves. Moreover, the situation was resulting in the deaths of Hatch's men, in this case Privates Jeremiah Owsley and Moses Turner of G Troop. Hatch complained of this situation in a letter to Department of Texas headquarters, on February 3, 1875.[1]

Headquarters Ringgold Barracks, Tex.
February 3d, 1875

Assistant Adjutant General
Department of Texas
San Antonio, Texas

Sir:

I have the honor to report that during the full moon of the latter part of January the cattle thieves have been unusually bold, and have succeeded in crossing several small herds of cattle, ranging from twenty to forty.

On the night of the 26th of January a small scouting party consisting of one Corporal and four privates of Company G, 9th Cavalry were attacked when on the march about ten o'clock P.M., eighteen miles below the post; two of the men were killed, and two escaped to the hills, being closely pursued, they did not reach the post until the next evening. The Corporal who behaved gallantly, owes his escape to his coolness and courage, was pursued within a few miles of the post, where he arrived about mid-night. I proceeded at once to the vicinity of the attack with sixty men of Companies B & G, 9th Cavalry, and by day-light in the morning had captured all suspicious characters for some twenty-five miles on the river, two of whom were wounded in the attack on the soldiers. I at once sent for the Sheriff of the County, and Coroner, and turned over the prisoners. The Coroner's Jury found nine men (Mexicans) guilty of the murder of the two soldiers, seven of whom were present among the prisoners, these men with others were sent to jail at Rio Grande City, Texas.

The soldiers killed were robbed and mutilated, the attacking party is estimated at from twenty-five to forty men, and live on both banks of the river, most of the party escaped into Mexico, some of the money taken from the soldiers killed was spent in Camargo the following day, the man when offering it boasted he had obtained it from the pockets of the dead soldiers; all the arms of the soldiers killed were also taken.

The facts developed by the examination are, that these marauders live on both sides of the river, that all river ranches are engaged in or connive in the stealing of stock and that the Civil authorities who are usually engaged in trade know the parties, and that, not to tolerate it is to take away the greater part of their revenue, there has never been a cattle thief arrested by the Civil Officers since coming to this station. Of these men committed for murder I have not the slightest assurance that any Jury in this County will ever convict them, and the result will be that the Bands of thieves will be bolder than ever. The troops of this garrison will be less effective in checking depredations as stronger patrols will be required, and these troubles will never end here under the present arrangements. If the state authorities wish the stealing to cease there is only one way and that is by assigning the territory on the Rio Grande to the Military. These thieves are aware now that they can ambush a party of soldiers and should they escape punishment at the time, there is no court in the country from which there is the slightest probabilities to them of convictions.

Yours Respectfully
Your Obedient Servant
Edward Hatch
Colonel 9th Cavalry
Commanding

Chapter Nineteen

Borderland operations: depredations and refuge

Captain Louis H. Carpenter of the 10th Cavalry, who had led H Troop to the rescue at Beecher Island in 1868, still commanded the same unit in 1875. At the end of 1875 he led his men and thirteen soldiers of the 25th Infantry across the Rio Grande river in a search for Indians. Carpenter's scouting expeditions, on which he reported from Fort Davis, illuminate the problem of operations along the international border, at a time when relations between the United States and Mexico were chaotic and tense, with Porfirio Díaz overthrowing the Mexican government in 1876, reinforcing the perception in the United States that Mexico was a shambles and that relations along the border would soon dissolve into a full-blown crisis. In such a situation, which the Indians were surely to exploit, cross-border raids on settlements and ranches would increase and citizens of both countries would suffer.[1]

Report of a scout in November 1875:2

Ft. Davis, Texas
Dec. 2d, 1875

Post Adjutant
Fort Davis, Texas

Sir:

I have the honor to make the following report of the scout ordered by S.O. No. 158 Hdqrs Ft. Davis, Texas, Nov. 5, 75.

The detachment consisted of the available force of Co. H, 10 Cavalry, 33 enlisted men and 1 officer and 13 enlisted men of the 25 Infantry, 1 guide, 1 packer, and 3 wagons containing 4 days forage and 25 days rations. Lieut. H. H. Landon 25 Inf. was detailed as acting Engineer officer. The command left Ft Davis, Tex., about 1 P.M. Nov 6/75 and proceeded in a southerly direction to Favers Ranch, distance 64 miles, arriving there on the 9 Nov.

Being disappointed here in obtaining forage, I was unable to leave the wagons here at this point, as I had intended in order to search the country in the neighborhood and therefore marched to Del Norte, Texas.

On the 13th the detachment left Del Norte and followed the Rio Grande upwards, reaching Russel's Ranche in 45 miles. Here I found a large settlement, and upon inquiring learned that no Indian depredations have been committed in that vicinity for a long time and that no Indian Ranchero exists between that point and the "Viejo" and "Capote" ranges to the south of "El Muerto," the country having been traveled lately by parties belonging [to] Russel's ranche and not being favorable in its features.

I returned to Del Norte on the 18th and on the 21st of November proceeded down the Rio Grande to the Tervino Canon in the Mocasin range, about 35 miles without discovering any sign which would indicate that the Indians have been in the immediate vicinity of Del Norte lately. I returned to that place on the 24th of November and left on the 26th returning to Fort Davis, via Davis ranche, reaching the post on the 1st of December, having marched on the scout 340 miles.

While at Del Norte I learned from reliable American residents on the Mexican side that a band of Mescalero Apaches under a chief named Alsate effected an agreement with the Mexican Government some time since amounting to a truce under which they have been trading continually in the Mexican town of Presidio del Norte, residing for the most time, however, in the Sierra Blanca, near the town of San Carlas, Mexico.

I am satisfied from what I have learned from various sources that these Indians have been constantly depredating on the American side and carrying stock and other spoils to Mexico to trade with impunity at San Carlas and Presidio del Norte.

By reference to the report of my scout from Fort Davis to the Guadalupe, Sacramento, Smoke and Eagle Mountains, dated Oct. 24 1875 it will be seen that 1150 miles of country were examined including the line of the Rio Grande to a point south of the Viejo, about 80 miles south of Fort Quitman, and in the late scout a farther distance on the Rio Grande to a point about 35 miles below Del Norte, without discovering any sign which would indicate that Indians have made any stay in the country for over 6 months.

The deputy Indian Agent at the Fort Stanton reservation assured me that it was known positively that other bands of the Apaches beside Alsate's were absent from the Reservation to which they properly belong and that they were, or are, in Texas. I therefore conclude that these bands are also below Del Norte, since I have been unable to discover any trace of them above and before leaving Del Norte. I made further inquiries which led to the information that Alsate had lately made application to the Mexican government for a "Pass" for other bands of Apaches who wish to be admitted to the same trading privileges enjoyed by his own. There is also a report that these bands have lately joined Alsate.

As Alsate is known to have in his own band 60 fighting men, it is safe to reckon that they have now at least 100 available warrior and perhaps more. A short time since Colonel Tarrassus[3] of the Mexican federal Army notified Alsate that the Mexican government desired his band to move to a designated locality in the interior. This, Alsate refused to do and fearing some coercive measures from Tarassus, I learned that a short time since he left the Sierra Blanco with his party and crossed the Rio Grande to the American side in the vicinity of Sierra Chisis in the upper part of the Horsehead Hills. As these Indians have made their homes in one of the most rugged and broken regions in the country, it will be necessarily extremely difficult to dislodge them. A single detachment proceeding against them can hardly hope to be successful, for as soon as alarmed the Indians will at once fly across the Rio Grande, where they find friends and protection, or have heretofore. I would therefore respectfully recommend the following for the consideration of the proper authority.

1. A detachment consisting of the companies of Cavalry at Fort Davis and Fort Stockton, with a company of Infantry, to start from Fort Davis at such time as may be deemed best, carrying supplies in wagons, as far as the Fislingha Creek, a point near the upper portion of the Horsehead hills (which I think is practicable), thence with pack animals to scout the country down towards the mouth of the Pecos, as far as possible.

2. A detachment at least 100 strong from Fort Clark on the same date as the above, and crossing the Pecos near its mouth to scout the country up the Rio Grande as far as possible.

3. To request Colonel Tarassus to cooperate with a Mexican force on the Rio Grande, below San Carlas, and to arrive at that locality about the time that our forces should be at the mouth of the Pecos and upper part of the Horsehead Hills. Each column should have at least 100 men, for these Indians number as many, if not more, and may have an immense advantage among their rocks and cañons, and are well armed.

Very respectfully,
Your ob'dt Servt.
L.H. Carpenter
Capt. 10 Cavalry
Comdg Scouting D'tchm't
from Fort Davis

Report of a scout in February–March 1876:4

Fort Davis, Texas
March 22, 1876

Post Adjutant
Fort Davis, Texas

Sir:

I have the honor to submit the following report. In obedience to S.O. No. 34 Hdqrs Fort Davis, Texas, Feby 29.76, I left the post of Fort Davis Texas Feby 29.76 in command of Companies H, 10 Cavalry, 31 enlisted men, and H and K, 25th Infantry, 53 enlisted men, with instructions to scout the vicinity of the Smoke Mountains. AA Surg S.S. Boyer accompanied the detachment as medical officer, 2 guides were furnished, 20 days rations and the necessary transportation. The command marched on the El Paso road to El Muerte, and then across the country to the Fresno Springs in the Carisso Mountains, and from this point proceeded along the east side of the Smoky Mountains to the Carrisito springs. Here, on the morning of the 7th of March, I struck a trail 3 days old, of almost 300 head of stock and quite a large number of Indians, going from the Smoke Mountains, in an easterly direction, towards the Guadalupe Mountains. As it seemed to me probable that the Indians were unaware of our presence in the country, I thought that there was a chance to surprise them in some rancheria in the Guadalupes, and therefore started on the trail with Company H 10 Cavalry and Compy K 25 Infantry with Lieuts Pratt, Ord, and Scott 25th Infy and Ayres 10 Cav and Dr. Boyer.

Lieut Stivers 25 Inf with Co H 25 Infy was left with the wagons with instructions to proceed northward to the overland route, and through the Guadalupe pass to Independence Springs, where he was to wait for the rest of the command.

The trail led us across the valley on the east side of the Smoke Mountain and entered the Guadalupe range. Just as we reached the latter mountains, a signal smoke was started by Indian scouts on the highest portion of the Smoke Mountain, evidently for the purpose of alarming the Indians in our front. In following the trail we were led through difficult canõns and over rocks and high mountains and very frequently our trailers found their skill and experience severely tested. On the second day the trail divided up, showing that the Indians had scattered, and we endeavored to follow a few tracks which led us over some of the most broken country in the Guadalupe range, and over a very stony and rocky soil, where it was almost impossible

"Troopers in Hot Pursuit" (From W. F. Beyer and O. F. Keydel, eds., *Deeds of Valor* [Detroit, MI: Perrien-Keydel, 1903], 204.)

to follow the trail. After losing all traces of it a number of times, I finally gave up the pursuit, convinced that the Indians were thoroughly alarmed, and that it would be impossible to overtake them, and came into Independence Springs after a march of over 70 miles through this portion of the Guadalupes. Six horses were found, abandoned by the Indians, but they were broken down and worthless. From the direction of the trail, I think that the Indians struck the Pecos higher up, and passed again into the Guadalupe Mts, near the Sacrimentos in New Mexico. From the sign, the guides were confident that the Indians were Apaches. Upon rejoining the wagons at Independence Springs, Lieut. Stivers reported that, immediately after separating from me, and while proceeding along the east side of the Smoke Mountain, he saw 5 or 6 Indians and a dust beyond, which indicated a small quantity of stock being driven. (This party went up the valley towards the Sacrimentos and the reservation near

Fort Stanton.) Having nothing but a small force of Infantry, he was unable to pursue them. From Independence Springs the command proceeded on the east side of the Guadalupe Range to the head of Toyah Creek, from there to the El Paso road and arrived at Fort Davis, Texas, on the 19th of March 1876, having marched 365 miles. Lieut. Ord 25 Inf was directed to keep the journal of the march, and it will be forwarded as soon as completed.

Very respectfully,
Your obedient Servant,
L. H. Carpenter
Capt 10 Cavalry
Comdg Scouting Detachment
from Fort Davis Texas

Chapter Twenty

A chaplain's report: discipline, morals, and education

Chaplain George G. Mullins of the 25th Infantry and his counterparts throughout the Army reported monthly on discipline and morals in their units to the Adjutant General in Washington. Mullins's report from Fort Davis, Texas, dated January 1, 1877, also included education, because chaplains of black units were responsible for teaching basic subjects to their men. Mullins and all of the other chaplains of black regiments were white until the appointment of Allen Allensworth as the chaplain of the 24th infantry in 1886.

It is clear from this report that Mullins had a generally positive view of the soldiers in his flock.[1] He boasted of the excellent state of discipline, the importance the men put on being exemplars for black Americans, and the difficulty of training for combat with so many other kinds of duties required of them. He had few complaints: the nights were cold, wood was insufficient, the mails were erratic, and although the quantities of whiskey consumed were not excessive the quality of frontier rotgut was very low.

General: I have the honor to submit the following report for the last month on "morals and general history" of the command at this post.

The peaceful industry and excellent order, which we may claim to be characteristic of our garrison, have prevailed among the enlisted men. There is no such thing as utter drunkenness; and the small quantity of ardent spirits consumed could not be pronounced a serious evil, were it not frontier and Texas whiskey. It would perhaps be a good moral and sanitary measure to compel the post trader to keep only the purest and most costly liquors for sale, and mete them out in very small quantities. The officer and soldier should be restrained by an iron hand from ever visiting the low dram shops and gambling dens that surround a military post. Our men gamble little, do not steal, and are not at all given to quarreling and fighting among themselves. Morally considered, they have certainly made slow but constant improvement during the year just ended. Viewed as soldiers they do, for the most part, present the appearance of being as thoroughly drilled and disciplined as the circumstances will permit. With the frequent scouting excursions, guarding the mail stations, building, and repairing the adobe houses, escorting trains, etc., our men have really had to learn "arts military" under trying difficulties. However, such as they are, the most ambitious officers might well be proud of the command. It is a fact deserving honorable mention that at the beginning of last month, of the whole number of enlisted men (395) in the 25th regiment only three were under arrest or in confinement. It is also due to state that Co. H, 10th Cavalry, now numbering seventy men, have conducted themselves admirably during the last two months, and are included in my words of praise.

The ambition to be all that soldiers should be is not confined to a few of these sons of an unfortunate race. They are possessed of the notion that the colored people of the whole country are more or less affected by their conduct in the Army.

The Chaplain is sometimes touched by evidence of their manly anxiety to be well thought of at Army Headquarters and throughout the States. This is the bottom secret of their patient toil, and surprising progress in the effort to get at least an elementary education. Their interest in school is unabated, and upon public Divine service the attendance large. In my vaguely defined mission as chaplain, often a very trying one, I would gratefully report that I have had from the Commanding Officer, the Adjutant, and some other officers very strong moral support. We have been blessed with good health. There have been but few cases of sickness during the month, and only one death. The weather this winter has been thus far severely cold. Inasmuch as it must be subversive of good morals and gentle speech to have to live in quarters and barracks, without fire enough to keep from shivering with cold, we should undoubtedly be allowed more wood. Because in the South, it does not follow that we are in a hot climate. Our mail line demands some attention. Whether we may get our mail with any promptness and certainty or not, has become vexingly problematic. Whether papers, packages, and registered letters shall come, or go in safety, seems to depend altogether upon the very capricious humor of Texas postmasters and carriers.

Very respectfully, etc. Geo. G. Mullins
Chaplain 25th Infantry

Chapter Twenty-One

Lieutenant Henry Flipper's competence, character, and treatment by other officers

Henry Flipper, United States Military Academy class of 1877, was the first black officer commissioned in the Regular Army after the Civil War. He was assigned to the 10th Cavalry and served with the regiment in Texas for nearly five years before he was dismissed from the Army for his failure to account properly for government funds for which he was responsible. While his dismissal from the service was clearly the work of white officers who were eager to see him go, Flipper was not blameless in the matter. His effort to cover up mistakes in his financial accounts included false statements and a bad check, written in desperation to cover up deficiencies. Basically, his efforts to cover his problems gave his enemies the opportunity to drive him from the Army.[1]

Flipper's undoing involved his duties as the regimental quartermaster, but he also served as a line officer with troops. In the field, he led his men in the normal routine of patrols and scouts. His report of a four-week expedition from Fort Sill south into Texas during the late winter of 1880, reproduced here, suggests that he was a diligent, observant, and articulate small-unit commander.

Captain Nicholas Nolan was born in Ireland, enlisted in 1852, and rose from the ranks during the Civil War. Throughout Henry Flipper's brief military career, Nolan remained his staunch friend and supporter. His letters to a former officer of the 10th Cavalry, Robert Newton Price, reflected his affection and respect for Flipper as well as his naiveté regarding the attitudes of other officers toward the black lieutenant.

Lieutenant Flipper's report of a scout in February–March 1880.[2]

Fort Sill, I. T.
March 28th, 1880

Post Adjutant,

Sir:

I have the honor to submit the following report of the scout, made from this post under my direction in compliance with Special Orders No. 31, C.S. [Current Series], dated February 25th.

Leaving Fort Sill on the morning of the 26th, ultimo I proceeded to Baldwin's Springs, Texas, arriving there early in the morning of February 29th, and camped at a point near Doane's Ranch in obedience to instructions from the commanding officer to that effect. My instructions were to intercept all Indians, not in the service of the United States, found south of Red River, with a view to preventing depredations by them in Texas; also to keep a strict watch over the ranch at Baldwins Springs and to endeavor to ascertain whether or not Indians from the Fort Sill reservation are in the habit of trading there for arms, ammunition, or other supplies. My instructions have been strictly complied with and I have the honor to report that no Indians whatever have visited Doane's Ranch during the period of my encampment at that place, and I am informed by Mr. Doane that none have been there since the fourth of July 1879, except Blackbeard, a Comanche, who was sent as guide to the escort in charge of grain for Captain Nolan's command in February last.

On March first a detachment of one noncommissioned officer and five privates was sent to the mouth of Pease River to ascertain whether any Indians were then or had recently been in that vicinity. The sergeant and party returned on the 3rd, instant, and reported that section of country entirely free of Indians. The settlers there informed him that no Indians had been there during the past fall and winter except one small party of Indian police, which was camped about February 10th, near to and just south of the mouth of Pease River. The settlers had no complain[t]s to make against this party.

I learned that fifty five head of cattle had been killed during the past winter between Red and Pease Rivers, which were supposed to have been killed by Indians from this reservation. It was discovered that one Suttles, a white man owning a ranch near the mouth of the Pease River was the man. He was forced to leave the country only a few days previous to my arrival at Baldwins Springs. Cattle have been driven into the territory by white men and killed. Cattle have also been driven across the line for sale to the Indians. A gentleman living at Camp Augur informed me that he had himself followed a party into the territory and found them in the very act of killing some of his own cattle. The same gentleman informed me that he knew of no instance where Indians from any place had killed cattle in Texas during the past winter and fall.

On the 7th, instant, with twenty two men of my command, I proceeded to Cañon Blanco by way of Wanderer's Creek and Pease River. I crossed Pease River at a point nearly south of Prairie Dog or Medicine Mounds and proceeded thence up Pease River to the Staked Plains and thence to the canon, where I arrived

March 15th. The country I marched over is full of settlers. Diligent enquiry was made of all who were visited along the route and all assured me that no Indians whatever had been known to be in that section of country, all reports from whatever source to the contrary not withstanding. The same section of country is full of horse thieves, white men, who wander from ranch to ranch ostensibly in search of work in the approaching general round up of cattle, but really to steal horses. There is a party of white men on the south side of Red River above Baldwin's Springs hunting wolves who openly say that as soon as the grass will permit it they intend stealing Indian ponies. They have their headquarters at or near Curtis' Ranch which is about fifteen miles nearly due west from the second monument on the hundredth meridian going north from Red River.

My inquiries have elicited the information that many of these reports of depredations by Indians are fictions for which the cattle men themselves are directly responsible. They make them to keep the settlers out of the country in order that they may preserve their cattle ranges entire as they have them now.

I returned to Baldwin's Springs on the 20th, instant and on the 23rd started for this post which I reached on the 26th of March.

I am, Sir,
very respectfully,
your obedient servant,

Henry O, Flipper

2nd Lieut., 10th Cavalry,
Comdg., Co. "G"

Captain Nolan's letters.[3]

The Color Line.—Forney's *Progress* publishes the following extracts from letters from Capt. Nicholas Nolan to a friend of his in that city, Mr. Robt. Newton Price:

Fort Elliott, Texas, September 4th, 1879.

. . . Now, my dear Price, in the Class of '77 Lieutenant Henry O. Flipper graduated in the Halves, and by so doing, had the privilege of selecting the arm of the service he preferred. He selected the 10th Cavalry, and was assigned to

Company A of that regiment, commanded by the representative Paddy of the regiment. Mr. Flipper reported to me at Fort Sill on my arrival from Fort Concho, and I immediately extended to him the hand of fellowship. I have ever since been intimately associated with him, and have found him to be all that West Point turns out. It appears that the lady of some officer, who, I presume, never smelt powder, has written from this post to some Northern papers, commenting on myself and family for receiving and entertaining Mr. Flipper. This, evidently, is done on account of his color, and no allowance is made for his grand attainments. The only thing that I regret is that I do not know the husband of this lady, in order to hold him responsible for her action in this matter. I am pleased that Mr. Flipper is an officer of my company, and I am satisfied that he does not consider that all Irishmen are opposed to his race, but are willing to take the hand of all who have been oppressed like themselves. . . .

Fort Elliott, Texas, September 18th, 1879.

. . . In reference to my former letter about Mr. Flipper, the statement was made at a dinner-table at San Antonio by a lady who had just returned from New York. I am certain that some of the New York papers published something about it, as a statement to that effect was made at the table above mentioned. . . . Mr. Flipper's standing with the officers is of the most friendly nature, and the more he comes in contact with them the better he proves the worthiness of his position. He is a universal favorite in the garrison.

Chapter Twenty-Two

Complaint about discrimination in selection of sergeants to noncommissioned staff positions

Black soldiers appreciated the significance of military service as a way to stake their claim on citizenship. However, they also recognized that they were being treated unfairly in being denied opportunities for advancement, and they voiced their objections publicly. This letter from Fort Stockton, Texas, the duty station of elements of the 25th Infantry as well as companies of the 24th Infantry, articulated some of their concerns.[1] During the rest of the century and the early decades of the twentieth century, they would not be reticent about airing their grievances in print. To publicize their views, they used the pages of the *Army and Navy Journal*, the black press, or locally produced broadsides.

Colored Men on the General Staff

Fort Stockton, Texas, July 17, 1879

To the Editor of the *Army and Navy Journal*:

Sir: Allow me, through the columns of your paper, to speak a few words with regard to the appointment of colored men on the General Staff of the Army. I myself am not possessed of much solid information on the subject as I should like, and yet my feelings prompt me to the penning of this article. I believe it to be a well known fact of long standing that not more than two or three colored soldiers have ever been rewarded for "their meritorious conduct, soldierly bearing, unceasing endurance, and eternal faithfulness to the United States government," with an appointment as either ordnance sergeant, commissary sergeant or hospital steward, although several have been made to perform some of those duties from time to time, with no other compensation than that of a private soldier. In fact, in most cases where they have had these duties to perform, they have executed them to the entire satisfaction of their superiors. Now, if these man [sic] can and do perform this work, and if they do it intelligently and satisfactorily to all concerned, and that, too, without any compensation, does it not look very reasonable to infer that these same men would do the same work just as well when paid for it? I think it does. At any rate, we here all believe that there would be more satisfaction on the part of the persons doing these duties.

A duly appointed commissary sergeant, hospital steward or ordnance sergeant, if on duty at any Post, would find it greatly to his own personal interests to see that nothing went amiss, for he would think, "I would lose my rank, appointment, and money also." But if a private is doing these duties, he does not naturally have that care that an appointed General Staff N.C.O. would have. He would say, "I have no stripes or appointment to lose, and they may give me the benefit of a church meeting (general court-martial) if they want to." So you see there is an advantage to the Government to see that none but duly appointed non-commissioned officers are allowed, or compelled, to perform these duties. It would also be an encouragement to the enlisted men of the Army to try and become well qualified for the appointments.

The four regiments of colored troops now in the field have been, I think, very unjustly treated in regard to this subject. According to the Revised Statutes of the United States, sections 1103 and 1107, there are supposed to be about 1,700 enlisted men in the 9th and 10th Regiments of Cavalry and the 24th and 25th Regiments of Cavalry, inclusive, and out of this number I believe there are only two who have been put on the General Staff—Commissary Sergeants D. B. Jeffers and Sullivant. I must say that there is either too much prejudice against the colored man in the Army, or else his officers are not sufficiently interested in him to see that the men are justly rewarded. In the four colored regiments there are many more such men as Sullivant and Jeffers, and I believe they just as earnestly deserve, and would as highly appreciate, an appointment, if they only had some one of influence and sufficient interest to advocate their cause.

[Signed] Knife

Chapter Twenty-Three

Colonel George F. Hamilton's chronology of the 9th Cavalry during the campaign against Victorio and Nana

George Hamilton served with the 9th twice, as a lieutenant just after he graduated from the Military Academy in 1894 and later as a captain. His father, Colonel John M. Hamilton, commanded the 9th in Cuba during the 1898 war with Spain and was killed in battle while leading the regiment at San Juan Hill.

George Hamilton's manuscript covered the history of the regiment from its formation until 1906. Hamilton's record of the campaign against Victorio and Nana during 1879–1881 was based largely on the regiment's monthly returns, reproducing their terse reports on days in the saddle, miles covered, horses lost, casualties hostile and friendly, and occasional incursions into Mexico.[1] During the campaign, the regiment never operated as a single force, but deployed in company-sized or smaller elements for independent patrols from different posts. There was occasional escort duty, even law enforcement, and for one company involvement in the conflict with the Utes, but the main focus was the long harsh war with Victorio's band of Apaches. By the summer of 1881, with Victorio dead and Nana leading the small number of Apache fighters who remained, a combined force of almost one thousand black cavalry, white infantry, and Indian scouts were combing New Mexico for an Indian raiding force that probably numbered closer to twenty than to one hundred.

Taken together, the reports compiled by Hamilton add up to a matter-of-fact portrait of the most severe operational environment and most tenacious foe that the 9th Cavalry ever faced. The portion reproduced here contains Hamilton's regimental summary for each of the three years, the lists of the stations of each of the troops at the end of each year, and the specific entries for I Troop. Chapter 24, following this document, provides details on one of I Troop's battles, showing the ferocity of the combat and the bravery of the soldiers.

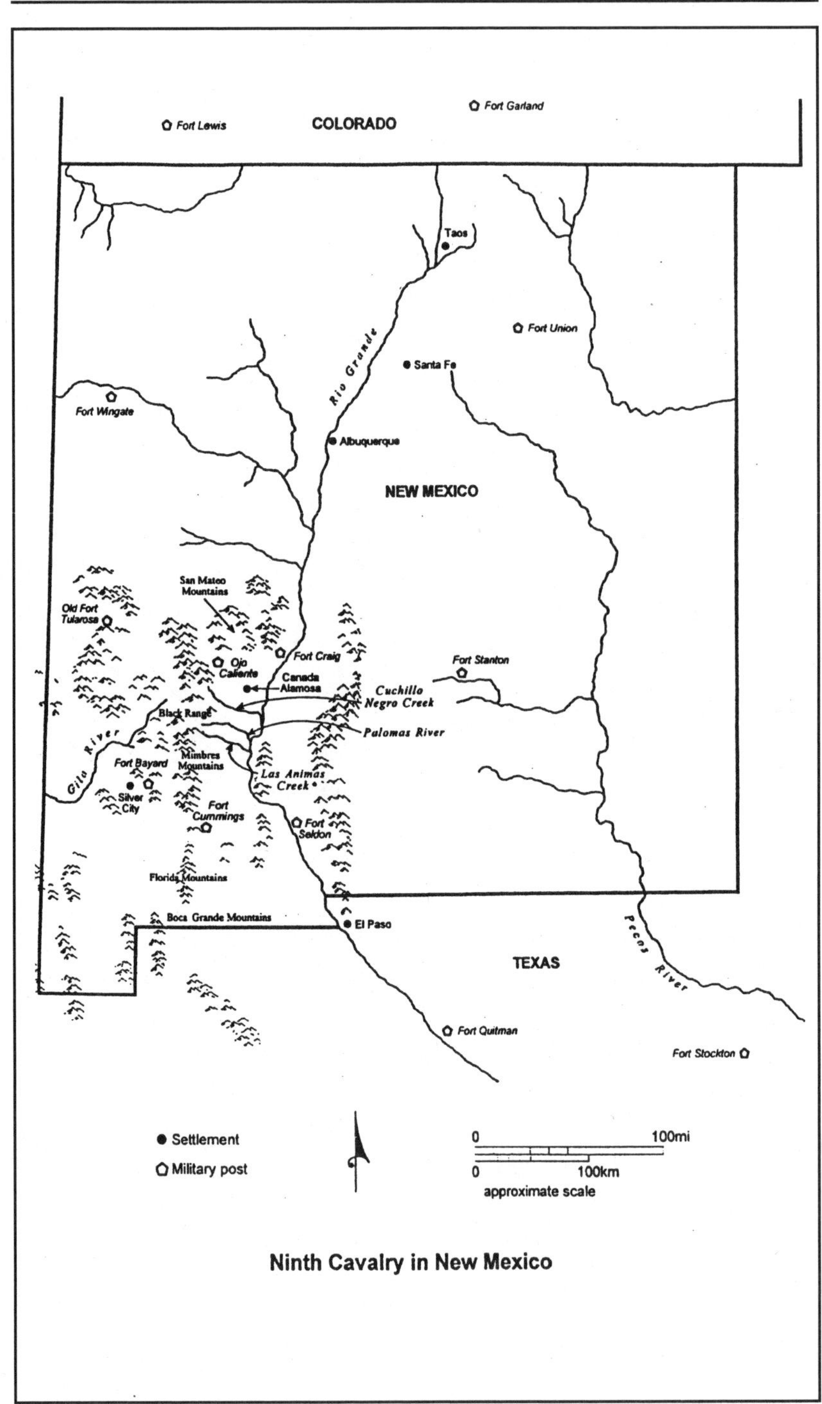

Ninth Cavalry in New Mexico

"History of the Ninth Regiment U.S. Cavalry."

1879

This year "Victoria," the famous Apache Chief, after surrendering with twenty-two of his band to Lieutenant Merrett (9th Cavalry) escaped and fled, closely followed by our troops, across the line into Old Mexico, and from there made frequent inroads back into the country and terrorizing the settlers and then returning beyond the border.

The history of the Regiment for the period covers almost constant campaign against him and his murderous band. . . .

Company "I":—The Company remained in the field at Ojo Caliente until the 10th of June, when it rejoined from Fort Wingate. On the 25th of August, Lieut. Cary, 15th infantry, with a detachment of fifteen men of the Company, took the field, returning on the 1st of September, after scouting one hundred and fifty one miles. On the eighth of October, Lieutenant Cary, with most of the available men of the Company (37), took the field, scouting after the Ute Indians on the San Juan River, and remained in the field for the remainder of the year, scouting three hundred and sixty six miles. . . .

Stations of Companies, December, 1879

"A" - - - - - In the field, Fort Cummings, N. M.
"B" - - - - - Fort Bayard, New Mexico
"C" - - - - - Fort Bayard, New Mexico
"D" - - - - - In the field near Fort Bayard
"E" - - - - - Ojo Caliente, New Mexico
"F" - - - - - Fort Bayard, New Mexico
"G" - - - - - In the field, Fort Cummings, N. M.
"H" - - - - - Fort Bayard, New Mexico
"I" - - - - - In the field, Animas River, Colorado
"K" - - - - - In the field, Farrington, N. M.
"L" - - - - - Fort Bliss, Texas
"M" - - - - - Fort Bayard, New Mexico

1880

Practically the whole of this year was spent in the field and nearly every company of the Regiment had engagements with the Indians. The wily Victoria was the cause of most of the trouble as he continued to rob, burn, and kill, escaping with marvelous sagacity to his fastnesses in the mountains or over the Mexican border. . . .

Company "I":— The Company remained in the field until the 23rd of July and scouted two thousand seven hundred and seventy six miles during the year. The ground covered was in the vicinity of Animas City, Farrington, Santa Fe, Ojo Caliente and Fort Wingate. . . .

Stations of the Regiment, December 31st, 1880

Headquarters - - - - - Santa Fe, N. M.
Band - - - - - - - - - - - -Fort Marcy, N. M.
"A" and "G"- - - - - - -Fort Stanton, N. M.
"B" and "H"- - - - - - Fort Stanton, N. M.
"C," "F," and "K" - - - In the field at old Fort Cummings, N. M.
"D" - - - - - - - - - - - - -Fort Craig, N. M.
"E" - - - - - - - - - - - - In the field, Colorado, N. M.
"I" - - - - - - - - - - - - Fort Wingate, N. M.
"L" - - - - - - - - - - - - Fort Bliss, Texas
"M" - - - - - - - - - - - Fort Selden, New Mexico

1881

This year was a strenuous one in the history of the Regiment. In July "Nana" with fifteen warriors, the remnant of Victoria's band, reenforced by about twenty five Mescalero Apaches, reentered New Mexico and whirled through the territory, plundering and killing a number of settlers.

It is difficult to describe the horror and dismay which the names of the bloodthirsty and relentless Geronimo, Victoria and Nana struck to the hearts of the settlers of the Southwest in those days. Their atrocities were such as to warrant to them no mercy if caught, and they and their followers seemed to realize this, and in their desperation no outrages were too abominable for their hands.

Nana and his gathering roused the other Indians of the region this year, and the troops were led a merry dance. The Indians usually sought refuge in the mountains of Old Mexico, the troops following them to the border and abandoning the trail only to be called out again by some new outbreak of these same Indians who re-crossed the border line as soon as the soldiers withdrew.

On the 17th of July, at Alamo Canyon, New Mexico, a small body of these Indians ambushed Chief Packer Burgess and one man belonging to a detachment commanded by Lieutenant Guilfoyle, 9th Cavalry, wounding Burgess and capturing three mules. On the 19th of July, Lieutenant Guilfoyle, with his detachment of the 9th Cavalry and some Indian scouts, following a trail westward of Cañon del Perro, New Mexico had a skirmish with some of the hostiles near Arena Blanca where they had just killed two Mexicans and a woman. The party, numbering about thirteen braves, succeeded in making its escape. On the 25th of July, Lieutenant Guilfoyle again struck the hostiles encamped in the San Andreas Mountains, New Mexico, capturing two horses, twelve mules and all the Indians' provisions. Two of the hostiles were shot and believed to have been killed. The others escaped, crossing the Rio Grande six miles below San Jose, killing two miners, and a Mexican in their flight.

On August 1st, a party of thirty six citizens under command of a Mr. Mitchell, while at dinner in the Red Cañon of the San Mateo Mountains were surprised and defeated by the hostiles, losing one man killed, and seven wounded, besides all their thirty six riding animals. The Indians escaped. On August third Lieutenant Guilfoyle's detachment again struck this band at Monaco Springs, N. M. wounding two Indians and capturing eleven head of stock and some saddles, blankets etc. This band numbered twenty or thirty warriors, led by Nana, had killed another Mexican while escaping from Red Cañon.

At Las Savoya, N. M. on August 11th, Lieutenant Guilfoyle found that two Mexicans had been killed and two women carried off by the hostiles.

On August 12th, Captain Parker, with a detachment of nineteen men of the 9th Cavalry, struck Nana's band twenty five miles west of Sabinal, N. M. losing one soldier killed, three wounded and one missing, but reported an equal loss inflicted on the hostiles, who then drew off. Captain Parker's small detachment, encumbered by their wounded, was unable to pursue. On August 16th, Lieutenant Valois, with Company "I" 9th Cavalry, had a severe fight with a band of about fifty Indians near Cuchillo Negro, N. M. in which Lieutenant Burnett 9th Cavalry, was wounded twice, and two men and six horses killed. The hostiles lost several killed. The same day, Lieutenant Taylor, with a detachment of the Regiment, also had a fight with the hostiles, capturing some horses and recovering some stolen property, himself losing a few horses killed. The hostiles were pursued toward the Black Range.

On August 19th, Lieutenant G. W. Smith, 9th Cavalry, with a detachment of twenty men, struck the hostiles about fifteen miles from McEwer's Ranch, N. M. The Indians were defeated after a severe fight, in which Lieutenant Smith and four men were killed.

A party of men under George Daly joined Lieut. Smith in the fight, and Daly was killed.

Altogether, eight companies of cavalry, eight companies of infantry, and two companies of Indian scouts under the command of Colonel Hatch of the Regiment were now in the field in pursuit of these Indians. Although no decisive engagement took place, the hostiles were persistently driven from one point to another, until they fled across the Mexican border, the chase being then abandoned under instructions from the War Department.

In the latter part of the year, the Regiment was relieved from duty in New Mexico, and ordered to Kansas and Indian Territory for station. . .

Company "I":— Until 15th March, the Company was in the field at Ojo Caliente scouting. On the latter day, they marched to the North Fork of the Cuchillo Negro where they remained scouting till June 6th, when the Company rejoined Post. On August 6th, left Post by rail for Fort Craig, arriving on the 7th. On the 15th, left Fort Craig and overtook, and engaged a band of hostiles for 2 hours at Rio Cuchillo Negro, the Indians retreating; two men wounded, and six horses killed. The Indians were severely punished. Their trail was followed to the Mexico border, whence the Company returned to Fort Craig on the 26th, scouted in the field near Fort Craig until the 5th when it returned to the Post. Took the field again on the 11th and chased hostiles in the vicinity of Fort Apache, A. T., and Black River country. In October, it spent most of the time scouting in the field, and on November 15th, arrived and took station at Fort Reno. Remained at Post during the remainder of the year. Total recorded distance two thousand nine hundred and seventy six miles. . . .

Stations of the Regiment, December 31st, 1881

Headquarters, and Cos. "D," "H," "L," & "M," Fort Riley.

Co, "A." . . . . .Fort Elliott, Texas.

Cos. "B" & "E." . . . . Fort Hays, Kansas.

Cos. "C" & "G." . . . . Fort Sill, I. T.

Cos. "F" & "I." . . . . Fort Reno, I. T.

Co. "K." . . . . .Cantonment, I. T.

Descriptive List, etc., of Private Henry Johnson, U. S. A., Retired.

Name, Henry Johnson
Rank, Private
Age, 49 5/12 years
Height, 5 feet 5 inches
Complexion, C Dark
Eyes, Brown
Hair, Black
Where born, Boydton, Virginia
Occupation, Soldier

Description.

Last enlisted.
When, March 26th 1898
Where, Fort Robinson, Nebraska
By whom, Lieut H S Wood, 9th Cavalry
Period, Three (3) years
Character, Good

Due soldier, $4.00 per month, for Fifteen years' continuous service.

Last served as Private of Co. K, Ninth Regiment of Cavalry

Retired August 29th 1898, in compliance with par. 34, Special Orders No. 180, Hdqrs. of the Army, A. G. O., dated August 2nd 1898

Signature of soldier Henry Johnson

Subsistence furnished to include September 2nd 1898

Final Statements furnished August 29th, 1898

I certify that the above is a correct transcript from the records furnished by the Comdg. Officer Troop K. 9th Cavalry

Station, Fort Robinson Nebr.

Date, August 29th 1898

A. E. Dalton.
2nd Lieut 9th Cav. Commanding Detachment
9th U. S. Cavalry

"Descriptive List" for Henry Johnson, a 9th Cavalry soldier who received the Medal of Honor for his bravery during the fight with the Utes on Milk River, Colorado, in October 1879 (Courtesy National Archives and Records Service)

Chapter Twenty-Four

Lieutenant George R. Burnett's account of a firefight between the 9th Cavalry and Nana's band in August 1881

Although a general summary such as that of George Hamilton shows the overall level of activity of the 9th during the Apache wars, such a narrative does not provide the detail needed to understand the individual acts of professionalism and bravery that marked the long, fierce struggle. The reports of small-unit commanders, such as this one by Lieutenant George Burnett, provide the details. Burnett commanded part of "I" Troop during the firefight of August 16, 1881, for which he, Sergeant Moses Williams, and Private Augustus Walley all eventually received the Medal of Honor.

Burnett wrote this letter in response to the request of Ordnance Sergeant Moses Williams, who used the letter as the basis for his own application for the Medal of Honor. Williams's letter to the War Department and the official approval of his application are also reproduced here.[1]

Lieutenant George R. Burnett, letter to Ordnance Sergeant Moses Williams, Fort Stevens, Oregon.

Consulate of the United States of America

Kehl, Germany, June 20, 1896

Ordnance Sergeant,

Moses Williams, Fort Stevens, Oregon

Sergeant: I reply to your communication of a recent date asking for the favor of a letter in your interests to the Adjutant General of the Army. I take pleasure in stating that some years ago I gave such a letter as you desire to your Colonel, Edward Hatch 9th U.S. Cavalry, in urging with other officers of your regiment your promotion from 1st Sergeant of Troop "I," 9th Cavalry, to your present position. However, if I can further serve you, it will be a source of gratification to see a faithful and meritorious old soldier deservedly rewarded, and I here cheerfully reproduce as nearly as I am able the substance of my former letter which was made in the form of a personal report to our Colonel. On August 16,

1881, we (that is Troop "I" 9th Cavalry under the command of Lieut. Valois) were lying in Camp at Cañada Alamosa N.M. when just about noon an alarm was given that the Indians had attacked Chavez Ranche about two miles distance and murdered the husband, wife and two children and two sheep herders. The command to "saddle up" was given at once, and Lieut. Valois directed me to proceed with the first dozen men ready, and take up the trail and that he would follow as quickly as possible. We found the facts as reported at Chavez Ranche and shortly afterwards sighted the Indians deployed mounted and apparently waiting for some one. I counted forty odd and some of the men claimed as high as sixty. They were for the most part dressed as Mexicans with blankets over their shoulders and wearing sombreros, which they waved for us to come on. We had been joined by a considerably party of Mexicans, dressed similarly and at first glance I mistook the Indians for Mexicans and supposed that they had sighted the Indians and were signaling to their friends to hurry up. I immediately deployed my men placing the Mexicans on the left and started forward at a fast gallop. The Indians remained mounted and allowed us to get within a thousand yards of them when they opened fire on us. I immediately dismounted my men and returned the fire. When they shortly broke and ran to the nearest ridge and dismounted and made a stand I immediately mounted and kept up a running fire till I reached an intermediate ridge where I was again obliged to dismount. I then sent 1st Sergeant Williams—who had received especial permission to ride ahead and join me—with a few men to try and turn their right flank, at the same time sending some Mexicans to the left for the same purpose. In the meantime I was keeping up the fire from the center. As soon as they were compelled to break, Sergt. Williams signaled me. I hastily mounted and charged them till they sought cover behind the next ridge and I was obliged to take shelter behind their old position. The country being hilly and rolling I resorted to the same tactics as previously and with the same result. So it was practically a running fight and this continued for several hours and we had driven the Indians eight to ten miles into the foot hills of the Cuchillo Negro Mountains when they made a final and determined stand. So hard did we push them however that they were obliged to abandon a large portion of their stock and captured plunder and that they suffered a large number in killed or wounded. I am assured for we could plainly see them carrying or dragging to the rear, between two riders their unfortunates and a number of bodies were found the next day concealed among the rocks, besides any quantity of bloody bandages and trails along the route subsequently followed up to the line that the Indians made their final stand about 4 P.M. Lieut. Valois had not as yet come up. I found the position of the Indians too strong for me and that I could not dislodge them by a direct attack and in fact there was serious doubt of my being able to hold my own, so I sent a courier to hasten Valois to my assistance with the request that he take the hill to my right which commanded the Indians position and I made endeavor to get around the left flank to the Indians rear and keep them out of the mountains so that we could have a better shot at them. Valois received my message and proceeded as requested. I made a wide detour to the left and on approaching the rear of the Indians my attention was called by Sergt. Williams to a dark object probably a 150 yards directly in front of me, and he remarked that he believed it to be the head of an Indian peeping over the rocks. We were riding in "column of files." I sprang from my horse and took deliberate aim at point blank range over my horse's saddle for an instant. The object did not move and not willing to risk giving an alarm I was on the point of withdrawing my carbine when I perceived a slight movement and firing instantly I had the satisfaction of feeling that I was responsible for at least one "good Indian." Immediately the Indians opened up on us from all along the ridge. I at once ordered my men to dismount and take shelter among the rocks, but in the excitement my horse broke away and started to the rear riderless on the dead run. Someone started the cry "they've got the Lieutenant, they've got the Lieut." and with this the whole outfit proceeded to follow suit—with the exception of 1st Sergt. Williams and Private Aug. Walley, who remained by me. I called to Sergt. Williams to go after them and bring them back. In the meantime myself and Walley under a heavy fire took shelter among the rocks and returned the fire till joined by Sergt. Williams and the rest of the detachment, he having quickly succeeded in rallying them. Finally we succeeded in dislodging the Indians and a number of them mounted started along the base of the mountains to the left toward the Rio Grande. My first impulse was to follow them, when my attention was attracted by heavy firing on our right, and the remark by Sergt. Williams that he "believed the main fight was there and that our Indians were only a decoy." On this supposition I gave up the idea of getting to the Indians rear and mounting my men I moved as rapidly as possible to the right. On coming over the intervening plateau I saw at a glance that there was not a moment to be lost for the Indians were concentrating from all directions on Valois who in his efforts to reach the hills referred to above, had been anticipated by the Indians who got there first and gave him a very warm reception. They killed or wounded nearly all of his horses and wounded some of his men and when we came up he was making his way to the rear as well as possible and the Indians were in hot pursuit. There was nothing for us to do but charge them, which I did mounted, and drove them back to cover and dismounting held them long enough for Valois to collect his scattered men and get his wounded to the rear. Believing the Indians to be too strong for him, Valois ordered his men to fall back and sent word to me to follow. I had given the order for my men to take up a position behind a ridge on our left and rear and the movement had begun when my attention was attracted by one of Valois men, whom I believed to be dead, calling to me "Lieutenant please, for God's sake don't leave us, our lives depend on you." I then discerned that Valois in falling back had left three men Privates Glasby, Wilson and Burton behind some prairie dog mounds about two hundred yards from the Indians and midway between their line and mine. When my attention was attracted by Glasby I was again alone with Sergeant Williams and Private Walley—"my striker"—the two men who were always by me in every danger, the rest of the detachment being considerably to the rear and left. I called to the men to crawl to the rear and in this would try and protect them. The answer came that Burton was hurt and could not walk. I then told Walley to see if he couldn't help him in some way to the rear. Without further ado, Walley mounted and galloped to him, dismounted, helped him in the saddle, mounted behind him and rode to the rear without getting injured. In the meantime myself and Sergt. Williams were exposed to the fire of at least 25 or 30 Indians at a distance of less than 400 yards and without the slightest shelter whatever but we had the advantage that the Indians had to fire downhill with the result that most of the shots went high. They however struck my horse twice, my new cavalry equipment making a good target of him; for the same reason they seemed to concentrate their fire on me, easily recognizing me by my color and uniform as the commanding officer. Myself and Sergt. Williams were both armed with carbines and being very fair marksmen, Williams especially so, and being cool and deliberate, we made the Indians respect us and enabled Glasby and Wilson to crawl to a place of safety—although it was about half an hour before the Sergeant and myself were enabled to reach the command. It was then nip and tuck with us trying to prevent Valois' abandoned horses from falling into the hands of the Indians. This we succeeded in doing, and as it was getting dark and our ammunition was about exhausted we went back to Cañada Alamosa for supplies and took up the trail the next morning at day-break, having had three men wounded, ten horses killed and several wounded. The Mexicans suffered some loss but I was unable to learn exactly how much. During the fight the men as a rule behaved splendidly and displayed much bravery. A notable exception was Private Martin of Valois' command who having been dismounted was making his way to the rear when I noticed some Indians sneaking around trying to cut him off. I immediately rode to his assistance and opened on them with my six-shooter, during which they shot my horse, when they broke for cover and I took Martin back with me to the command. A short time afterwards seeing Private Wilson in the same predicament I ordered this man Martin to go to his relief but he had had enough and was afraid to do so, and I had to take him with me almost at the muzzle of my six shooter. I have recommended Private Walley for a Medal of Honor for his rescue of Burton & Trumpeter Rogers for carrying my message to Valois under the peculiar circumstances stated—for a Certificate of Merit. I write this long letter in the interest of 1st Sergeant Moses Williams in his application for a transfer to the Ordnance Department and I further recommend him for a Medal of Honor for his bravery in volunteering to come to my assistance, his skill in conducting the right flank in a running fight of three or four hours, his keensightedness in discovering the Indians in hiding and which probably prevented my command from falling into a trap, for the skill and ability displayed by him in rallying my men when I was dismounted and unable to reach them, and lastly for his coolness, bravery and unflinching devotion to duty in standing by me in an open exposed position under a heavy fire from a large party of Indians, at a comparatively short range and thus enabling me to undoubtedly save the lives of at least three of our men.

I am, Sir,
Very respectfully,
Your obedient Servant
George R. Burnett
1st Lieut. USA, Ret.
formerly 2d Lt Troop "I" 9th Cavy

Fort Stevens, Oregon
July 29th 1896

(Through Headquarters Dept of the Columbia)
Sir:

In compliance with paragraph 175, A.R., I have the honor to forward herewith an application requesting to be awarded a medal of honor for distinguish bravery in action with the hostile Apache Indians in the foothills of the Cuchillo Negro Mountains, New Mexico, August 16th 1881. I enclose herein recommendation of 1st Lieut. Geo. R. Burnett, who was my immediate commanding officer during the engagement and who was an eye witness to all of my actions. I forward an application at this late date because I have just been informed that two of my comrades have received medals of honor for their bravery in the same engagement. The enclosed recommendation will show that I am also entitled to be recognized for a medal of honor.

I am Sir,
Very respectfully,
Your obedient Servant

Moses Williams

Ordnance Sergeant
U.S. Army

War Department
41940 A.G.O. Adjutant General's Office
Washington, November 23, 1896

Ordnance Sergeant Moses Williams,
Fort Stevens, Oregon.
Thro. Headquarters Department of the Columbia,
Vancouver Barracks, Wash.

Sergeant:

I am instructed by the Assistant Secretary of War to transmit to you the accompanying medal of honor, awarded to you by direction of the President of the United States for most distinguished gallantry in action with hostile Apache Indians in the foot hills of the Cuchillo Negro Mountains, N. M., August 18, 1881, while serving as 1st Sergeant Troop "I" 9th Cavalry.

The remarks of the Assistant Secretary of War in making this award are as follows:

"This soldier rallied the detachment when his commanding officer was dismounted and unable to reach it; he skillfully conducted the right flank in a running fight for three or four hours; his keen-sightedness in discovering the Indians in hiding probably prevented the command from falling into a trap; and his coolness, bravery, and unflinching devotion to duty in standing by his commanding officer in an exposed position under a heavy fire from a large party of Indians was undoubtedly the means of saving the lives of at least three of his comrades."

Very respectfully,

(1 Incl.) Assistant Adjutant General

Inventory of the effects of Moses Williams, late an Ordnance Sergt ~~of Captain~~ U.S.A. Retired ~~of the~~ ~~Regiment of~~, who died at Vancouver Wash., on the 23rd day of August, 1899, by reason of Heart failure, and was buried at Vancouver Barracks, Wash. No. of grave 393

INVENTORY.

ARTICLES.	No.	ARTICLES.	No.	ARTICLES.	No.
Bedstead & Spring	1	Gold rim spectacles	1	[illegible]	5
[illegible]	[illegible]	[illegible]	[illegible]	[illegible]	[illegible]

MONEY: Specie $23.00; Notes $

I certify that the above Inventory comprises all the effects of Moses Williams, Ord. Sergt. Ret., deceased, and that the effects are in the hands of [illegible], at Vancouver Barracks, Wash., to be disposed of by a Council of Administration.

Walter C. Sweeney
2nd Lieut 24th Infty
~~Commanding the~~

Station: Vancouver Barracks, Wash.
Date: NOV 18 1899

[A. G. O. March 21, 1898, No. 13.] [TRIPLICATE.]

Inventory of possessions of Ordnance Sergeant Moses Williams made after his death (Courtesy National Archives and Records Service)

Chapter Twenty-Five

The 10th Cavalry in the Campaign against Victorio

The 9th Cavalry bore the brunt of the fighting against Victorio, but the 10th also contributed significantly to the successful end of the campaign. Lieutenant John Bigelow described some of the regiment's actions in this grueling operation.[1]

In 1880 the regiment was engaged in what was known as the Victoria campaign, a series of operations directed against the Mescalero Apache chief Victoria, who, with his whole band, had escaped from the military authorities in New Mexico. On the 30th of July Colonel Grierson, with a party of only six men, was attacked by this band between Quitman and Eagle Springs. Lieutenant Finley with fifteen men of Troop G came up, engaged the Indians, and held them in check until the arrival of Captains Viele and Nolan with Troops C and A. In an engagement, which lasted four hours, seven Indians were killed and a number wounded. On the side of the troops one soldier was killed and Lieutenant Colladay wounded. The hostiles were driven off and pursued to the Rio Grande. In the course of the pursuit a running fight of at least fifteen miles was maintained near the Alamo by a detachment under Corporal Asa Weaver of Troop H. Private Tockes, Troop C, was killed. His horse went to bucking and then ran directly into the Indians. When last seen alive this devoted trooper had dropped his reins, drawn his carbine, and was firing to the right and left. His skeleton was found months afterwards. For his gallant conduct in this affair, Corporal Weaver was promoted to a sergeant on the ground. The same day Captain Lebo, with Troop K, followed an Indian trail to the top of the Sierra Diablo, captured Victoria's supply camp of twenty-five head of cattle, and a large quantity of beef and other provisions on pack animals.

The decisive blow of the campaign was struck a few days later by Colonel Grierson. Being on the trail of Victoria, heading northward through the Carriso Mountains, Grierson switched off to his right, and, by a forced march of sixty-five miles, swung around the flank of the unsuspecting Apaches and struck them in front, forcing them southward, across the frontier. Victoria never went raiding again on American soil. He was subsequently killed by Mexican troops near Lake Guzman, Mexico.

Chapter Twenty-Six

Colonel George Andrews pleads for a change of station for the 25th Infantry

Black regiments tended to serve very long periods in the most remote locations. The 25th Infantry was no exception: its companies served at out-of-the-way Texas posts for a decade, from 1870 to 1880. As far as the regimental commander, Colonel George Andrews, was concerned, this was entirely too long, and the effects of such isolation were profound. Officers were going native, marrying into local families, and assimilating into a culture of questionable morality. The enlisted men were employed more as laborers than soldiers,[1] and they were spending their time and money in disreputable border towns. In addition, a very nasty court-martial concerning accusations of incest by one officer against another had just run its course.[2] Besides, being stuck in the remote parts of western Texas was not enhancing Andrews's career either. He wanted to move his regiment to a more civilized environment as quickly as possible.

Army officialdom wasted no time in granting Andrews's request for changes of station. Less than two months after his letter of March 22, 1880, reproduced below,[3] on May 17, 1880, his regiment started to leave Texas. The 25th moved north, and established its headquarters at Fort Randall, on the Missouri River in southeastern Datoka Territory. The companies of the regiment were assigned there and at two other Dakota posts, Hale farther up the Missouri and Meade in the Black Hills. The improvements represented by the transfer may have been questionable. As the regimental historian, Captain John Nankivell, wrote, "Opinions may differ as to the 'vicinity of civilization' that this latest move of the regiment entailed, but at least it was a change and as such was welcomed by the regiment."[4]

Headquarters 25th infantry
San Antonio, Texas, March 22nd, 1880

Assistant Adjutant General
Department of Texas
San Antonio, Texas
Sir,

I have the honor to respectfully request that the stations of the headquarters and Companies of my Regiment may be changed.

In this connection, I desire to invite the attention of the Department Commander, to the following short *resumé* of facts, which constrain me to make this request.

The headquarters of the regiment were established at Fort Davis eight years ago this spring; some of the companies were stationed at Forts Davis, Stockton, Quitman, and Bliss, as long ago as 1870, and although some changes have taken place, all the companies, with perhaps one exception, have served in the section of country where the posts named are located from five to six years.

The result of being stationed so long in a country having the peculiar characteristics which pertain to this section, is that the Regiment is becoming localized; two officers have already married into families residing contiguous to the posts, and rumor promises one, if not two more alliances of the same kind. What the entanglements of the enlisted men may be, it is impossible to tell, the experiences of the Commanding General will suggest what they may be.

I do not hesitate to state that the duties devolved upon the Regiment, during this long stay in one locality, have been onerous in the extreme, more so than that of any other Infantry regiment serving in this Department. Speaking from memory (the records are not accessible to me at this time) the garrison of Fort Davis during the sixteen months ending with the year 1875 marched over 8000 miles, each company averaging over 108 miles per month, while scouting maps of over 1500 miles of country were made and forwarded.

Upon an examination of the Report of the Department Commander for 1879, I find that during the year the Infantry troops (not mounted) in the Department marched 4552 miles, of this distance the companies of my regiment marched 3700 miles, or over 81¼ per cent. I also find, that during the year, troops commanded by officers of Infantry, marched 6573½ miles, of this distance, 3121 miles, or 47⅝ per cent, were accomplished under the command of officers of my regiment, or omitting Lieut. Bullis, 24th infantry, who with his command are virtually cavalry, the percentage amounts to nearly 72½ per cent.

The amount of labor performed by the companies of the Regiment, during the past year in building roads, is well known to the Department Commander to have been Herculean.

Several times during the eight years referred to, has the garrison of Fort Davis been depleted by detached service, that for months at a time, it has been difficult to obtain two guards, and I presume the other posts have been similarly situated. Drills even of squads, in most of the companies, are almost matters of tradition.

I am confident that the records of your office will show that during the last five years, there have been fewer desertions, fewer men in confinement, and less Court Martial cases in this regiment than in any other regiment serving in the Department.

I have good reasons for believing that both officers and men are becoming discouraged and disheartened; one officer has already resigned, in my opinion as much from these causes as any other.

I am led to believe that the men of Company "E," are longing for their terms of enlistment to expire, with a determination not to reenlist, and they include some of the best men in the Regiment, others, including non-commissioned officers, I find are reenlisting in other regiments, heretofore a rare occurrence.

In a word, the regiment as a whole feels that it is no longer a body of soldiers, but "hewers of wood and drawers of water" ostracized and ignored by all.

In addition to the foregoing the recent notorious Court Martial case of an officer of the regiment has added its baneful influence towards completing the trials of the Regiment, and to assist in its demoralization.

Another matter, which as it now stands, is not without great influence for harm to the regiment, viz., the equivocal position occupied by its Colonel. Of the Colonels belonging in this Department, I am now the third in rank but from appearances am expected to occupy a subordinate position, while those who are my juniors by many years have comparatively independent commands, and of much greater importance than that of a post only.

I am therefore placed in a false position, and subjected to criticisms, which so far as I am aware are undeserved, and against which I cannot defend myself.

Very respectfully,
Your obt servt,
Geo. S. Andrews
Co. 25th Infy, Comdg

Chapter Twenty-Seven

A borderland love triangle: white officer, black soldier, and Latino woman

This affair, while it did not involve members of the 25th Infantry, may have been the kind of thing Colonel Andrews had in mind when he argued the negative influence of borderland service on his regiment.

General Court-Martial — War Department
Adjutant General's Office
Orders No. 50 — Washington, August 23, 1880

I. Before a General Court Martial which convened at Fort Clark, Texas, June 2, 1880, pursuant to Special Orders No. 99, Headquarters Department of Texas, San Antonio, Texas, May 24, 1880, and of which Colonel D. S. STANLEY, 22th Infantry, is President, was arraigned and tried—

2d Lieutenant *Theodore Decker*, 24th Infantry.

Charge I.—"Conduct unbecoming an officer and a gentleman, in violation of the 61st Article of War."

Specification 1st—"In this: that he, Second Lieutenant *Theodore Decker*, 24th Infantry, while dressed in the uniform of an officer of the United States Army, was drunk, and did visit the premises of a Mexican prostitute, one Refugia Estrada, *alias* Cuca, the mistress of an enlisted man, Private John Rollins, Company F, 24th Infantry. This at or near the town of Eagle Pass, Texas, on or about April 12th, 1880."

Specification 2d—"In this: that he, Second Lieutenant *Theodore Decker*, 24th Infantry, while dressed in the uniform of an officer of the United States Army, did, upon the premises of a Mexican prostitute, one Refugia Estrada, *alias* Cuca, the mistress of an enlisted man, Private John Rollins, Company F, 24th Infantry, engage in a disgraceful shooting affray with said Rollins, during which affray said Refugia Estrada was shot and killed, and said Lieutenant *Decker* was shot in the face and shoulder. This at or near the town of Eagle Pass, Texas, on or about April 12th, 1880."

To which charges and specifications the accused, Second Lieutenant *Theodore Decker*, 24th Infantry, pleaded "Not Guilty."

Finding.

The court, having maturely considered the evidence adduced, finds the accused, Second Lieutenant *Theodore Decker*, 9th Cavalry, as follows:

Of the 1st *Specification,* "Guilty."
Of the 2d *Specification,* "Guilty."
Of the Charge, "Guilty."

Sentence.

And the Court does therefore sentence him, Second Lieutenant *Theodore Decker*, 24th Infantry, "*To be dismissed from the service.*"

II. The proceedings in the foregoing case of Second Lieutenant *Theodore Decker*, 24th Infantry, having been approved by the proper reviewing authority and the record forwarded, in accordance with the provisions of the 106th Article of War, for the action of the President, the following are his orders endorsed thereon:

Executive Mansion, Washington, August 20, 1880

The sentence in the foregoing case of Second Lieutenant *Theodore Decker*, 24th U.S. Infantry, is hereby confirmed.

R. B. Hayes

III. By direction of the Secretary of War, the sentence in the case of 2d Lieutenant *Theodore Decker*, 24th Infantry, will take effect September 4, 1880, from which date he will cease to be an officer of the Army.

By Order of General Sherman:

R. C. Drum
Adjutant General

Chapter Twenty-Eight

Encounter with Racism: The 10th Cavalry at San Angelo, Texas

In the late 1870s and early 1880s, more than a decade after the end of the Civil War, Texas remained an unpleasant and unaccommodating assignment for black soldiers. One of the worst spots in this generally hostile environment was Fort Concho, near the small town of San Angelo, where elements of the 10th Cavalry served during the period of the campaign against Victorio.

At San Angelo, local residents repeatedly insulted, menaced, and harassed soldiers of the 10th Cavalry. The soldiers made plain early their willingness to retaliate. In 1877 and 1878, the soldiers responded twice to civilian harassment by going to town saloons in force and shooting up business establishments in which they had been threatened.[1] The second of these episodes is described by Frederic Remington in the article called "How the Worm Turned."[2]

Remington used as a vehicle for his story a conversation in Cuba with a black veteran that took place just before the fighting started at the end of June 1898. The old trooper disingenuously claimed to have heard about the shooting in a town saloon but not to have been present. Coming as it did during the period of the spread of Jim Crow legislation and racial violence incited by whites, this article reminded readers of *Collier's* that, when provoked and abused, black soldiers would defend their dignity and retaliate.

In addition to telling a good story, Remington's article had two noteworthy characteristics. It highlighted the role of a "Sergeant Gadsby" as leader of the soldiers. This soldier was actually Sergeant George Goldsby, who deserted shortly after leading the attack on the saloon, probably in fear of his life. Goldsby, who was the father of legendary Indian Territory outlaw Cherokee Bill, became something of a legend himself.[3] More than thirty years after he disappeared from the Army, rumors circulated that he had been seen and that he was in reality Pancho Villa, the Mexican revolutionary.[4]

Remington's article also said something very important about soldier violence. The troopers did not riot, run amuck, or strike out randomly. They did not ride through town, terrorize citizens, and vandalize property in an indiscriminate fashion. They focused on places where they had met affront, planned their responses carefully, selected appropriate objectives, and acted in a disciplined military fashion. Even when responding to civilian insults and outrage, they remained soldiers.

Finally, in 1881, just months after the 10th Cavalry had played a significant role in ending the Apache conflict in western Texas, a white sheep rancher shot and killed Private William Watkins in a San Angelo saloon. At that point, the soldiers issued their ultimatum and once again took direct retaliatory action. The ultimatum, signed "U.S. Soldiers," was the work of white and black soldiers alike, both of whom had been reviled and victimized by the civilians they were assigned to protect. Colonel Benjamin Grierson, who commanded the regiment and the post, dutifully tried to control his men but was unable to prevent their retaliatory raid.

"How the Worm Turned," *Collier's*, May 4, 1901

". . . You say you have fought white men. You are not old enough to have been in the Civil War; so how could that have been?"

"This wa'nt no civil war—this was out in Texas, whar Ah fo't white men. Say, Cap'en, be yu a Texas bown—Ah reckon not?"

Knowing that Texans were not in need of my sympathies, I protested my thoroughly judicial frame of mind concerning them.

"Well—Ah don't tell 'bout fightin' white men much. White men don't seem to want to heah 'bout it. Come to think 'bout it, Ah didn't fight that time. Ah only heared 'bout it. Yu see, Cap'en, thar's all kinds of white men. Some of them is good to people of ma colah, and agin, some of 'em is pizen, and the pizenest kind of white men used to live out on the plains of Texas. Them punchers and buffalo hunters and whiskey men didn't think no mo' of shootin' a po' nigger man than yu would of lightin' a cigarette. Ah have had one of them men set to shootin' at me soon as Ah come into town, and keep it up till Ah could get out of range, and my horse jus' a burnin' the grass too. He didn't hit me 'cause he was tanked up, Ah s'pose. In them days, Ah was a-servin' in the cavalry. Say, Boss—yu needn't tell my Cap'en that—Ah don't let on Ah evah served in the cavalry.

Being reassured, he continued: "Well—Ah didn't fight, Boss—Ah only heared 'bout it. Ah reckon we'll both forget this Texas fight befo' day aftah to-morrow, when we gets tangled up with tham Span-yards. Say, Boss—when all these yah cannons and balloons and that squirt-gun down to the Rough Riders gets to goin' and everybody is done pumpin' his Kraig—Say! that Texas fight won't cut no mo' ice than a sheep-tick in a buffalo herd."

"Go on with your Texas fight."

"Well—Ah was a-servin' in the cavalry, way back yondah at Fort Concho in Tom Green County, Texas, and them Texicans use' to shoot at us nigger soldiers on sight. They use' to run us out of town whenevah we'uns would go in to get a drink."

"Good thing," I interpolated, laughing, "keep you away from bad places."

"No, sah—Boss, yu don't think every man with a thirst ought to be shot, do yu? Reckon we'd both be shot right now. We soldiers was a-gettin' hot 'bout it, but the officers wouldn't stand fo' us goin' to town nowhow. One day Peter Jackson was orderly to the Cap'en, and he was sent into town with a note to carry. He was a-ridin' into town, 'cordin' to orders, when a bad white man come out of Bill Powell's saloon, and, drawin' his gun, he done shoot Peter off his horse. He hit him here"—pointing to his own thigh—"and Peter lay in the middle of the road, a-mo'nin."

"His horse come back to the post a-runnin', with blood on the saddle. The guard went down, and got Peter, and brung him back to camp, where he died that night. The officers tried to get the Law on some one, but the peace officers was all in cahoots with the Powell gang, and there was nothin' doin'. We soldiers was mad 'nough tu eat railroad iron. What du yu think 'bout that—shootin' a poor soldier, what was only 'beying' orders, jus' fer fun?"

"Outrageous—perfectly outrageous."

"Well, that was what Sergeant Gadsby of F Troop said—'perfectly outrageous,' said he. We held a meetin' in the quarters, and the Sergeant he made a speech, and the soldiers was wild. He ended up by sayin', 'If we was men, to come on.' We was all ready to 'come on,' so Gadsby took twenty-one of us—Ah didn't go—with two six-shooters apiece, and after dark we run the guard. He tole us he was a goin' down to clean out Bill Powell's saloon or die. He tole us jus' what we was to do.

Say, Boss, Ah wasn't thar—Ah only heared 'bout it from men what was. Ah get to thinkin' Ah was thar sometimes, but, honest, Ah wasn't. The men walked the three miles to Powell's in the dark, and when we got there, Sergeant Gadsby opened the do', and the twenty-one soldiers walked right in—single file—and faced the bar. The room was full of men—must have been thirty-five or forty Texicans in the room. They was might'ly surprised to see us—the soldiers, Ah mean. The Sergeant was the last man to come in, and he locked the do' and put the key in his pocket. We'uns was all facin' the bar: 'What will yu have, gen'lemens?' says Gadsby. 'Whiskey,' says we. Say, boss—yu could hear you heart beat in that room, while we was a-pourin' our drinks.

"Every man bein' fixed, 'How,' says Gadsby, and we drunk.

"As we put the glasses down, Gadsby says—''Bout face—give 'em hell!' and every nigger turned his guns loose. Ah don't know jus' how it all was. Yu couldn't hear your own gun go off, and yu couldn't see nothin'. Pretty soon, Ah got to the do' by slidin' 'long the bar and thar was Sergeant Gadsby, who had it open. By this time they was only a shot now and then in the room back of the smoke, but the gro'nin' and cussn' on the flo' was awful. One white man come a crawlin' tro' the smoke toward the do', and the Sergeant shot him as he lay. When we done got outside, we reloaded and waited, but only seven colored soldiers come out of Bill Powell's saloon, and some of them was bleedin'. Then we went back to the post.

"We didn't know what to do, and we lay all night a talkin'. We knew the Law would be on us. We knew the Texicans had the Law all right, so after 'stables,' we got on our horses with our arms, and we got whar ther' wa'n't no Law,'" concluded the narrator.

"How many white men were killed in the fight?" I asked.

"Ah don' jus' know, Boss; but Ah heared they swept up thirty-five Texicans next mornin, besides de col-lod sojers."

"Why—you didn't run away with Gadsby, did you? You say you were not in the fight."

"No, sah—Ah didn't fight, but Ah quit the cavalry so soon after that Ah didn't heah jus' how that was. Ha—yu talk 'bout Yabor City—that wasn't no red licker in that Powell fight. That was a dead squar' shake. Say, Cap'en, Ah've often wondered how many holes thar was in Powell's saloon next mornin'," laughed the horse-tender, as he got up to go over to his charges.

As he had said, "When the cannons and balloons got to goin'," I forgot all about that Texas fight for a time, but it ought not to be forgotten. When the great epic of the West is written, this is one of the wild notes that must sound in it.

Ultimatum, February 3, 1881[5]

Fort Concho, Texas
February 3, 1881

We, the soldiers of the U.S. Army, do hereby warn cow-boys & c. of San Angela, and vacinity [sic] to recognize our right of way, as just and peaceable men.

If we do not receive justice and fair play, which we must have, some one must suffer, if not the guilty, the innocent.

It has gone too far, justice or death.

U.S. Soldiers
One and All

Colonel Grierson's reaction

Headquarters, Fort Concho
February 3, 1881

General Augur
San Antonio, Texas

The foregoing was shown to me about nine P.M. this date. Myself and Adjt immediately investigated the matter, which resulted in finding that Private Cregan 16th Infantry wrote it, and induced the printers Privates Mitchell 10th Cavly and Kruel 16th Infty to print it. They have been arrested and confined.

Two soldiers, one of Company "F" 16th Infty and one of Co. "E" 10th Cavly have within a short time been murdered at the town of San Angela. The first murderer being furnished with a horse, and assisted by citizens to make his escape, the last one was arrested by the military, and turned over to the civil authorities, Since which time a strong guard has been placed about the post under charge of the officer of the day with a Lieut. of the Guard.

Grierson
Colonel 10th Cavly
Commanding

Headquarters Fort Concho Texas
February 8th 1881

Assistant Adjt General
San Antonio Texas

Telegram relative to trouble between citizens and soldiers at this post received.

The facts are as follows: On the night of the 19th ultimo, Private Hiram E. Pinder, Co. "F" 16th Infty, was murdered in the town of San Angela, by a citizen without any cause or provocation whatever, and the murderer was furnished with a fast horse, by citizens to enable him to escape, and has not been arrested.

On the 31st of the same month Private Wm. Watkins, Co. "E" 10th Cavly was also mercilessly murdered in the town of San Angela, by another citizen, who, attempting to make his escape, ran against one of the sentinels near the barracks, and was arrested; he having a pistol in his possession from which one shot had just been fired.

The next day he was turned over to the civil authorities and guards were at the same time placed about the garrison to prevent soldiers from leaving the post to visit the town.

Later in the evening the guards were further increased and check-roll-calls ordered. At the first check made it was discovered that nearly all of the company of the 16th Inf. to which Private Pinder belonged were absent with their arms, as were also parties from the other infantry companies, and a few men from company "E" 10th Cavalry, to which Private Watkins, murdered the night previous, belonged.

Immediately upon the discovery of the absence of the men, the alarm was given and the long-roll sounded. The officer of the guard proceeded rapidly to the town with the main force of his guard, as did also some of the officers of the companies to which the absent men belonged.

In the mean time the soldiers had arrested Sheriff Spears, and made demand for the murderers.

From the best information obtainable, it is believed that in arresting Sheriff Spears, the soldiers mistook him for a man named Thomas, a constable of the town, and who had previously brutally murdered a soldier in front of the Post-Trader's Store at Fort Concho Texas without any cause whatever, and for which offence he was arrested, released on bail, kept on duty as a Deputy Sheriff, and never punished.

Since, however, he has been made constable, and on repeated occasions of late he has waylaid and robbed soldiers, and still retains his position as constable in the face of all the facts as stated.

The men remained but a short time in town, and upon hearing the call immediately returned, and within fifteen minutes time every man was reported as being present and no injury inflicted upon persons or property.

Additional guards were placed in each company over the guns in the arm racks, and patrols kept moving throughout the night. This manner of guarding the garrison was continued the 2nd, 3rd, and 4th of the present month on account of prevailing excitement pending the examination before the civil authorities which was not completed until the afternoon of the 4th, on which day the Sheriff sent me word through one of my officers, that he feared an attempt would be made by armed citizens to rescue the prisoner, that they were assembling in the town for that purpose, and that he had heard that one thousand dollars had been offered by the murderer's friends to secure his release, and at the same time the Sheriff requested me to send him a company of troops. As I could not do this without violation of the law, and without a fear of the movement being misinterpreted by those not acquainted with the facts and true condition of affairs, as to do so, at such a time, would have the appearance of an attempt to overawe the civil authorities.

I however sent a discreet officer to confer with the Sheriff and at the same time held a company in readiness to move promptly and in a short time the officer, sent to town, sent back word to send his company down to the crossing of the river midway between the post and town, which was done accordingly.

In about one hour and between 3 and 4 P.M. the sheriff passed by the post with the prisoner, I having previously ordered a company to Benficklin (county seat) to prevent soldiers from going there and to arrest any who might attempt to do so. The sheriff and the company proceeded at the same time, the company returning after the prisoner was lodged in the county jail.

Shortly after the Sheriff with the prisoner and the company had proceeded towards the jail, 5 armed citizens rode rapidly past the party in the same direction.

In the evening about dusk, a report, said to be made by citizens from the town, reached the enlisted men, to the effect that the murderer had been taken from the jail and again taken to San Angela. Shortly before tattoo, five armed citizens rode from the town to the river bank, dismounted from their horses and deliberately fired upon the picket guard, which had been placed on the reservation, near the river to keep the soldiers from crossing into the town, and as a precautionary measure for the protection of the citizens and their property.

At Tattoo roll-call no absentees were reported, all being present or properly accounted for.

In a very few minutes and between tattoo roll call and taps, men mostly from the three companies which had not been involved and who were all present on the previous occasion made a rush through their barracks, extinguishing the lights, pulling open the arms racks in the darkness and confusion, many of

Frederic Remington's view of the shooting at San Angelo (From Remington, *Done in the Open* [New York: P.F. Collier & Son, 1898, 1902].)

them seized their arms and rushed for the town. This was at once reported by the men on duty in the barracks, the alarm promptly sounded, two companies [were] sent rapidly in pursuit, but reached there only in time to see and fire upon the last men seen leaving the town, and in a few moments from the time the alarm was given, all were back.

Three non-commissioned officers and two privates, who, upon investigation, are believed to be the leading spirits in this matter, were arrested, the non-commissioned officers immediately reduced, and all confined. Charges are being prepared, and the matter is still under consideration.

A good many shots were fired in the vicinity of the Hotel, but fortunately only one person slightly wounded.

The number of soldiers reported to have been in the town, is greatly exaggerated, there not being over seventy men absent the first time and from thirty to forty the last time.

For three nights, the 4th, 5th, and 6th, a suitable guard in charge of an officer was sent to the town and remained there during the night, notwithstanding

Capt. Marsh and twenty rangers arrived on the 5th. The Captain at once came over to consult with me, and we have been cooperating to insure quiet and order and to prevent further disturbance.

There are now on guard, two officers, 5 non-commissioned officers and 41 privates, with 13 posts regularly established.

Since the commencement of this business, most of the officers have been on the alert, day and night and everything possible has, and will be done, to prevent further trouble.

In addition to the cold blooded murdering of soldiers which occurred lately, a great many others have been killed by citizens and up to this time the murderers have invariably escaped punishment, which the records will show that soldiers are constantly arrested and severely punished for slight offenses by the civil authorities.

I do not make this latter statement as an excuse for the wrong done by soldiers as the guilty ones will be punished, but simply to show under what difficulties the officers are placed to control men, when their comrades are shot down without any punishment being inflicted upon the guilty parties.

I request that a copy of this telegram be furnished his Excellency Governor Roberts in order that suitable measures may be taken by the state authorities to prevent citizens from murdering U.S. soldiers.

Grierson
Col. Comdg

Chapter Twenty-Nine

A SOLDIER'S LOVE LETTERS

Some aspects of buffalo soldier life differed little from the lives of all soldiers at all times. Private Charles Cook of A Company, 24th Infantry, at Fort Supply, Indian Territory, wrote these letters to Miss Anna Payne of Dodge City, Kansas, during 1882–1883.[1] They combined affection, longing, and frustration over their relationship with family news and even a little poetry.

Fort Supply, IT,
Dec. 4th 1882
Miss Payne

Dear friend. I received your missive today and was glad to hear from you. But I must say with which I am sorry that I will have to cease corresponding with you for it is not my desire to correspond with a lady that is afraid to trust me to my gentlemanship and I hope you will send me my letters and photograph and I will send you your letters and I hope you will not think hard of me for so doing. Here is the letter you requested of me to send you. I will send you the present as I said for I am a gentleman of my word. And I hope you will accept of it.

For I have not seen a lady that I thought as much of as you and if ever I come in your presence again I will state to you the reason. I hope you don't hate me if you do feel like a manhater for I tried to act as a gentleman as near as I could and comply with your desire as near as possible. But to show my letters I do not and am sorry you think so.

Now I must close.

From a friend, I remain and always will be when ever I meet you.

Charles Cook

I am all but crazy to think this must be done but I cannot help it.

Charles Cook
Company "A," 24th United States Infantry

Fort Supply, Indian Territory, January 15, 1883

I have been an orphan now for nearly nine years. My mother died when I were sixteen and my father died when I were one year and four months old.

You asked me to let you know when I were coming to Dodge City. It is impossible for me to say for if my letters make you sick to read them why my presence may cause you to get worse and that I would not like to hear.

Anna dear the only way you can prove your love to me is to comply with the question which I before asked of you.

And I hope you will state to me in what way I can prove my love for you as you told me that you would tell me in your letter of the 11th but you neglected to do so as I desire to know. I hope I shall before a great while.

Why is it Anna you wish to see me. Cannot you state it as well with pen and ink as you could with face to face.

I will come if you think you can stand the shock of the questions with which I am going to present to you and I hope that you will not take them as hard as the last one I approached you with. For if I come to Dodge City it will be expressly to see you and I would not like to go to that trouble to be disappointed in my undertaking but I will tell you when I can come in my next letter.

Dear Anna

My heart is bound
With a viewless chain
I see no wound
But I feel its pain.
Break my prison and set me free
Bondage though sweet
Has no charm for me.

I think it is time for me to stop speaking so foolish but it is all true but I guess that you are tired of reading a letter from one that makes you sick to receive so I will close.

I hear that one of your brothers got frost bitten is it true.

My regards to your sisters but my love for you.

Mr. North desire to know whether Miss Fruzann Leyth is in Dodge City or out for he has not heard from her for some time.

No more at this time present.

But please excuse my bad writing for my hand trembles today as I write also correct all errors if there are any.

Please answer as soon as possible for I am always glad to hear from you.

I remains as ever yours,
Charlie

Fort Supply
June 7th 83

Dear Anna

I received your most kind and loving letter of the 6th this evening & was more than glad to hear from you.

When did you think I wanted you to come to Supply.

Why no darling even if you had of meant to come I would have told your mamma not to let you for I don't think it any place for persons of society & especially the ladies.

Dear you say if you did not see me for a year you would not come to Supply.

I believe that to be true my dear for I think your love is so great that you could remain out of my sight a great deal longer but you don't wish to say it now.

O Dear you say you are tired of Dodge City & you don't know what to do.

Well Anna when I get tired of a place I go some where else and I guess that is the way with you for I understand you are going to Topeka Kansas in a few days.

Dear you say you don't understand the word minutest. Well if I am not wrong I think it meaning is small very minute. And the word matrimony I guess you know its meaning if not I will tell you as near as I can.

I think the meaning of the word is marriage.

And what I want to ask you was this. Will you tell me the smallest secret of your heart in regards to marriage. Anna I may be wrong for asking you such a question as that but as I wanted to know and learn your heart & mind and that is the reason I asked you.

I am sorry there are no Birds around there for sale but if I hear of any around here I will get them and send them to you. Dear it is very true you are young but foolish. I cannot say for I guess you are aware of the words that I spoke more so than myself as you have a book with the meanings of all such words spoken but as I have not any you must allow for me if they have the wrong meaning and correct it for me.

You say you are tired of the town what would you do if you had a Husband

and he wanted to live there after marrying you.

Good bye loving one for all I can say is a kiss for you. With my regards to your mamma and sisters & sister Bettie especially.

Yours as ever.

Charles Cook

To Miss Anna Payne

Chapter Thirty

John Howerton's escape from slavery

John Howerton served one five-year enlistment in L Troop of the 10th Cavalry, from September 1882 to September 1887, the period of the 10th's involvement in the pursuit of Geronimo. However, many years earlier he had already had a great and risky adventure, fleeing slavery as a child with his mother. This statement, made when Howerton was over seventy years old and in search of a pension for his Indian War service, provides details of that experience.

A Statement made by John C. Howerton, Late of Troop L, 10th U.S. Cavalry, made under oath by the request of the Hon. Commissioner of Pensions, Washington, D.C., Chicago, Cook County, September 10, 1927.[1]

Chicago, Cook County, September 10, 1927

My full name is John Calvin Howerton. I was born April 16th 1854, a slave & belonged to William B. Bruce, who lived on a farm 5 miles north of Brunswick, Missouri, Chariton County. My mother was also a slave and belonged to the said Mr. William B. Bruce and lived on the said farm. My mother's full name was Mary A. Bruce until she married my father, whose full name was Henry Howerton, also a slave and belonged to Joseph Howerton, who lived in the same neighborhood. My father was sold by his owner and was taken with others down south in 1860 or 1861. About a year after, we heard that he died down there. Now kind sir you asked me to state where I was from 1860 to 1870. 1860–61, 62, 63, I was at home there with my old master William B. Bruce and on the farm. In October or November in 1864 my mother concluded to take us children & run away from her owners. So one night my mother put us children (whose names will be given later) into a wagon that she hired & got the man to drive us to Laclede, Missouri. After arriving there, we were taking [sic] in charge by a white gentleman, and he put us in his cellar under his house & fed us there for 2 or 3 days & nights. Then he put us, mother & her children, & some others, on the train on the old Hannibal & St. Joe R.R. to St. Joseph, Mo., and gave us advice to cross the Missouri River as soon as we could over to Kansas. My mother had with her at the time 4 children, myself included. Their names were John Calvin, Eliza, Polly, and Henrietta. Eliza died young. After hiding in St. Joe, Mo., a couple of days & nights, we was put on to a ferry boat run by a Capt. Blackston & crossed to Kansas. There we were taken out on a farm that belonged to a Mr. Bryant and given a cabin to stay in. That was one or two miles west of Wathena, Doniphan County, Kansas. From latter part of 1864 to 1869, I was on that home farm. In the summer of 69, I went to St. Joe, Mo., and went to Omaha, Nebraska, and got work out on a farm 19 miles west of Omaha & 3 miles south of Elkhorn Station on the U.P.R.R. The farmer's name was John [?]. I remained there until 1871.

Chapter Thirty-One

Moses Green's court-martial, Fort Reno, Indian Territory, 1883

Private Moses Green tried to bash the skull of his first sergeant, the feisty, aggressive Emanuel Stance. Green was convicted of conduct to the prejudice of good order and discipline. He was fined and jailed for nine months.[1]

The record of Green's trial for conduct prejudicial to good order and discipline provides much useful evidence on the nature of life in the barracks. It also shows that a new generation of black soldier was emerging in the 1880s, a group of men who would not tolerate the bullying leadership style of men like Stance.

Fort Reno, I.T.
Sept. 14/83
1010 oc'k A.M.

The Court met pursuant to the foregoing order [HQ, Department of the Missouri Special Orders No. 51, March 10, 1883].

Present

Capt. R. M. Taylor, 20th Infy
1st Lieut. L. A. LaGarde, Med. Dept., USA
2d Lieut. E. P. Pendleton, 23rd Infy
2d Lieut. C. W. Taylor, 9th Cavy
2d Lieut. J. S. Rogers, 20th Infy
2d Lieut. C. J. Stevens, 9th Cavy
Judge Advocate 1st Lt. Palmer Tilton, 20 Infy

Absent

Capt. F. T. Bennett, 9th Cavalry on detached service
Capt C. O. Bradley, 20th Infy on sick "leave"
2d Lieut. J. H. Waters, 20th Infy on detached services

The Court then proceeded to the trial of Private Moses Green Troop "F," 9th

Cavalry, who being called before the Court and having heard the order appointing it read, was asked if he had any objection to any member present named in the order to which he replied in the negative. The accused having no objection to offer, the Court and the Judge Advocate were then duly sworn in the presence of the accused.

The accused Private Moses Green Troop "F," 9th Cavalry, was then duly arraigned upon the following charge and specifications.

Charge: Conduct prejudicial to good order and military discipline.

Specification I. In this that he, Pvt Moses Green Troop "F," 9th Cavalry, did behave in a disorderly and unsoldierly manner in the squad room of his Troop.
This at Ft. Reno, I. T., August 31, 1883.

Specification II. In this that he, Pvt. Moses Green Troop "F," 9th Cavalry, did deliberately procure and provide a deadly weapon, in the form of an oak club, studded with large protruding nails, for the purpose of attacking therewith a Sergeant of his Troop, and did with said club strike Sergeant Emanuel Stance Troop "F," 9th Cavalry.
This at Ft. Reno, I. T., August 31, 1883.

Specification III. In this that he, Pvt. Moses Green Troop "F," 9th Cavalry, did in a deliberate and cold blooded and cowardly manner attack Sergeant Emanuel Stance Troop "F," 9th Cavalry and did strike said Stance several powerful blows over the head and body with a heavy club thereby producing severe injuries.
This at Fort Reno, I.T., Aug. 31, 1883.

Specification IV. In this that he, Pvt. Moses Green Troop "F," 9th Cavalry, did deliberately plan and execute an attempt to kill or inflict serious bodily harm upon Sergeant Emanuel Stance Troop "F," 9th Cavalry.
This at Fort Reno, I. T., Aug 31, 1883.

To which charge and specifications the accused pleaded as follows.

To the 1st specification—Guilty.

To the 2nd Specification—Guilty.

To the 3rd Specification—Guilty, excepting the words "cold blooded," and "cowardly manner," and of the excepted words Not Guilty.

To the 4th Specification—Guilty, excepting the words, "attempt to kill," and of the excepted words Not Guilty.

To the Charge, Guilty.

Sergt. Emanuel Stance Troop "F," 9th Cav. a witness on the part of the prosecution, being duly sworn, testified as follows.

Question by Judge Advocate: What is your name, rank, regt, and station?

Ans: Emanuel Stance, Sergt, Troop "F," 9th Cav. Fort Reno, I. T.

Quest: by J. A. Do you recognize the accused and if so as whom?

Ans: Yes sir. Moses Green, Pvt. Troop "F," 9th Cav. Ft. Reno, I. T.

Quest: by J. A. Did anything occur between you and the accused in the barracks of Troop "F," 9th Cav. on or about Aug 31, 1883, and if so state the facts in detail.

Ans: Yes sir. On that date I was ordered from my squad into the 1st Sergts room Troop "F," 9th Cavalry, on a matter of business, when I returned to my squad and approached the middle door of the barracks. Pvt. Moses Green stepped from behind the door and struck me with a club, as near as I can remember twice. He knocked me senseless. When I recovered consciousness I found my arm broken and my head cut.

The accused declined to cross-examine the witness.

Cross Examined

Question by Court. When you were struck over the head was that the first knowledge you had of the presence of Pvt. Green, or did you see him before this?

Ans: When I first saw Green he had his club to strike then. I had no chance to defend myself.

Private William Green Troop "F," 9th Cav. a witness on the part of the prosecution, being duly sworn testified as follows.

Question by Judge Advocate. What is your name, rank, regiment and station?

Ans: Private William Green, Troop "F," 9th Cavalry, station Fort Reno, I. T.

Quest: by J. A.: Do you recognize the accused and if so as whom?

Ans: Yes sir: Private Moses Green Troop "F," 9th Cavalry, station Fort Reno, I. T.

Quest: by J. A.: Did any disturbance or quarrel occur in Troop "F," 9th Cav. barracks on or about Aug. 31, 1883, between the prisoner and any member of the Troop, state in detail what you know of such disturbance.

Ans: Yes sir, it took place then Aug. 31/83 between Sergt. Stance and Private William Davis, both of "F" Troop, and while this was going on the accused went out of the door, and while Stance and Davis were fussing Stance dropped his pipe. Sergt. Hope parted them and Stance returned to the barracks and went up to Moses Green and asked him if he had kicked his pipe. Green said "No," he hadn't seen his pipe. Stance replied to Green that he thought that Green had seen his pipe over there, and Green said that he (Stance) needn't come into the quarters starting a fuss with him, and Stance replied that he needn't think that when Davis tried to bluff that he could, and Stance brought his sabre down on the accused, and told him that for two cents he would plunge that sabre through him and send him to the hospital.

The accused told Stance to put down his sabre and give him a man's show. Stance said "No," he'd fight him with what the government issued to him.

I heard no more of what passed between them then. I saw them both quit and go out of the quarters.

I was sitting in the saddler's room about half an hour after this disturbance when I saw the accused come from a pile of lumber in rear of the kitchen, towards the upper end of the kitchen with a stout club in his hand.

Quest. by J. A.: I have a club here which I will show you; do you recognize it as the club which the accused had?

Ans: Yes sir, this is the same club. I went into the quarters about fifteen minutes after and was cleaning my pistol. The accused was standing near his bunk, and was fixing his belt, the accused's bunk was right behind the door, the door of the barracks shut right on his bunk. Stance was coming in the quarters, and I saw the accused raise a club while he was standing by his bunk near the open door. This was the door Sergeant Stance was coming through. I saw the accused strike Sergt. Stance with a club several blows, three or four as near as I can recollect. The Sergt. fell at the first blow.

I took the accused away from Stance, the accused said that Stance must not attempt to run him through with a sabre anymore. I took the club away from the accused and threw it down.

Cross examined

Question by Accused. Did Sergt. Stance state when he said that he would use the arms the government issued him that he would be "backed" in it?

Ans: I don't know. I don't remember hearing him say so.

Quest. by Accused: When I "quit" when Stance was quarreling with me and threatening to use his sabre, what was I doing that I "quit," was I doing anything?

Ans: He was not doing anything to Sergt. Stance.

Question by Court: Did the accused hit Stance (when Stance entered the barracks) without any warning?

Ans: Yes sir, he did, he never warned him.

The Judge-Advocate announced that the prosecution here rested.

Private William Lee, Troop "F," 9th Cavalry, a witness for the defense being duly sworn, testified as follows:

Question by Judge Advocate: What is your name, rank, regiment and station?

Ans: Private William Lee, Troop "F," 9th Cav. Fort Reno, I. T.

Quest. by J. A.: Do you recognize the accused and if so as whom?

Ans: Yes sir, Private Moses Green, Troop "F," 9th Cav. Fort Reno, I. T.

Question by accused: Was there any provocation for a quarrel between myself and Sergt. Stance, Troop "F," 9th Cavalry, Aug. 31, 1883?

Ans: There was no cause for a quarrel that I know of.

Quest. by accused: Did you hear Sergt. Stance make any threats to injure me?

Ans: Yes sir. I saw Sergt. Stance draw a sabre on the accused and threaten to thrust it through him, the accused asked the Sergt, to give him a man's show, Stance said he wouldn't give him a show but would fight him with what the government issued him.

Quest. by accused: If you were present at the commencement of the quarrel between myself and Stance, and also when I struck Stance, do you think I had any cause or provocation for what I did, and if so what?

Ans: Yes sir, because he (Stance) threatened to run a sabre through the accused first, when the accused was not bothering Stance at all, Stance wounded the accused's finger with a sabre.

Private Curtis Rouse, Troop "F," 9th Cavalry, a witness for the defense being duly sworn testified as follows:

Question by Judge Advocate: What is your name, rank, regiment and station?

Ans: Curtis Rouse, Private Troop "F," 9th Cavalry Fort Reno, I. T.

Quest. by J. A.: Do you recognize the accused and if so as whom?

Ans: Yes sir, Private Moses Green Troop "F," 9th Cav. Fort Reno, I. T.

Quest by accused: Have you ever heard Sergt. Stance make any threats against me, if so, what were they, and when made and where?

Ans: Yes sir, I heard Stance tell the accused the he'd run his sabre through him, about two weeks ago this occurred. I know of no other threats. I heard Stance say "I'll run this sabre through you. I'll kill you with it."

The accused having no further testimony to offer, made the following sworn statement in his defense.

The Sergeant said in Oklahoma, "I'll bet I'll take my carbine and stow you away in the hospital, God damn you, you'd better stop your fooling and go to soldiering," and again on the 31st of August 1883, he cut my finger with a sabre and threatened to kill me.

I went and got a club and struck him twice, once on the arm and once on the head. I did this because I was afraid of him, as he had made such desperate threats against me.

I did not intend to kill the Sergt., but only to lay him up to prevent his injuring me. I knew that if I hadn't struck Stance a strong blow he'd injure me as it is his habit of striking men with a carbine and I knew that if I didn't give Stance a good strong blow he'd get up and injure me, because it is his custom to strike men.

Cross examined

Question by Court. How do you know that Stance is in the habit of striking men?

Ans: Because he struck Private Abe Washington Troop "F," 9th Cav. who lays now in the guard house with his back injured, and he struck me with a sabre and injured me with it. I know of no other case.

Quest. by Court: Simply because Stance struck you and another man do you solemnly swear it is Stance's habit to strike men?

Ans: I solemnly swear that I think so, he has made threats against me to strike me, and I never gave him any cause for fear that he would.

I've been in the Company with Sergeant Stance about eleven months only.

The Judge-Advocate submitted the case without remark and the Court was closed for deliberation, and having maturely considered the evidence adduced, finds the accused, Private Moses Green Troop "F," 9th Cavalry, as follows:

Of the 1st Specification, Guilty.

Of the 2d Specification, Guilty.

Of the 3rd Specification, Guilty.

Of the 4th Specification, Guilty, excepting the words "an attempt to kill," and of the excepted words, not guilty.

Of the Charge, Guilty.

And the Court does therefore sentence him, Private Moses Green, Troop "F," 9th Cavalry, to be confined at hard labor, under charge of the guard, at the post where his Troop may be serving, for the period of nine (9) months, and to forfeit to the United States ten ($10.00) dollars per month for the same period.

The Court is thus lenient on account of the unreasonable and ill advised conduct of Sergeant Stance towards the prisoner.

R. M. Taylor
Capt. 20th Inf. President

Palmer Tilton
1st Lt. 20th Infy Judge Advocate

Headqrs, Department of the Missouri
Fort Leavenworth, Kas, Oct. 10th 1883

The proceedings, findings and sentence in the case of Private Moses Green, Troop F, 9th Cavalry, are approved and the sentence with be duly executed.

John Pope
Major General,
Commanding

Chapter Thirty-Two

Statement by Private Edward Hamilton, Troop C, 9th Cavalry[1]

Like Moses Green, Private Edward Hamilton also reacted negatively to abusive behavior by his first sergeant. Stance may have been an archetype, but he was surely not the only noncommissioned officer who led through fear. In his statement to the general court-martial, convened at Fort Sill, Indian Territory, in August 1884, Hamilton added his voice to that of Green's, sending a signal to the regiment's officers that intimidation would be resisted. Colonel Hatch and his offciers never got the message, and the deteriorating relations between privates and sergeants finally led to the death of Emanuel Stance in 1887.[2]

Sirs:

I have the honor respectfully to submit the following statement in extenuation of my case:

I am brought before the Court for violating the 62d Article of War, with four specifications thereto setting forth insubordinate, insulting, blasphemous, and threatening language etc. against my 1st Sergeant, also engaging in an altercation with the cook, and refusing to obey the lawful orders of the 1st Sergeant of my Troop, which accusations I deny (as set forth in my pleas before the Court), and respectfully state that before this occurrence the 1st Sergeant of my Troop was always pecking after me and using abusing language toward me, and did ill treat me in various ways, and when I asked him to allow me to speak to my Troop Commander, he would refuse to give me permission to see him, so that I may tell him my grievances, and being a young man in the service less than a year, being treated in such a manner, I began to think that there was no justice, or that I had no rights that he (the 1st Sergt.) was bound to respect, and became discouraged and did not know what to do, and what I said was said, but caused to be said by being driven to desperation by ill treatment. As I have said before, I have been in the service only a very short time, and when I enlisted I was told that as long as I behaved myself and performed all duties required, which I have always done to the best of my ability, I would be treated as a man. So when I was treated inhumanly, and persons with authority seeing such going on each day and countenancing such by silence and not saying a word to stop it, I had to speak at times in my own behalf.

Gentlemen: It is very hard for a man to be called a Black-son-of-a-bitch, threatened with bodily injury, and to have your brains knocked out, and not allowed to speak, such treatment I received, and when I spoke or tried to assert my rights, I was placed in confinement and charged with being insubordinate etc. while the one that abuses me is encouraged and allowed to go free. Such is my case, and I earnestly ask the Court to consider my case in its true light and deal justly with me.

Very respectfully,

Your obedient servant

His
Edward X Hamilton
Mark
Pvt, C Troop, 9th Cavy

Chapter Thirty-Three

Lieutenant Powhattan H. Clarke and the rescue of Corporal Edward Scott

In letters that he wrote home during the fighting against Geronimo in Arizona, Lieutenant Powhattan H. Clarke described the action in which he saved the life of Corporal Edward Scott. Clarke received the Medal of Honor; Scott lost part of his leg. Clarke referred to the troopers of the 10th Cavalry as "nigs," "darkies," and "Chasseurs d'Afrique," but his letters show that he respected their ability, dedication, and toughness.

Letter, Nogales, May 4, 1886:[1]

"My dear Father . . . The day before yesterday (2) evening followed an awful trail 27 miles in mountains. Yesterday broke camp at 6 A.M., struck remains of a large camp. Walked all day over the worse trail I ever want to see. Spotted Indians in a saddle of very high mountains, drove them off the saddle but caught flank fire from inaccessible rocks on our left at 200 yds while the Indians from the same place let our horses have it and stampeded the whole of them. One man was killed and a Corporal shot through both legs. I had some close calls while I was trying to pull the corporal from under fire and succeeded in getting him behind a bush and you can be sure it was a very new sensation to hear the bullets whiz and strike within six inches of me and not be able to see anything. Our men were played out to begin with and from the position we were in all of us would have been struck had it not been for the proverbial cowardice and excitability of the Apache. . . . The Captain is hard to beat and how he came out alive is a wonder to me as the bullets rained in on him, one striking the rocks not over three inches from his foot but he has the nerve of an old nick. I think we dropped two of the Indians for certain. As have been on the walk and ride 6 A.M. yesterday and it is now 3 A.M. to day I am weary. . .

Letter, Camp of Troop "K" 10th Cavalry, May 10th, 1886:

"My dear Mother . . . Our troop has been very highly complimented and the

Corporal Edward Scott, after his amputation (Courtesy Armed Forces Institute of Pathology)

Captain is the hero of the hour. Do not tell me about the colored troops there is not a troop in the U.S. Army that I would trust my life to as quickly as this K troop of ours. I have seen them only once but it was in a place where a stampede would have meant massacre. The firing was at 200 yards from rocks nearly over our heads. No men could have been more determined and cooler than these same darkies were and as for their officers they like them and will risk themselves for them. The wounded Corporal has had to have his leg cut off, the ball that shattered it lodging in the other instep. This man rode seven miles without a groan, remarking to the Captain that he had seen forty men in one fight in a worse fix than he was.[2] Such have I found the colored soldier.

Chapter Thirty-Four

Fifteen hard years: Sergeant John Casey's service in the 10th Cavalry

John Casey served from 1872 to 1887 against the Kiowa and Comanche tribes in Indian Territory, and then later in the campaigns against the Apache leaders Victorio and Geronimo. He also participated in the pursuit and capture of one of the last holdouts from Geronimo's band—Mangus with two warriors, and eight women and children—in October 1886. In the official record, the latter effort appeared to have been the work of Captain Charles Cooper and the men of H Troop. Both Lieutenant Bigelow and later Major Edward Glass, both of whom gave the capture of Mangus one sentence in their regimental histories, mentioned only Cooper, who according to Casey was too overweight to be of much use.[1]

Casey wrote this account of his service in the autumn of 1919, as part of his effort to obtain an increase in his pension from the $6 per month he had received since 1905. The letter of Captain Charles Ayres of the 10th Cavalry corraborated Casey's story of a fall from a horse during a patrol from Fort Davis, Texas, in 1877.[2]

Sergeant Casey's account:

The Partial Military Record of John F. Casey
Late 1st Sergt. Troop H., 10th U.S. Cav.

John F. Casey, late 1st Sgt., Troop H, 10th U.S. Cav. enlisted at Kansas City, Mo., Sept. 28, 1872, was assigned to Troop H, 10th U.S. Cav. at Ft. Gibson, I.T. Served in several military campaigns at Parker, Kansas in pursuit of horse thieves and renegades. Troop transferred to Ft. Sill, I. T. in 1873. Several Indian campaigns in 1873. Red River, 2nd Campaign, Washita Agency, 1873 in pursuit of Kiowas and Comanche Indians. In the spring of 1873 the Kiowa and Comanche Indians surrounded the post of Fort Sill, which caused the command to keep their horses saddled and to arms for the consecutive days. The number of Indians were supposed to be between five and six thousand surrounding the post, which were Kiowas and Comanches, whose chief was Lone Wolf. At that time the Indians were going on the war path so they called for volunteers. Col. B. H. Grayson [Grierson], commanding the post, called for a volunteer to carry a dispatch to the

Indian agent who was about two and one-half or three miles east of the post. Out of nine troops of cavalry and three of infantry and two U.S. Indian scouts none would volunteer, so the Sergeant Major, having known me personally before I entered the army, came to my troop and asked me would I volunteer to carry a dispatch for the colonel to the Indian agent. I told him I would, if they would permit me to ride my captain's horse. He complied with my request and the orderly brought the horse to my barracks at once and I reported to the Adjutant for orders. He gave me a sealed envelope which contained the orders of the commander to carry to the Indian agent. I charged right through the Indians who lined the road and all the surrounding country, clear to the Indian commissary, got the dispatch OK'd by the Indian agent and returned safely without firing a shot, which would have been futile for me to do, as the Indians were in great numbers and had their bows and arrows pointing at me as I rode through, but they did not fire a shot. I returned safely, delivered the message to the Adjutant and in about two and one-half hours the Indians began moving away from the post. This was not entered on my discharge, because at that time my captain had been promoted or was on leave and I was discharged by a young West Pointer, C. G. Ayres, who did not know my military career, therefore gave me no mark of distinction.

In a very short time, probably ten or twenty days, the regiment was moved out on a campaign in pursuit of Chief Lone Wolf and the Kiowa and Comanche Indians who had gone on the war path. This campaign lasted about one and one-half years, from 1873 to 1875. In this campaign the regiment was for ten days snowed in without rations but one hardtack a meal and very little coffee because our supply train was lost in the snowstorm. For ten days they wandered across the plains and could not find our camp. In the meantime I was detailed under the lieutenant with twenty men from my company to go to the rescue of a band of buffalo hunters who were surrounded by a band of Indians and had asked for reinforcement and we were sent to relieve them. During this trip each man was only allowed to carry one blanket and his poncho and we had to drive our picket pins between the pommel and cantle of the saddle. In this way we had to sleep with our heads on our saddles and the horses kept us awake and uncovered most of the night. It was very cold and we nearly froze. After five days out we got orders to return to headquarters. On our return trip two days before we had reached camp it rained and snowed and we had nothing to eat as we had no fuel for cooking. We had to burn buffalo chips and they were wet and would not burn and there was no wood within twenty miles. When we returned to camp the command had moved, but they had left a wagon with hardtack, bacon and beans and coffee, which we came upon after being without food for two days and nearly froze. After we had eaten our meal and fed our horses we started to find headquarters, which was about twenty miles away.

It rained and snowed continually all day and night and we had no overcoats only our ponchos. When we reached headquarters, about 12 o'clock at night, the snow was six or eight inches deep. In this we had to lay down to sleep with our clothes and blankets wringing wet and the weather continued very cold during the entire time we were there, which was ten days or more. In the meantime we were on half rations or less. Our horses had no forage; as the train was lost in the snow storm and we could get nothing due them or ourselves. We had to go one-half or a mile to cut down cottonwood trees and carry the limbs for the horses to eat. This was all the food they had during the whole ten days and we had to carry wood and build log heap fires in the rear of our horses, night and day, to keep them from freezing to death. We had no tents to sleep under only shelter tent halves. We lost between three and four hundred horses and mules for the three regiments, which were two of cavalry and part of one infantry in this camp. Gen. Schofield was in command as near as I can remember. This ends this campaign of 1873, 74 and 75, which to the best of my knowledge ended along about Feb. 1875 at Fort Sill.

When we arrived at Fort Sill there were orders waiting for our regiment to be transferred to Ft. Davis, Tex. We arrived at Ft. Davis, Tex. May 1, 1875, from which post I was on continuous scouting from ten days to thirty days, and from that to a year and a half at a period. At this post we were stationed ten years. From this post we were continuously scouting either as a whole company or in detachments from ten to twenty men in each. In May, 1877, at 12 o'clock at night we were called out to go to the rescue of a band of men who were besieged in Musquiz Canyon. When we got to the canyon we had to file in and charge the Indians in columns of fours, the canyon being so narrow we couldn't deploy. It was so dark we could not see one from the other and there was danger of falling into a subterranean lake. On this charge my horse fell into a partly filled up well or spring and two horses fell on top of me, which knocked my left shoulder out of place. In this condition I continued on the drive for six days until I received relief and returned to the post.

In the years 1879 and 1880, I was on another campaign which is known as the Victorio campaign, in pursuit of Mescalero Indians which came from New Mexico to Texas, murdering and pillaging as they went, about four hundred strong. My company and several other troops in fact a whole regiment or parts of regiments were sent in pursuit of them. This campaign lasted about a year and four months. During this campaign we tracked the Indians from Texas into Old Mexico and the Mexicans drove them back into Texas crossing the Rio Grande near El Paso, Texas. We first intercepted them at Eagle Springs, Texas, had a running fight about dark on the following day, and drove them back in toward Mexico and the Copoka [sic] Mountains and thence into the Crecey [sic] Mountains in the Salt Lake Valley where we engaged in a battle and drove them from the Salt Lake Valley into the mountains again, and two companies of them kept them engaged all day until about 3 o'clock in the afternoon when our ammunition ran out and we were called to the reserves and other troops took our place on the firing line. Shortly after the Indians retreated going in the direction of Old Mexico and between 4 and 5 o'clock in the evening my company was ordered to flank them on the west and keep them out of Old Mexico. While traveling over an unknown trail over sage brush, sand and alkali we became very thirsty and very nearly perished from lack of water, as we had no fresh water, nothing but salty water for two days. About 7 o'clock that evening a cloud appeared in the horizon and in about twenty minutes the rain commenced pouring down in torrents which gave us fresh water for the first time in 24 hours. We got water and watered our stock and kept up the trail to Old Mexico. We arrived too late to keep the Indians off. We followed on the trail until we came to the Hot Springs in the bed of the Rio Grande, where the Indians had crossed into Old Mexico. The Mexican soldiers, who were on the opposite side, took up the trail and followed them into the Candelaria Mountains, Mexico, and there captured all of the band except about eight, including Chief Victorio, who was chief of the tribe. They beheaded him and carried his head to Mexico City. This ended this campaign.

In 1885, April 1st, our regiment was ordered from Fort Davis, Texas, to Fort Grant, Arizona, which was also headquarters at this time of the 1st U.S. Infantry. Sometime in July we were ordered on a campaign in pursuit of Geronimo, chief of the Chiricahua Indians. This campaign lasted about one year and a half, which ended in the capture of Geronimo and his entire band of Indians in Skeleton Canyon, Old Mexico. While on this campaign, we had our supply camp in Rock Canyon, twenty miles south of Fort Bowie, Ariz. And from this camp which was our headquarters we continued scouting at various times from ten to twenty days at a time, down to the border of Old Mexico and as far as Silver City New Mexico and into the Chiricahua Mountains. On this campaign in the fall of 1885 we encountered a very severe snow storm, rain, sleet, and snow.

We got lost in the mountains for four days being snow bound and we could not get out on account of the snow. While in this camp we were not able to build a fire on account of the rain, sleet and snow which continued for four days. Neither could we lay down on the ground, so we had to cut down brush and lie on logs. There were only two blankets to a man. On this campaign I contracted a cold which developed into catarrh, which caused the captain to send for the doctor from Fort Bowie when we arrived in camp, and in the meantime a great many of our men developed symptoms of scurvy. The doctor gave us medicine, what it was I do not know, but it caused me and a great many of our men to suffer great pain and lose our teeth. This campaign ended in the capture of Geronimo and his entire band of Indians, in Skeleton Canyon, Old Mexico, in 1886. During all of these campaigns I lost my health on account of my company being without water half of the time as we could only find water in the mountains and would have to make dry camp and travel all day in the hot sun and dust without any water to drink either for ourselves or our horses. On account of the many campaigns I was on at the end of my term of service in 1888 I was completely broken down physically. When I came off the campaign of 1886, I never was myself again, as I had to frequently have my teeth worked on and be excused from duty by my doctor or captain, because I suffered with neuralgia of the head. In the winter of 1887 I contracted what the doctor called the catarrh. This confined me to my office for two weeks. Shortly after my time expired in March 1888, with no objections to re-enlistment, I then went to St. Joseph, Mo and there took a back set of the same disease with which I suffered at Depcha [sic], which the doctor in St. Joseph called the Grippe, which settled in my eyes, back and jaws, which caused me to lose my teeth and also my eyesight. I was almost totally blind for two months or more, from which I have only partly recovered by good medical treatment. When I was in the service I had been sharp shooter for several years and have been with three department rifle teams. From this you can see that at that time I had very good eyesight, but now my eyesight is very bad and I suffer with the neuralgia in my head so severely that I was compelled to stop working at my trade, which was a barber, and am now in the Military Soldiers Home at Leavenworth, Kansas, because I am no longer able to work and make a living for myself and family. I will further state that I never drank a drink of whiskey or beer in my life. My military career is per excellent, with three fine discharges.

We were ordered back to our post at Fort Grant, and from there my company moved to Fort Apache, Arizona. After we had been in Arizona but a short time, about October 17th, 1886, our commanding officer received word that a band of Chiricahua Indians which had been on the war path for about five years, and had been in and near the Candelaria Mountains in Old Mexico all this time, were on their way back to the United States and were committing depredation as they returned. Orders were received to send out detachments of one officer and twenty men each to intercept them as they tried to get back to the reservation. About six o'clock the evening of October 17th my detachment, consisting of Captain C. L. Cooper, twenty men, and two Indian scouts, sighted the Indians. We went into camp and put out a chain guard. Next morning we took the trail and followed it. In the meantime our two Indian scouts became sick and the Captain detailed me as trailer and scout and I selected Sergt. Cole to assist me in Trailing. In this way we followed the trail without difficulty, and about twelve o'clock we came in sight of them going down the mountain. We waited until they got to the foot of the mountain and we followed them. The mountain was so steep we had to hold the horses back to keep them from falling down. When we arrived at the foot of the mountain the Indians had not yet detected that we were following them and they were going up the opposite side, going west, making for the reservation, supposing that Geronimo was still on the reservation, not knowing that he had been captured. Chief Mangus was supposed to be Geronimo's half brother. Now we struck out on the trail and followed them to the side of the canyon and waited until they had all gotten to the top of the mountain. This way we had to walk and lead our horses, as the mountain was so steep we couldn't ride. Of course, me being the guide and trailer, had to go ahead with Sergt. Cole. While climbing this mountain there would be places where two or three horses could pass each other on the trail. In this way six of us men got ahead of the command and followed on the hot trail up the mountain. While the captain and the remainder of the company followed on behind. The captain being a very large man, had to stop and rest very often and of course we arrived at the top of the mountain one half hour ahead of the command. When we arrived, at the top of the mountain we held a council of war of six men, Sergt. Cole and myself. Blacksmith Boyer, Corp. Foster, Pvt. Sparks and C. E. Miller, and we all swore to each other that we would follow the trail without the command because we knew if we would wait for the command they would get on the reservation and get mixed up with the other Indians and we could never capture them, so we mounted our horses and followed the trail on walk, trot and gallop, until we came to the rear of the renegades. We were then going down into a canyon which formed the letter "T," the canyon running due north and south. In this way they went in from the East and we hemmed them into the canyon. Two men went to the South, two to the North, Sergt. Cole and myself closing up the gap behind them. At a certain signal they commenced firing, but not to hit them, but to intimidate them, and one of them returned about twenty shots, which was Mangus' young son, and they all surrendered to us six men, except the chief, his wife and his interpreter. When the captain arrived we had them all captured and their ponies all corralled. That night the captain had to negotiate with Mangus' aged mother, and as I spoke Spanish, I induced her, by giving her something to eat and sending food to induce them to come in and surrender the next morning at eight o'clock, which they did. This capture occurred at about 4:30 P.M. Oct. 18, 1886. For this service my captain promoted me to 1st Sergt. I had held this rank off and on in the company for twelve or fourteen years, but had been reduced, then reinstated for this service. At this time I was corporal, but I was promoted by my captain to 1st Sergt. for distinguished service in the capture of Chief Mangus and his entire band of Chiricahua Apaches and also was commended by Gen. N. A. Miles, and given the honor of taking them to Florida under the command of a lieutenant.

My time expired in this troop in the last military service March 6th, 1888, with character excellent on two of my discharges and very good on one. Time of service 15 years.

I am drawing a pension of only $6.00 per month since 1905, for fracture of left shoulder and nasal catarrh.

J. F. Casey
Late 1st Sergt. Troop H, 10th U.S. Cav.

Captain Ayres's letter:

Ft. Assiniboine, Montana
Feb. 28th 1893

John F. Casey
St. Joseph
Mo.

Sir

Your letter of the 24th inst. just arrived and I am very glad to be able to do anything in my power to assist you [to] get a pension which I think you are entitled to. I well remember the night in Musquez cañon and your falling into the well with three or four other men and horses on top of you, and the wonder is you were not killed. I also remember perfectly well your coming to me and reporting to me that you were seriously hurt, and someone had his carbine stock broken. I do not remember just who. At the time you were a sergeant under my command in troop "H" 10th Cav. and we were endeavoring to overtake some Indians in the spring of 1877. This to be used as you wish.

Your obt. servt.
C.G. Ayres
Capt., 10th Cav.

Chapter Thirty-Five

24th Infantry soldiers censure some of their own

At a meeting held in the garrison of Fort Elliott, Texas, the soldiers of "F" Company, 24th Infantry, voiced their public disapproval of the conduct of some of their fellows. In fact they went so far as to offer resolutions of censure, thereby taking on themselves the disciplinary function reserved to the chain of command. The soldiers showed familiarity with parliamentary procedure, demonstrated organizational skills, and showed the ability to express their concerns. The senior man among them, William Rose, paid a stiff price for his participation in this extralegal proceeding, but came back to a successful career as an ordnance sergeant. Others escaped, probably because it was impossible to manage an infantry company without such competent non-commissioned officers.

Jacob Clay Smith, the instigator and secretary, never had a problem with shyness. He too seems to have escaped the wrath of military justice. Smith was the one who recommended fellow sergeant Edward Baker for the Medal of Honor that Baker ultimately received for the rescue under fire of a wounded comrade. After twenty years in the Army, Smith settled in Washington, D.C., where he supported himself as a real estate agent.

Fort Elliott, the site of this remarkable meeting, had been established in 1875 during the climactic fighting on the Southern Plains. It was the northernmost post in Texas. Built in the panhandle on the headwaters of the Red River near the town of Mobeetie, it blocked routes into Texas from reservations to the north in Indian Territory, discouraging Indians from leaving the agencies and returning to western Texas.

The meeting:[1]

(Correspondence of the *Army and Navy Journal*)
Fort Elliott, Texas

December 15.

Pursuant to a call of Corporal Jacob C. Smith, of Co. F, 24th Inf., a rousing meeting of the enlisted men of said company was held on the evening of Dec. 15, 1886, for the purpose of expressing contempt at the conduct of Sergt. Chas.

Conner and party, two privates, one of Co. B and one of Co. F, 24th Inf., who, while being detailed, armed and provided with proper orders from this post, and en route to Fort Leavenworth, Kas., Military Prison, as guards to two military convicts, did suffer themselves to be disarmed in broad daylight by two unmasked highwaymen on the Fort Worth and Denver Railroad, notwithstanding notice had been given the sergeant and party that the robbers were on the train. The meeting was called to order by Sergt. M. Wilcox, Acting Chairman. Corpl. J. C. Smith was appointed Acting secretary. Sergt. Wm. Wilkes was elected to the Chair. Corpl J. C. Smith was elected Secretary. 1st Sergt. Wm. Rose, Pvt. A. L. Lewis and Sergt. John D. Spurling were elected as a committee on resolutions.

The committee offered the following resolutions which were enthusiastically received:

Resolved, That we, the undersigned members of Co. F, 24th Inf., as a committee of the same, do hereby each and all of us condemn the action of Sergt. Chas. Conner and party, consisting of one private of Co. B and one private of Co. F, of the 24th U. S. Inf., who did suffer the train, through cowardice, to be robbed by three unmasked highwaymen, on which the party were traveling as armed Government passengers.

Resolved, that the cowardly and unsoldierly conduct of Sergt. Conner in allowing himself and party to be disarmed did bring disgrace on himself, his company, regiment, and U.S. Army in general, and shame to the faces of all lovers of the military.

Resolved, That the cowardice of Sergt. Conner was instrumental in bringing about a loss to the taxpayers of this country (to the extent of the losses of that class on board the train at the time of the robbery) whom it should have been, as their servant, his aim to protect, if necessary, with the blood of himself and party.

Resolved, That Sergt. Conner has, in our opinion, belied his warrant as a non-commissioned officer.

Resolved, That as our action is based on the report published in the Fort Worth (Tex.) *Gazette*, a copy of our action be sent to that paper and to the *Army and Navy Journal*, and ask that it be published to the world.

W, Rose, 1sr Sergt. Co. F
Asia L. Lewis, Pvt. Co. F. Committee
John D. Spurling, Sergt. Co. F.
William Wilkes, Sergt. Co. F, Chairman.
J. Clay Smith, Corpl. Co. F, Secretary.

The reaction:[2]

A Breach of Discipline

To the Editor of the *Army and Navy Journal*:

Of all extraordinary things we hear and read of concerning the Army the meeting of the enlisted men of Co. F, 24th Inf., at Fort Elliott, Texas, which is reported in your issue of Dec. 25, as having been held on the evening of Dec. 15, is the most extraordinary. It is almost incredible that such a thing could be allowed by either company commander or post commander, and the proceedings was, without doubt, one of the most open violations of par. 5, Article I., Regulations of the Army of 1881, that was probably ever heard of in the Regular Army. National Guard people and militia may do that sort of thing, but for a company of Regular Infantry to hold a "rousing meeting" and pass resolutions thereat, is a most extraordinary breach of discipline.

The outcome:[3]

Court-Martial Cases

Before a G.C.M. at Fort Elliott, Texas, was tried Sergt. Chas. Connor, Co. F, 24th Infantry, for allowing himself and guard to be disarmed by train robbers while en route from Fort Elliott to Fort Leavenworth while in charge of a military prisoner. Sentence "to make good to the U.S. $26, being the money value of two Colt pistols, the property of the U.S., for which Lieut. A. A. Augur, 24th Inf., is responsible, by such monthly stoppage of his current pay not to exceed one-half of his pay per month, as will reimburse the Government for the loss, and in addition to be reduced to the ranks as a private soldier, and then to be dishonorably discharged the service of the U.S. with loss of all pay and allowances now due or to become due, and to be confined in such military prison as the proper authority may designate for two years." In his remarks on the case, Brig. Gen Wilcox says: "So much of the sentence as relates to stoppage of pay is disapproved, being inconsistent with the findings on the second charge and specification. The remainder of the sentence is approved and will be duly executed. The Leavenworth Military Prison is designated as the place of confinement. The prisoner being now in the hands of civil authority awaiting trial on a charge of murder, the confinement awarded in the sentence will take place when he again comes under military control."

Before the same court was tried Sergt. William Rose, Co. F, 24th Inf., on the

Jacob Clay Smith, one of the authors of the resolution of censure (From Herschel Cashin, *Under Fire with the Tenth Cavalry* [London: F. Tennyson Neely, 1899], 312.)

following charge: "Did, while first sergeant, permit a meeting of enlisted men to be held in the company barracks and did participate in such meeting, said meeting being held for the purpose of denouncing the conduct of a sergeant of the company and others in the Military Service; knowing that a meeting was to be held in the company for a purpose forbidden by he Regulations, did fail to report the fact to the proper authority; and did in violation of Army Regulations cause to have sent and published in various newspapers resolutions condemning the action of a sergeant and party in allowing himself and party through cowardice to be disarmed by highwaymen and permitting the said highwaymen to rob the train on which his party were passengers at Fort Elliott, Texas, Dec. 20, 1886." He was found guilty and sentenced to be reduced to the ranks, and to forfeit to the U.S. $10 per month of his monthly pay for six months and to be confined at hard labor under charge of the guard at the post where his company may be serving for six months. (G. C. M. O., Dept. Mo., 1887.)

Chapter Thirty-Six

Don Rickey's notes on interviews with Simpson Mann

Don Rickey was a distinguished frontier historian, whose best-known book, *Forty Miles a Day on Beans and Hay: The Enlisted Soldier Fighting the Indian Wars*, was first published in 1963, and before his death in September 2000, went through sixteen printings. The following notes derive from interviews with Simpson Mann, who had served in the 9th Cavalry at Fort Robinson, Nebraska, between 1888 and 1891.

February, 1965

Simpson Mann (Wadsworth V.A. Hospital, Leavenworth, Kansas)

First joined the Army in 1888. Enlisted at Cincinnati. Came from Mickles Mill, Monroe County, West Virginia; born in 1861. Joined Army because he was "doin' wrong." Incident involved "moonshine" from neighbors. His mother caught him, objected, and "whomped me twice." As a result he went to Cincinnati and enlisted. He was (27 years) old, relatively, when he enlisted. Walked down the old C. and O, to Cincinnati. "Devilment" prompted him to join Army. At one time, he went to live with Hyer Peck and Will Peck and their mother. Then went back again. After last time went into Wyoming on the railroad, hired by a contractor who wanted men to run a coal mine.

A soldier at the recruiting station in Cincinnati told him how good it was in the Army when he joined.

Wyoming coal mining experience: he was a shooter. He was greatest shooter known, and taught white men to shoot.

West Virginia again, on Wolf Creek, went back to Wyoming to ? Stayed there a long time. Then to Montana on B. & M(?). "Just runnin' around."

Army: Went from Cincinnati to Jefferson Barracks. Then to Fort Robinson,

Nebraska. Thought he had his time, when he took his discharge in 1891. They gave him "a piece of paper with an eagle on it." Rode around on horses most of the time in the Army. At Pine Ridge in 1890, in Troop F, 9th Cavalry. Didn't know Charlie Creek.[1] Worked in Captain Steadman's wife's garden and yard at Fort Robinson. Hardly ever stayed down with troop, but slept with troop in Barracks. Sergeants and Corporals had mostly been in Army a long time. Some of the Sergeants were pretty friendly with soldiers. Just before he went to 9th two or three soldiers (a mob) killed a Sergeant who had beaten soldiers and told the Captain lies about them.[2] This occurred near Crawford. The Sergeant was "dirty mean." The Captain didn't know as much of the soldiers as he should. Didn't take time to find out for himself, but he believed what his non-coms told him. Sgt. Fletcher replaced the man who was killed. He was better, but "all were about the same." Few of the soldiers were married, it was not allowed in the Army. They were not very young men however.

Had laundresses (Chinamen, "down in the hollow.") They took clothes in on Saturday, got them back on the next Saturday evening. Chinese and Mexican men and women did this. Stayed on a "line," not in the barracks. $3.00 a month for laundry.

Soldiers gambled quite a bit, played faro (in Crawford), monte. Won $100.00 once almost before he could turn around. Crawford had a big gambling house. Many soldiers wouldn't have any money 15 minutes after the paymaster had paid them. Soldiers often gambled right in the barracks. Mann didn't know whether this was legal or not. Played lots of poker, not much dice. Few dominoes. "A man could win a sack full of money after the paymaster had been there." Men were often "cleaned out"—"we didn't have a penny." "A man could win so much money it would 'take a horse to carry it in to town.'," i.e., fairly big games. No, he never had any civilian clothes in his possession. They used to go to the Lake Ranche and have a big time. Music: soldiers played guitars and all kinds of banjos and fiddles. Mann played the guitar. Learned to play it in the Troop. He could play anything. Lots of fun. Dances: there were a good many dances. Soldiers danced their heads off in the barracks.

The soldier in Cincinnati had asked him if he drank when he enlisted. Mann said yes. This information went right into Washington (on his records anyway), for his Captain knew he drank. Soldiers had or put on no shows among selves.

Free time: shot craps in barracks. Very few wrote letters. Some couldn't write. Mann can't. Carried water and ties on the C. and O. when a little boy. His father left his mother[;] he had to go to work as soon as he could. Later he broke rocks with a sledge and drove spikes on the railroad. "Them boys thought I was a lump of coal."

Guard duty: he never had any (?) Why did he leave Army?: tired of it, and he wanted to marry a girl he met in Chadron, Nebraska. As a child worked for farmers for 25 cents per day and board. Wouldn't have left home if mother hadn't whomped him. Bigger he got, the more work the old farmer would give him. Once met Grover Cleveland in Des Moines.
Wyoming, Kemmerer.
Montana, Butte, Anaconda, Fort Custer.
Fort Custer: A man couldn't get his horse by the cemetery (Custer Battlefield). The horse say what the man couldn't. Mann told him to look through the horse's ears and he would see ghosts of men who got killed there.

Old soldiers didn't talk much about old days, or their previous service.

Jefferson Barracks: Drillin' on foot not on horseback. Ran around to look at Mississippi River. Lots of places to go—to farms south where there was beer and food. Farmers brought baskets of pies and cakes. Supper was three prunes and a piece of bread.

Once had an altercation with an officer. At Cincinnati they told him that they wanted him to fight. He didn't care who he fought.

Was with Miles. (1891) Miles picked him to be his orderly. Mann was a private. 18 picked later as escort.

Dress parades: had these all the time, too much for me. Guns and sabers had to be kept clean. Done quick. Sunday was inspection day. No special cartridges were put in their cartridge boxes for inspection. Mann had a gallon of whiskey hidden in his foot locker. Lieutenant told the Captain. Captain's wife said, "No you don't, you ain't gonna put Simpson in." Mann felt that since he'd told them that he drank in Cincinnati, they hadn't ought to complain. He never was in the Guard House. He did some guard duty. Prisoners (22) in chains—he took them out and brought them back. Carried a pistol and carbine on guard duty. No saber. Prisoners didn't try to run away. Mann would have shot them if they had tried. Prisoners worked—hard but not fast. Washed, dug ditches, did everything. But had guards watching 'em. Tough men in Troop. "Some were hard as pig iron." Lots of old Army people. Didn't know if any had been in Civil War. Had lots of horseback riding. Horses often naturally mean. He broke horses in the Army. "Horses spent half their time on their hind legs." Many soldiers were city fellows.

Lots of deserters, but only one or two men deserted while he was at Fort Robinson. Old Sergeant was ornery. He tried to do the best he could. Soldiers took guns into town. Army guns were kept locked up in locker, but were sneaked out.

8th Infantry and 9th Cavalry got into it over a dog at Fort Robinson. Infantry fellows hit the dog, and this precipitated a fight. Infantry and Cavalry didn't get along at all. He didn't play on baseball team; he played on beer bottles. Good baseball players—didn't have anything to do but drill so they were good.

Mann was CO's orderly while on guard duty. Felt he did too much—duty heavy. Mrs. Steadman kept his saddle for him. Captain thought it was his saddle. Had a quarrel over it. Told Mrs. Steadman not to let anyone have it but him (Capt.).

Knew George Webb[3] in St. Joe. Worked at Swift's. Married his wife in Chadron, Nebraska, after he got out of the Army.

Eating: Ate in barracks at Fort Robinson. "Them soldiers cooked. One man cooked for 90 men." Good food. Sugar, flour, coffee, salt pork, bacon. Beef came out of the butcher shop early in the morning every day. Breakfast at 6:00 A.M. every morning. Biscuits, good cook. Very little sickness. Sent to Chadron as a soldier. Met wife in Army, wife working for another lady. Not much fighting among soldiers.

Interview II

Barracks: adobe buildings, the Infantry was down by the railroad track. 9th Cavalry had nine buildings. One for each Company. Smoother plaster inside; dove colored. Pictures in barracks: Only one, Abraham Lincoln, no girls, no family. No Indian souvenirs. (Indians smelled back of his head—said he was part Indian.) Lots of Indians hung around the barracks.

Beds: wire beds, iron, 1 high, side by side. Pillow had a cover. Laundresses did take care of these things. Had seven blankets on his bed. Clothing issue was on the 7th of the month, and you got issue as you wanted. When done, you paid for these when you were discharged. He had seven blankets—as many as you wanted.

Solders kept account of their tobacco, and government did too. Horseshoe, plug tobacco. More chewed than smoked. Had spittoons in barracks. Made own bed. Stacked bedding. Mattress and blankets folded twice back in daytime. Shoes and boots were to be placed under bunk. Drinking water: none in barracks. Company guidons kept in separate building. Bell at 6:00 A.M. to get everybody up.

Mrs. Steadman liked beer, and Mann got it for her at the canteen. Beds in straight row. Big stove. Wood burned at post. Sometimes coal. Two men had job of stoking stove. No pool table in barracks room. Had a dog, who slept in barracks, on a pillow. Name was Dick. Covering on barracks floor: no rugs. Swept with brooms. Curtains, yes—were particular about them. Men threw in money to get them. Cartridge belts and canteens kept in room, not in barracks sleeping area. Cartridge belts in room, made cartridge in another building. It was an extra duty punishment. Old guard fatigue too, to make re-load ammunition by an assembly-line technique. Saddle bags kept in with horses, not in the barracks, in tack room (plus saddles). Day room: none in barracks. No trash can. Barracks: "clean as a ribbon." Trash dumped about 1 mile up White River.

Carbines kept in rack in center of barracks building. Round and locked. 2nd duty Sergeant had key. Always used same carbine. Knew own by number of gun.

Wash room: Big tubs (iron) to bathe. One filled tub in evening and then let it freeze. Shaved with cold water. Shaved once a week on Saturday. Wash basins. Could get hot water if you wanted. Hot water piped under floor. Most used cold water.

Didn't know Col. Henry.[4] Saw 7th Cavalry at Pine Ridge. Saw Wounded Knee battleground. Took Indian prisoners to Pine Ridge. Treated well. Major Henry fed prisoners. Many were wounded. Got same attention (medical) as Colored soldiers. Soldiers treated them well. Buried Indians (soldiers). Lt. Mann from

Ft. Duchesne, Utah. Got in there evening, about 3 o'clock. Band playing. Dog on hand. Buildings (barracks) were full of bed bugs.

Soldiers and Cowboys got along fine. Men sometimes stole guns out of locker, to take to town. Cavalry got along pretty well in town. Sometimes fought—hardly ever killed one another. "Soldiers didn't have hard feelings against Indians, they were just people."

Pvt. Simpson Mann, Troop F, 9th Cavalry. Worked in Omaha building the main road from south to north when Grover Cleveland was President, worked here and there and in many places at many things—"and you know, I worked a long, long time!"

Chapter Thirty-Seven

Protecting the Payroll

In May 1889, paymaster Major Joseph Wham, with an escort from the 24th Infantry and the 10th Cavalry, was heading north from Fort Grant to Fort Thomas, Arizona Territory, when he was ambushed. The enemy, who delivered a very effective fire from well-concealed positions, was not an Apache war party but a band of white thieves. Wham's escort could not prevent the robbery but made such a valiant effort, as his report shows, that he recommended two of his men, Sergeant Benjamin Brown and Corporal Isaiah Mays, for the Medal of Honor.[1]

Major Wham's report.[2]

Pay Department, US Army
Tucson, Arizona, Sept. 1, 1889

To the Secretary of War,
Washington, D. C.
Thro Hdqrs. Dept. of Ariz.

Sir:

Referring to the fact that while en route from Fort Grant to Fort Thomas May 11 last, making payment on the April muster, my party was ambushed and fired into by a number of armed brigands, since estimated by U.S. Marshal Meade at from twelve to fifteen, but by myself and entire escort, two non-commissioned officers and nine privates, at from fifteen to twenty.

A large boulder, weighing several tons, had apparently, as is often the case, rolled into the road and stopped, my ambulance had almost reached this boulder when it slowly came to a halt, and to my question, "What's the matter, Sergeant?" came his immediate response from the box, "A boulder on the road, sir." The sergeant stopped, passing armed down the gorge, to the point to clear the way.

They were nearly all at the boulder when a signal shot was fired, which was instantly followed by a volley, believed by myself and entire party to be fifteen or twenty shots.

A sharp, short fight, lasting something over thirty minutes, ensued, during which time the following named non-commissioned officers and privates, eight of whom were wounded, two being shot twice, behaved in the most courageous and heroic manner.

Benjamin Brown, Sergt. Co. C, 24th Infantry
Isaiah Mays, Corpl. Co. B, 24th Infantry
George Arrington, Private Co. C, 24th Infantry
Benjamin Burge, Private Co. E, 24th Infantry
Thornton Hams, Private Troop C, 10th Cavalry
Julius Harrison, Private Co B, 24th Infantry
James Wheeler, Private Troop G, 10th Cavalry
Squire Williams, Private Co. K, 24th Infantry
James Young, Private Co. K, 24th Infantry
Hamilton Lewis, Private Co. B, 24th Infantry

Inviting attention to the following statement, I have the honor to recommend them to the President for the honors provided by pars. 175 & 176 A.R.

Sergeant Brown, though shot through the abdomen, did not quit the field until again wounded, this time through the arm.

Private Burge, who was to my immediate right, received a bad wound in the hand, but gallantly held his post, resting his rifle on his forearm and continuing to fire with much coolness until shot through the thigh and twice through the hat.

Private Arrington was shot through the shoulder while fighting from the same position.

Privates Hams, Wheeler and Harrison were also wounded to my immediate left, while bravely doing their duty under a murderous cross fire.

Private Williams was shot through the leg near my ambulance at the first volley, but crawling behind cover continued the fire.

Private Lewis, my ambulance driver, was shot through the stomach, but the noble fellow was undaunted, and while the blood gushed from his terrible wound, he insisted that my clerk, W. F. Gibbon, should allow him to take the wounded Wheeler's gun, instead of using it himself and buckling on the belt heroically continued to fight until all present were wounded except myself and Corporal Mays, then, without my knowledge walked and crawled two miles to Cottonwood ranch and gave the alarm to Barney Norton, who at that distance had distinctly heard the firing and estimated the first at fifteen to twenty shots.

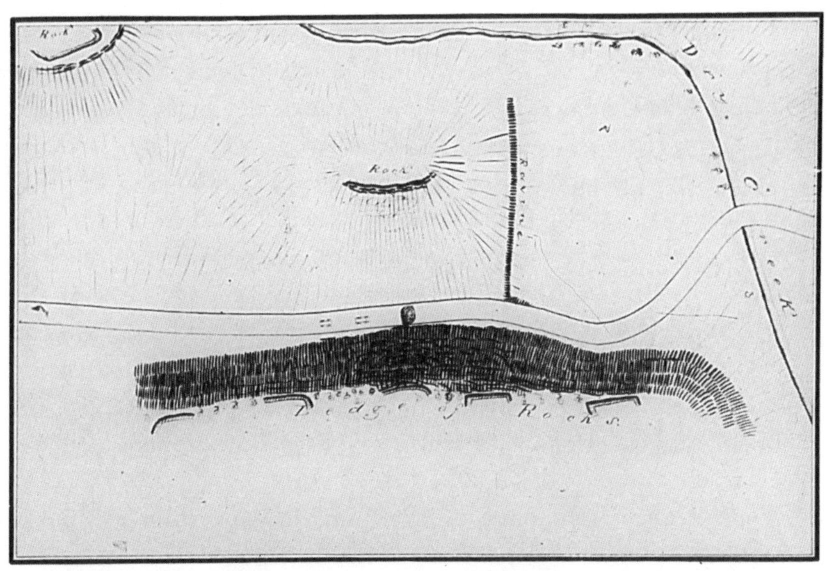

Major Wham's sketch of the site of the May 1889 ambush, showing the boulder in the middle of the road, and the bandits' positions on the high ground (Courtesy National Archives and Records Service)

Isaiah Mayes, one of the heroes of the attempt to save the payroll (Courtesy Library of Congress)

In frequent conversations with the sergeant and other members of the escort I have been convinced that two men did little or no fighting and almost immediately left the field, which reduces the number actually engaged, excluding my ambulance driver, to nine, making a casualty list of nearly 89per cent, but including my ambulance driver it makes a casualty list of 80 per cent of the number actually engaged, and including the ambulance driver and myself it makes a casualty list of near 79 per cent of numbers actually engaged, either of which is larger than any open field fight heretofore authentically reported.

The brigands fought from six well constructed stone forts; the arrangements seemed thorough, the surprise was complete. The leader was, as is almost certainly shown by Marshal Meade, Gilbert Webb, a reputed member of the "Mormon Legion," "Destroying Angels," and participated in the "Mountain Meadow Massacre."

While my men were forced to fight from such poor cover as could be instantly found, the Sergeant, who in the melée became detached with Privates Young and Short, made his entire fight from open ground. However the position which I occupied with the main party was but little better being enfiladed by both the robber flanks, but it was the only unoccupied cover; yet with all this against us, the men behaved as previously stated. The lowest estimate placed on the number of brigands by U.S. marshal Meade is twelve. A cartridge belt worn by one of the robbers and from which there was apparently forty rounds fired, brings the probable number of shots fired from the robber position to 480. I was a soldier in Grant's old regiment during the entire war, it was justly proud of its record of sixteen battles and of the reflected glory of its old Colonel; the "Great Commander," but I never witnessed better courage or better fighting than shown by these colored soldiers on May 11, 1889, as the bullet marks on the robbers' positions today abundantly attest.

I am, Sir, very respectfully,
(Sigd) Jos. H. Wham
Paymaster, U.S. Army

Chapter Thirty-Eight

William Wilson, courage under fire, and desertion

Corporal William Wilson's troop of the 9th Cavalry was one of many sent into the field in the autumn of 1890 in response to the panic that spread among white settlers in northwestern Nebraska and southeastern Dakota. Desperation among the Indians, caused by the disappearance of the buffalo, crop failures, pervasive assaults on Indian culture and society, and confinement to reservations had provided fertile ground for the Ghost Dance religion, which promised an Indian rebirth and triumph over the whites. The popularity of the Ghost Dance among the once-warlike Dakota tribes struck fear in the hearts of ranchers and townspeople throughout the region. Thousands of troops, almost one fourth of the entire Army, deployed in response. Before the campaign ended, about 150 Miniconjou Dakota people of Big Foot's band lay dead, killed by soldiers of the 7th Cavalry on December 29, 1890, at Wounded Knee Creek.[1]

On the next day, Corporal Wilson was part of the escort for a 9th Cavalry wagon train that was encircled by Indians. He braved heavy fire in dashing for help to relieve his comrades. His courageous act was recognized in a battalion order published very shortly afterward and later with a Medal of Honor. Lieutenant Philip P. Powell of the regiment testified to Wilson's courage at Corporal Wilson's later trial for desertion and forgery. Wilson's letter to President Grover Cleveland contained his explanation for his unauthorized departure from his troop, which was sufficiently convincing to have the charge reduced to absence without leave. The government never succeeded in proving the forgery charge, so after reduction to private, he was restored to duty.

Then in 1893, while on duty away from his regiment as a participant in a Department of the Platte marksmanship competition, he did in fact desert and return to his hometown of Hagerstown, Maryland, where he lived a long life and fathered seven children. There, the soldier who had once escaped conviction for forgery, came to be known as "the penman" because he produced elegant calling cards.[2]

Recognition in orders:[3]

Headquarters Battalion 9 Cav

Pine Ridge Agency, SD

Orders
No. 1

On the morning of Dec 30th 1890 the wagon train of this command was attacked by hostile Indians. To obtain assistance it was necessary to send word to the Agency. The duty to be performed was one involving much risk as the Indians, knowing what was intended, would endeavor to intercept the messenger and overwhelmed by numbers certain death would follow.

Corporal Wm. O. Wilson, Troop I, 9 Cav, volunteered for the above duty, and though pursued by Indians succeeded. Such examples of soldier-like conduct was worthy of imitation and reflect great credit not only upon Corpl Wilson but the 9th Cavalry. This order will be read to each troop.

A copy furnished Corpl. Wilson and one to Regimental Headquarters.

By order of Maj. Henry
John F. Guilfoyle
1st Lieut. 9 Cavalry
Battn Adjt

Lieutenant Philip Powell's testimony:[4]

[Corporal Wilson] came under my notice for the first time during the latter part of November at Pine Ridge Agency. He was A.Q.M. Sergt. of his Troop at the time, I think, and I was A.Q.M. of the Battalion. He impressed me as being an intelligent and well-behaved non-commissioned officer, always active in the interest of his Troop for which he drew rations and forage. He came more immediately under my observation on the morning of the 30th of December during an attack upon our wagon train by the Indians. Having conferred with

Captain Loud and Lieut. Bettens as to the propriety of notifying Major Henry of our position *and* the attack, we agreed that he should be notified. At the instance of Captain Loud I wrote a dispatch notifying Major Henry that we were being attacked, and not knowing the strength of the enemy in front of me and to our right, we thought he had better send another Troop to our assistance. Having written the dispatch I turned to the Indian Scouts we had with us, handed the dispatch and directed one of them to proceed to the agency with all haste with it. Both scouts refused to go stating that their horses were played out. Corporal Wilson, who was standing near at the time with several of the soldiers (all of us under fire at the time) walked up to me and said, "Lieut., I will carry that dispatch." I told him "I will not order you to go as it is very dangerous, but if you volunteer you can do it," and handed it to him. I told him to pick the best horse in the command. He took the dispatch, mounted his horse and started. He had not gone more than 50 yards from the point he started from when we observed a number of Indians, probably eight or ten, making an effort to cut him off. We turned our fire upon them and checked them as far as I remember; the Corporal proceeded and delivered the dispatch to Colonel Henry. I regarded the action of the Corporal as gallant and commendable.

Wilson's letter to the President:[5]

Fort Robinson, Neb.
May 30, 1891

To the honor of the
President of the United States
Washington, D.C.

Sir

. . . I will herein give my statement against the 1st specification in my charge of desertion. I became under the influence of intoxication and while under and in that condition I absented myself from detachment and was absent about 9 hours that is from the time I [was] at the Agency and to the time I was arrested at Chadron Neb. on the evening of March 20th 1891 about 5 P.M. when I was about 23 miles from Pine Ridge Agency. I had by hard riding become somewhat sober by this time. Then I began to realize what a rash step I had taken, and after I considered the matter over I had an idea that I would be looked for by Indian scouts and did not think that I would receive much mercy at their hands should they overtake me between there and Chadron.

So I concluded to go to Chadron Neb. and report to my detachment commander by telegram, which I did. When I arrived in Chadron I placed my horse in a livery stable to be taken care of, then I engaged a room in a Hotel, and I then put the remainder of my plan in action as to telegraphing to my commander. I was arrested by a sheriff on an order of Lieut. Williams 6th Cavalry as a deserter, a crime that had never entered my mind. It does not look much like deserting when a man enters a town equipped with Government property complete and riding a horse belonging to the same and equipped the same which was issued to me. I am not a habitual drinker and was never intoxicated before. I would respectfully beg of the authority to give the facts a consideration.

Having been constantly on duty for about 4 months as acting Commissary Sergt. at Pine Ridge Agency, and Battalion 9th Cavalry in the field which was the most mental strain to which I had been subjected to in my life.

I do not state these facts with a view to show that I was overworked or in any way mistreated, for I considered it an honor to hold the estimations of my superiors which is highly essential to a soldier and I am ever willing to do my duty no matter in what capacity, which I think my early days of soldierly [sic] will prove. Attention respectfully called to Orders No. 1, Hdqrs 9th Cavalry, Pine Ridge Agency, hoping this statement will meet a lenient consideration.

I am respectfully
Your obedient Servant,
William O. Wilson
Corpl Troop I, 9 Cav

Desertion:[6]

Endorsement, Captain E. D. Dimmick, Fort Duchesne, Utah, November 2, 1893, to the Adjutant General, U. S. Army, responding to query regarding omission of Wilson's name from the list of "Names Present" on troop roster:

> Respectfully returned (thru post headquarters) to the Adjutant General U.S. Army, Transportation Request (duplicate) was furnished Pvt. Wilson from Denver, Col., to Price Utah, by Major Atwood, A.Q.M., at a cost of $16.00 & commutation of Rations for 3 days $4.50 from Aug. 26th to Aug. 28th inclusive (en route from Denver), Col. To Fort Duchesne, Utah

William Wilson around the time of the Pine Ridge campaign, wearing a uniform embellished with 24th infantry insignia (Courtesy The Wilson family)

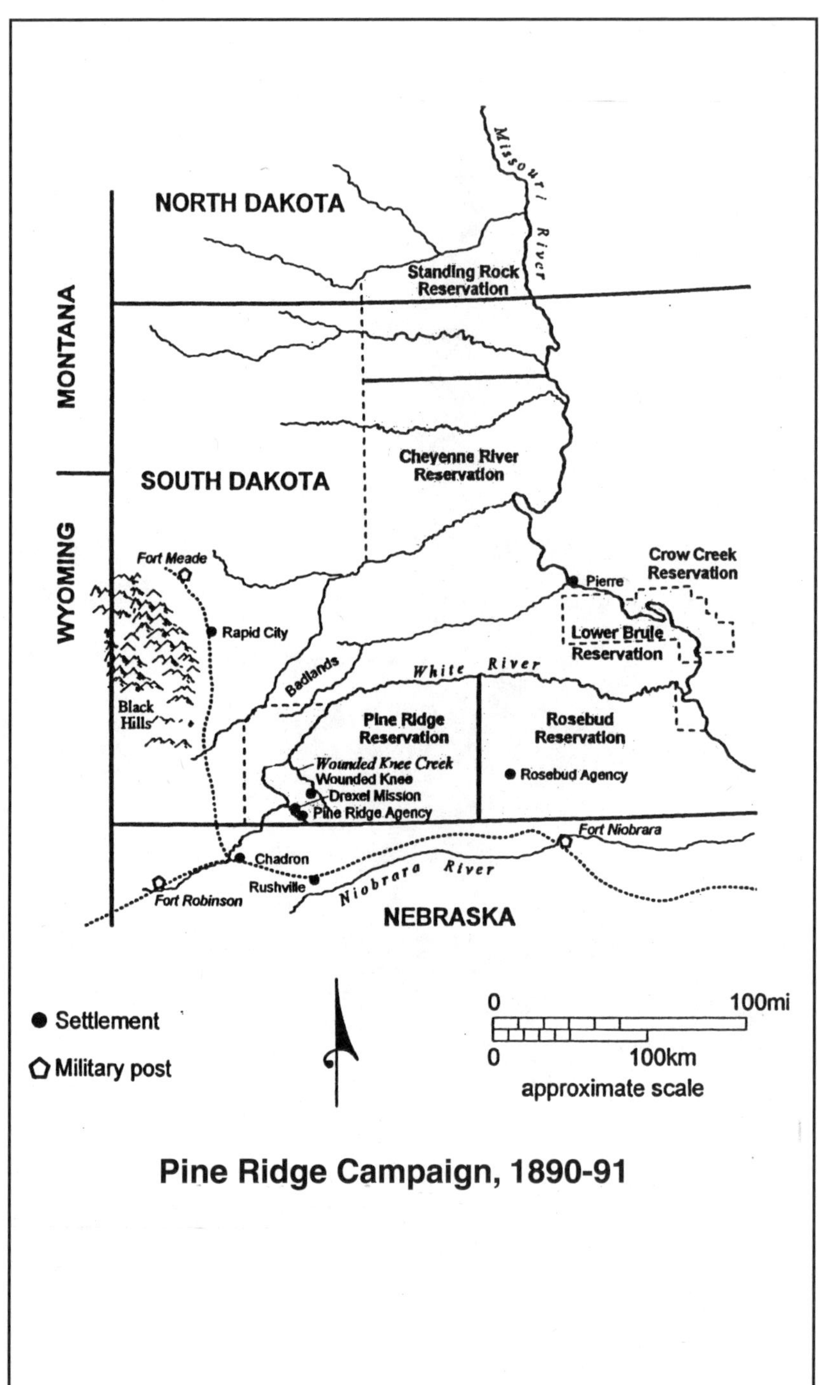

Pine Ridge Campaign, 1890-91

by Capt. Dravo, A.C.S. per S.O. # 23, dated Hdqrs. Dept. of the Colorado Aug. 22nd 1893. Wilson had been furnished with transportation thro to post from Bellevue Rifle Range & com. Of rations to include Aug. 25th 93, with permission to delay 5 days en route, arriving in Denver Aug 22nd, he reported to the A.A. Genl that he had lost his transportation request, covering travel from Denver Col. To Price, Utah. The Chief Q. M. was directed to furnish Wilson duplicate transportation, & the Chief Commsy com. of Rations, for 3 days, but Wilson never rejoined his station, & was dropped as a deserter Sept. 5, 1893.

E. D. Dimmick
Capt. 9th Cavalry, Comdg Troop H

Chapter Thirty-Nine

The poetry of Private W. H. Prather of I Troop, 9th Cavalry

Like Corporal Wilson, Private W. H. Prather spent the winter of 1890–1891 on the Pine Ridge Agency. The verses that he wrote based on that experience covered everything from the causes of the conflict to the specific role of the 9th Cavalry.

The first poem deals with the Ghost Dance religion, the mobilization of troops, and the fighting at Wounded Knee Creek on December 29, 1890.[1] Prather did not consider the actions of the 7th Cavalry on that terrible morning to be unwarranted or unreasonable. In fact, he seemed to view the episode as reflecting well on the regiment.

The second and untitled poem, first published in the *Army and Navy Journal*,[2] is unusual for its expression of empathy with the plight of the Indians. Despite an ironic sense of a common condition shared by the men of the 9th Cavalry, who endured the slashing snows and bitter cold of that brutal winter with only tents for shelter, and the Dakota residents of the Pine Ridge Reservation, the poem also showed an understanding that troops were still required in the event of a resurgence of the Ghost Dance and the panic that it engendered. Prather just wished that the duty had been assigned to some other regiment instead of his own.

The Indian Ghost Dance and War[3]

The Red Skins left their Agency, the Soldiers left their Post,
All on the strength of an Indian tale about Messiah's ghost
Got up by savage chieftains to lead their tribes astray;
But Uncle Sam wouldn't have it so, for he ain't built that way.
They swore that this Messiah came to them in visions sleep,
And promised to restore their game and Buffalos a heap,
So they must start a big ghost dance, then all would join their band,
And may be so we lead the way into the great Bad Land.

Chorus:
They claimed the shirt Messiah gave, no bullet could go through,
But when the Soldiers fired at them they saw this was not true.
The Medicine man supplied them with their great Messiah's grace,
And he, too, pulled his freight and swore the 7th hard to face.

About their tents the Soldiers stood, awaiting one and all,
That they might hear the trumpet clear when sounding General call
Or Boots and Saddles in a rush, that each and every man
Might mount in haste, ride soon and fast to stop this devilish band
But Generals great like Miles and Brooke don't do things up that way,
For they know an Indian like a book, and let him have his sway
Until they think him far enough and then to John they'll say,
"You had better stop your fooling or we'll bring our guns to play."

Chorus:
They claimed the shirt, etc.

The 9th marched out with splendid cheer the Bad Lands to explo'e—
With Col. Henry at their head they never fear the foe;
So on they rode from Xmas eve 'till dawn of Xmas day;
The Red Skins heard the 9th was near and fled in great dismay;
The 7th is of courage bold both officers and men,
But bad luck seems to follow them and twice has took them in;
They came in contact with Big Foot's warriors in their fierce might
This chief made sure he had a chance of vantage in the fight.

Chorus:
They claimed the shirt, etc.

A fight took place, 'twas hand to hand, unwarned by trumpet call,
While the Sioux were dropping man by man—the 7th killed them all,
And to that regiment be said "Ye noble braves, well done,
Although you lost some gallant men a glorious fight you've won."
The 8th was there, the sixth rode miles to swell that great command
And waited orders night and day to round up Short Bull's band.
The Infantry marched up in mass the Cavalry's support,
And while the latter rounded up, the former held the fort.

Chorus:
They claimed the shirt, etc.

E battery of the 1st stood by and did their duty well,
For every time the Hotchkiss barked they say a hostile fell.
Some Indian soldiers chipped in too and helped to quell the fray,
And now the campaign's ended and the soldiers marched away.
So all have done their share, you see, whether it was thick or thin,
And all helped break the ghost dance up and drive the hostiles in.
The settlers in that region now can breathe with better grace;
They only ask and pray to God to make John hold his base.

Chorus:
They claimed the shirt, etc.

Untitled

The rest have gone home,
To meet the blizzard's wintry blast.
The Ninth, the willing Ninth,
Is camped here till the last.

We were the first to come,
Will be the last to leave
Why are we compelled to stay,
Why this reward receive?

In warm barracks
Our recent comrades take their ease,
While we poor devils,
And the Sioux are left to freeze.

And cuss our luck,
And wait till some one pulls the string,
And starts Short Bull
With another ghost dance in the spring.

Chapter Forty

Chaplain Theophilus G. Steward on his relationship with the regimental commander

Chaplain Steward (1843–1924) was a distinguished scholar and minister of the African Methodist Episcopal Church. He served as chaplain of the 25th Infantry from 1891 until his retirement in 1907 and wrote numerous works of history and theology. His second wife, Susan Maria Steward, was one of the first women in North America to graduate from medical school.1

Letter, Chaplain Steward, Fort Missoula, Montana Territory, to Honorable John Wanamaker, Postmaster General, Washington D.C., October 8, 1891:2

I had been told that Army officers were not generally kind to chaplains, and that colored chaplains especially came under the ban of their disapprobation. I wish to say emphatically that my reception by the officers of this post and my treatment since has been all that any reasonable man could require. The officers themselves and their families freely accord to me all the civilities and courtesies to which my position entitles me, and do not seem wanting in respect for me personally. Certainly they have secured from me sincere respect and regard. The commanding officer and his noble wife set a brilliant example in this particular. On my arrival here they welcomed me to their home and entertained me with all courtesy until my own quarters were prepared. Indeed the Colonel telegraphed all the way to St. Paul inviting me to share his hospitalities. Both himself and wife appear to be decidedly Christian people. Mrs. Andrews leads the singing in our worship and takes a deep interest in the moral and religious welfare of the men. . . . One man told me a few days ago that if it had not been for Col. Andrews and one or two other officers he should not have been worth a dollar. Both the Colonel and his wife are beloved by many men of the command.

Chapter Forty-One

The Suggs affray, June 1892

This violent episode involved troopers of the 9th Cavalry, who were sent from Fort Robinson, Nebraska, to restore peace in the wake of the Johnson County, Wyoming, cattle war of 1892. Leaders of the Wyoming Stock Growers Association, which represented the largest cattlemen in the new state, demanded that Senator Joseph Carey arrange that black troops be sent to Wyoming, to exploit the antiblack feelings of their opponents and prevent any sympathetic relations that might develop between small ranchers and white troops. The War Department sent the 9th Cavalry, and one of its troopers, Private Willis Johnson, was killed as the result of a barroom confrontation in Suggs, a tiny "hell-on-wheels" community, one of many that temporarily sprang up at the end of track when a new railroad line was under construction. Other soldiers of the regiment returned to Suggs and shot up the bar where the original assault had taken place. Local whites called the action of the soldiers a riot, but it was focused on a specific objective and carried out in a typically deliberate, well-planned, and efficient military manner.[1]

Telegram, Frank Wolcott, Henry G. Hay, George H. Baxter, Henry A. Blair, John Clay, and Willis O. Van Devanter to Senator Joseph M. Carey, Washington, D.C., June 1, 1892:2

We want changes of troops made as follows. Headquarters of eighth infantry and three companies of that regiment not at Fort McKinney ordered to Sidney. Major Egbert of 17th Infantry and three companies of that regiment ordered from [Fort D. A.] Russell to McKinney. . . . We want cool level-headed men whose sympathy is with us. Order Major Fechet and the two companies of the Sixth Cavalry from McKinney to [Fort] Niobrara, anywhere else out of that country. He and his men have relations with the sheriff and his gang that make the whole command very undesirable for us. Send six companies of Ninth Cavalry from [Fort] Robinson to McKinney. The colored troops will have no sympathy for Texan thieves, and these are the troops we want. . . .

Chapter Forty-Two

Chaplain Henry V. Plummer on life at Fort Robinson and his religious and educational duties

Chaplain Henry Plummer was the first African American appointed to a chaplaincy in the Regular Army. He served from 1884 until his dismissal from the service ten years later after conviction by a court-martial of conduct unbecoming an officer.[1]

Shortly after Plummer's dismissal, all four black regiments had African American chaplains. Allen Allensworth had joined the 24th Infantry in 1886; Theophilus G. Steward had served the 24th from 1891; and William T. Anderson arrived in the 10th Cavalry in 1897. In 1895, George W. Prioleau replaced Plummer.[2]

Chaplain Plummer wrote this letter to the monthly newspaper of the U.S. Army Mutual Aid Association, which had been founded in 1879, to assist families of deceased members.[3] It was still active in 2001 as the Army and Air Force Mutual Aid Association, headquartered at Fort Myer, Virginia.

We have been receiving quite an addition to our post lately in the persons of recruits from Kentucky who have been especially enlisted for the 9th Cavalry by Capt. Joseph Garrard, 9th Cavalry, who is on special Recruiting duty for his regiment at Lexington, Ky. The young men that he is now sending out are a fine class of young fellows; robust and hardy and in appearance very intelligent, and it is believed they will make a fine set of soldiers.

Recently a fire broke out in the quarters of Lieut. Col. R. F. Bernard, 9th Cav. It was underneath the parlor and before it could be reached the flooring had to be all torn up and the basin flooded with water. The men worked very faithfully and hard until the fire was suppressed, although it was a cold and disagreeable morning.

Too much praise can not be given to our brave boys in blue, who not only defend their country when attacked, but protect property of a private nature as well when called upon to do so. Fires have been very frequent lately at this post, but on all occasions the men have worked faithfully to care for the property and comfort of others.

Only a few days ago we were somewhat startled by the news of the killing of four cowboys by some Indians at the Pine Ridge Agency. It seems to have grown out of a personal difference between the Indians and the cowboys and no further trouble is apprehended. The Indian police were promptly sent out to arrest the Indian murderers, and they did their duty well, for they killed several of the renegades who resisted arrest. Two Indian boys who were concerned in the murder of the cowboys have since been arrested and are now held by the United States civil authorities for trial.

We have been holding a series of gospel meetings at this post and much good has been accomplished. About seventy-five persons indicated a desire for a better life, and about nineteen joined the Christian Church.

The Sabbath school is well attended; so also is the day school and the interest manifested by the young men of the command in all matters, educational and otherwise, has been most encouraging indeed.

Thus far we have had a splendid winter in its mildness and only one real cold snap.

Your paper is always a source of much pleasure to me and many others at this post, and we hope it may live long and prosper.

Fraternally yours, etc.,
H. V. Plummer
Chaplain, 9th Cavalry

Chapter Forty-Three

Sergeant Barney McKay and "500 Soldiers with the Bullet or Torch"

The appearance of this incendiary sheet at Fort Robinson in 1893, with its promise of bloody retaliation for racist outrages, frightened the commander, Lieutenant Colonel Reuben Bernard. He thought Chaplain Henry Plummer was involved but could never prove it. All he could demonstrate was that Sergeant Barney McKay of G Troop had possessed a copy, and that was enough to convict McKay of "conduct to the prejudice of good order and discipline" and to have him packed off to the military prison at Fort Leavenworth.[1] The broadside itself was filed as an enclosure with the proceedings of the McKay court-martial.[2]

After his release from Leavenworth, Sergeant McKay applied for a pension based on a service-connected disability. McKay was an intelligent and articulate man, who made his living as a journalist and wrote Republican campaign literature. The Pension Bureau repeatedly rejected his claim, but McKay persisted. His "Declaration" of his service, written in 1917, still reflected his anger and sense of injustice at the events of 1893, while his appeal to Secretary of the Interior Franklin K. Lane in the following year, showed his enduring patriotism and appreciation of the battle against German tyranny abroad and American racism at home. He finally wrested a very modest stipend from the government, first $6 per month and later $20.[3]

Attention, Soldiers: The soldiers of Fort Robinson, Neb., and most especially the cavalry, are earnestly and urgently petitioned to boycott and remain away from the saloons of Deitreich, Myers, and Tische, of Crawford, Neb., as they not only keep and encourage fierce gamblers in their places of business to rob you, but have also given support and sanction to some recent would-be lynchers of our people.

On the night of April 17 these men and their henchmen joined in a chase after a colored man who had bowed to the decree of the law of the land and had submitted to a rigid preliminary examination as to the question of his guilt or innocence of an offense charged against him.

The prosecuting attorney, in behalf of the commonwealth of Nebraska, came from Chadron and appeared for the state and after he had carefully and officially sifted the flimsy and ex parte testimony that was brought against the accused, one Diggs, ordered his release and forthwith these human ghouls and blood fiends filled the night air with the cry of "nigger!!" "nigger!!" "let us lynch him" and they would have doubtless duplicated the savage and brutal horrors of Paris and Texarkana, Tex., and Fort Gaines, Ga., if they had caught Diggs who had been tried and acquitted.

To the eternal shame and disgrace of Nebraska, let it be stated that the town marshal, Morrison, the presumed and authorized conservator of the law, joined in this brutal hunt, together with such abandoned scoundrels as Newcomb, Tische, Deitreich, Butts, Foote, "Skinny" and others.

Too much praise and credit cannot be given to Messrs. Potts and Mooney, who were too manly and much to[o] civilized to participate in such a murderous and southern chase.

If you soldiers wish to respect yourselves and do not wish to see blood spots on your dollars and dimes, spend your money with Messrs. Potts and Mooney, who will treat you like men and soldiers.

Diggs is not the only man who has been cruelly treated in the town of Crawford, but American soldiers of the Ninth Cavalry have been beaten over their heads with six shooters by these thugs and "black-legs" and they have gone "unwhipped of justice," and still others have had pistols drawn upon them and have been subjected to the most abusive and disgusting ribaldry, and no redress has been furnished—no protection offered.

Diggs would have been lynched if friends had not got him to the post, and we give warning now to the town of Crawford that these things must cease. You lynch, you torture, and you burn negroes in the south, but we swear by all that is good and holy that you shall not outrage us and our people right here under the shadow of "Old Glory," while we have shot and shell, and if you persist we will repeat the horrors of San Domingo—we will reduce your houses and firesides to ashes and send your guilty souls to hell. "Who would be free must themselves strike the blow." We have spoken and we call upon the gods to witness that we are in earnest.

500 Men with the Bullet or the Torch

Barney McKay, Declaration, Subscribed and sworn before Jabez Lee, Notary Public, August 11, 1917.

ATTENTION!

SOLDIERS:

apr. 28/93

The soldiers of Ft. Robinson, Nebraska and most especially the Cavalry are most earnestly and urgently petitioned to boycott and remain away from the saloons of **DEITREICH, MYERS and TISCHE,** of Crawford. Neb., as they not only keep and encourage FLEECE GAMBLERS in their places of business to rob you, but have also given support and sanction to some recent would-be lynchers of our people.

ON the night of April 17 these men and their henchmen joined in a chase after a colored man who had bowed to the decree of the law of the land and had submitted to a rigid preliminary examination as to the question of his guilt or innocence of an offense charged against him.

THE Prosecuting Attorney, in behalf of the commonwealth of Nebraska, came from Chadron and appeared for the State and after he had carefully and officially sifted the flimsy and ex parte testimony that was brought against the accused, (one Diggs), ordered his release and forthwith these HUMAN GHOULS and BLOOD-FIENDS filled the night air with the cry of "NIGGER!" "NIGGER!!" "NIGGER!!!" "let us lynch him" and they would have doubtless duplicated the savage and brutal horrors of Paris and Texarkana, Tex., and Ft. Gaines, Ga., if they had caught Diggs who had been tried and acquitted.

TO the eternal shame and disgrace of Nebraska let it be stated that the town marshall, Morrison, the presumed and authorized conservator of the law joined in this blood hunt, together with such abandoned scoundrels as Newcomb, Tische, Dietreich, Butts, Foote, "Skinny," and others.

TOO much praise and credit can not be given to Messrs. Potts and Mooney who were too manly and too much civilized to participate in such a murderous and Southern chase.

IF YOU SOLDIERS wish to respect yourselves and do not wish to see blood spots on your dollars and dimes spend your money with Messrs. Potts and Mooney, who will treat you like men and soldiers.

DIGGS is not the only man who has been cruelly treated in that town of Crawford but American soldiers of the NINTH CAVALRY have been beaten over their heads with six shooters by these thugs and "black-legs" and they have gone "unwhipped of justice" and still others have had pistols drawn upon them and have been subjected to the most abusive and disgusting ribaldry and no redress has been furnished—no protection offered.

DIGGS would have been lynched if friends had not got him to the post and we give warning now to the town of Crawford that these things must cease. You lynch, you torture, and you burn Negroes in the South, but WE SWEAR BY ALL THAT IS GOOD AND HOLY that you shall not outrage us and our people right here under the shadow of "Old Glory," while we have shot and shell and if you persist, we will repeat the horrors of San Domingo—we will reduce your homes and firesides to ashes and send your guilty souls to———HELL.

"WHO would be free themselves mast strike the blow." We have spoken and we call upon the gods to witness that we are in eatnest.

Signed: **500 Men With the Bullet or the Torch.**

The broadside "500 Men with the Bullet or the Torch" (Courtesy Nebraska State Historical Society)

District of Columbia

Personally appeared before me, a notary public, in and for the District of Columbia, one Barney McKay who first being duly sworn according to law deposes and says, that: he is the same man who served in Company C 24th U.S. Infantry under the name of Barney McDougal, that: he served in that Company as private, corporal, and sergeant from Oct. 1881 to Aug. 31st 1886, that: he was discharged at Fort Sill Ind. Ter., on the above named date and after a lapse of about seven months enlisted for the general mounted service at St. Louis Mo., on the 12 day of Jan., 1887, that: he was stationed at Jefferson Barracks Mo., until about the First of April 1887 when he was assigned to troop C 9th U.S. Cav., stationed at Fort Robinson Nebraska, that: while serving in that troop he underwent a surgical operation on the left knee for a floating cartilage, that: the operation was not a success, part of the joint water escaping leaving the knee weak, partially stiff, and at times badly swollen and sore to the touch, that: said knee has been in that condition ever since causing him much pain annoyance and inconvenience, that: he is entirely unable to perform any manual labor at all, such as lifting, running, walking or anything requiring weight or pressure to be put on that knee, that: the continual swelling in the knee causes poor circulation and thereby causes the knee, leg and hip to break out with pimples and splotches which resembles neuritis or erysyplis, that: he has bought on an average of one bottle of liniment, Sloans, Omega or St. Jacobs oil every week since leaving the service, that: he has spent approximately one hundred and twenty-five dollars for such medicines during the last twenty-three years, that: he has besides spent over five-hundred dollars in doctors bills receiving treatment for lumbago, diarrhea, piles, deafness, dizziness, vertigo, and rheumatism all contracted in the army and in the line of duty, that: he was a young man in perfect health and physical vigor when he entered the army, never having had any serious illness or complaint of any kind or character, that: he was a puddler by trade working in the car works of Shickle and Harris at Jeffersonville, Indiana, receiving two-dollars and fifty-cents per diem for an eight hour day, and thirty cents an hour for over time work, that: his service in the army, especially that in the cavalry arm was hard, arduous and exacting, that: his company and regiment took the field in Oct. 1890, and remained out with only tents to live and keep warm in until May 1891, that: the winter was one of the hardest deponent ever encountered, the thermometer ranging anywhere from 10 to 40 degrees below zero, that: this service was in Wyo., Nebr., and So. Dak., that: the Sioux Indians were on the war path that winter and the 9th Cavalry was ordered out along with other troops to quell the uprising, that: in May 1892 he had the operation referred to above and in the following year, namely Aug. 1893, he was discharged by order of a general court martial after a trial that was the most sickening farce that ever disgraced the annals of the army, that: he was accused of trying to incite riot among the troops of Fort Robinson Nebr., against the Citizens of Crawford Nebr., that there was not the slightest foundation for the charge, that: it was wholly unsupported by the evidence adduced at the trial, that: the simple truth is that certain ruffians residing in Crawford Nebr. had undertaken to lynch and burn a colored man who had formerly served in the 9th U.S. Cavalry, that: the mob was foiled by Sergt. McKay and four other men, the man taken out of their hands spirited away and ultimately sent out of the state, that: later some men at Fort Robinson belonging to a secret society, to which McKay did not belong issued a circular denouncing the attempted lynching and threatening reprisals if such an attempt was ever made again, that: this action aroused the southern ire of Lieut. Col. Reuben F. Bernard who immediately threw out a drag-net in an effort to find some one to punish, that: finding no one to fasten the charge on he questioned McKay who could tell nothing of the origin of the circular, that: Col. Bernard made that circular the basis of charges against Sergt. McKay, tried, convicted, and sent him to Leavenworth military prison all because he had resisted lynch law, thus putting the government squarely on record as endorsing the mob, that: this has no place in this record, but some mobocrat in the pension office has seen fit to seek to poison the minds of Senators and members of Congress against deponent by insinuating that he has a bad record, [so] he deems it his duty to himself to give briefly the facts, that: he joined Troop C 9th Cav., in April 1887, was promoted corporal in May 1887, by Lieut. Ballard S. Humphrey, an officer who had known and served with him in the infantry arm of the service, that: he was promoted sergeant in Sept. 1888, and served as such until the date of discharge, that: he is a sergt now never having been legally nor lawfully discharged from the service, that: he tendered his service to the government during the Spanish American war and offered himself for enlistment, that: he was rejected by the medical authorities because of crepitus in the joints and lame knee, that: he has again tendered his service to the government in the present crisis and stands ready to lay down his life for the perpetuity of free government, that: this application for pension has been pending since Aug. 1897 and been rejected wrongfully several times, that: no medical board has ever given him a thorough examination such as he underwent when he enlisted in the army, that: the last board at Hartford Conn., last Jan., gave him a most casual and perfunctory examination, paying no attention whatever to the knee except to look at it and note the scar left by the incision, tho there [was] swelling and inflammation in and around the knee joint at the time, that: rheumatism is a disease of purely subjective symptoms and is hard to detect unless the patient is under observation a long time and carefully examined at intervals, that: the rheumatism was contracted in line of duty at various times while serving in the army, that: once, while at Fort Duchesne Utah he was ordered to Prices Station to meet and escort Chaplain Scott back to the Fort, that when he and his party reached the Uintah River he found it out of its banks with ice floes running in it ranging in size from 10 to a hundred pounds, that: he and his detachment erected and constructed a raft and ferried the chaplain, his family, and household goods from the mouth of the bridge to dry land a distance of about five hundred yards, that: this was in the month of March when the water was cold and the ice in the mountains just beginning to break up, that: on returning to the Fort he was sick with a severe cold which threatened pneumonia, that: rheumatism became aggravated from that time on and he has suffered continuously from the effects of it since, that: deponent knows he is entitled to receive from the government a pension and that if he does not get it a grave injustice will be done a man who has rendered faithful and valuable service to the government, that when he left the service he was a physical wreck, but has lived a temperate, abstemious life, observing strictly the laws of health and hygiene and has thus managed to preserve an appearance of health which is likely to deceive physicians making a cursory examination, as has been the case heretofore. Deponent, further states and avers that his eyesight is poor due to sleeping under the direct rays of an electric light while serving at Leavenworth military prison, that he is compelled to wear glasses a thing he did not have to do before he went there, that: he suffers from nervousness and weakness superinduced by hard, rigorous service while in the army, that: at times he is so weak and nervous that he cannot perform the slightest work either mental or physical, that: he was treated at various times for that weakness while in the service but does not remember the dates but the sick report record will show. And further, deponent hereby requests that his case No. 584182 be reopened and that I be given another examination here in Washington at the earliest practicable moment. And further deponent sayeth not.

Signed Barney McKay
Company C 24th U.S. Inf. and
Troop C, E, and G 9th U.S. Cavalry

Subscribed and sworn to before me this
11th day of August 1917
Jabez Lee
Notary Public

Barney McKay to Hon. Franklin K. Lane, Washington, D. C., August 15, 1918.

Hon. Franklin K. Lane,
Sec. of the Interior,

18th and F Sts., N.W.

Dear Sir:

I have the honor to submit for reference to the board of appeals the following, to wit:

I am an applicant for a pension under the law of 1890. I applied for pension July 8th 1897—21 years ago. My claim was rejected for the fifth or sixth time June third 1918. In a letter to Hon. J. S. Freylinghuysen, the honorable commissioner of pensions made statements which require explanation and amplification on my part. I, therefore, submit the following statement of facts to accompany the record.

I enlisted for the general dismounted service, at Indianapolis Ind., Aug. 16 1881. Was sent to Columbus Barracks Aug. 19 1881. Sept. 10 1881 was made lance corporal. Oct. 30 was sent with a detachment of recruits, under command of Capt. Patterson, to Camp Supply Ind. Ter. Was made a lance sergeant and placed in charge of the mess for the trip. Arrived at our destination Nov. 17 1881. The men were assigned to the different companies of the 24th Infantry, I to Company C, Capt. B. M. Custer. April First 1881, I was made company clerk of my unit. Served in that capacity for 18 months. April First 1883, I was made a corporal. July 15 1884 was promoted sergeant. Reduced to pvt., March 1 1886. Discharged Aug. 15th 1886, character "Very Good." My first enlistment was under the name of Barney McDougal. That was merely a boyish prank, which I afterwards explained to the Adjutant General in a letter of date Oct. 15th 1892.

If that is important, as having bearing on my right to a pension the letter is a matter of record in the archives of the government. Not deeming it relevant I shall not advert to it further as a part of the record. I enlisted again Jan. 12 1897 [sic], at St. Louis Mo., for the general mounted service and was assigned to the 9th U.S. Cavalry, at Fort Robinson Neb. Assigned to Troop C 9th Cav., at the request of First Lieut. Ballard S. Humphrey, March First 1887. Made corporal March 7th 1887. Sergeant Sept. 20 1888. Discharged Jan. 11th 1892 at Fort Robinson Neb., by Capt. Mathias W. Day, character excellent. Re-enlisted Jan. 12 1892, retaining the rank and status of sergeant. Served as such until July 31st 1893, when I was discharged by order of a general court-martial which is made the subject of a great deal of comment by the honorable commissioner of pensions. This court-martial record really has no place in the case, and ought not to have been referred to at all, but since it is in the case I shall tell the story just as the record shows it to exist. Race prejudice and passion played the leading role in my court-martial and dismissal from the army. Lynching, that monstrous crime so recently denounced by our great president was the cause. I was so unfortunate as to align myself in opposition to that peculiar pastime, and while no would be lyncher was hurt, yet certain officers of the 9th Cavalry felt that they had been threatened and some body had to suffer. Briefly, the facts are these. I was in the town of Crawford Neb. during the latter part of Feb. 1893 on pass, when an attempt by border ruffians to lynch and burn a colored man named James Diggs was made. The trouble occurred thru business rivalry, Diggs being a butcher was employed by a reputable business man. The methods employed by Diggs and his employer conflicted with the practices of the other gentry, who made a business of stealing cattle, killing and cutting them up on the prairies and huxtering them about the various settlements. Diggs was arrested and put in jail for assault on one of these ruffians, and while awaiting a hearing before a magistrate a mob visited the jail, broke it open, tied the victim, and dragged him to the public street where they intended to lynch and burn him. I with three other men interfered, by getting behind the mob and firing into the air to frighten them. We succeeded in scattering the mob and saving the life of their victim. We then spirited the man off to a place of safety and raised money to send him out of harm's way. We felt interested in Diggs, for the reason he had served ten years in our regiment and was still well liked by all. Besides, we looked upon lynching as a growing evil that ought to receive a check. The day following the attempted lynching the sheriff of Dawes County, Neb. visited Fort Robinson with a posse and demanded that I,

Sergt. McKay, be turned over to the civil authorities for trial on a charge of rioting. Col. James Biddle, the commanding officer of the garrison, and also of the 9th Cavalry peremptorily refused the request and told the sheriff that he ought to thank Sergt. McKay for saving his town and county the disgrace of a lynching. By the act of that sheriff the great state of Nebraska ranged herself on the side of lynch law. Later, the government of the United States did the same thing and is persisting in it to this very day. Commissioner Saltzgabber has by his reference to it, when it is wholly irrelevant and immaterial to any issue raised in my pension case put the government in the unenviable position of indorsing the action of the court-martial and condemning me. But, I was not tried by court-martial for my part in that affair, but on a trumped up charge of which I was in no sense guilty as the record of the court-martial garbled and distorted as it is will abundantly show. If this court-martial is to play a part in determining my right to a pension, why, then I demand that the record be sent for and examined by the board of appeals—fair minded men far removed from the unpleasant atmosphere of the time, and with no ax to grind. Now, for the trumped up charge. Soon after the attempt to lynch Diggs occurred, certain members of a secret society, to which I did not belong got together and issued a circular denouncing lynch law and warning the offenders not to attempt such tactics again. The circular was bitter and entirely improper, especially emanating from soldiers, but there was a reason for the issuance of that circular. Three men, all soldiers had been murdered by border ruffians prior to the Diggs affair. The first one, Jacob C. Smith, Troop G 9th Cavalry, suffered a most shameful death. He was hung to the limb of a tree with a placard across his chest reading "Niggers beware." The second, Edw. Moton, was a peaceable, unoffending fellow who was a model soldier without an enemy in the world, so far as anyone knew. He was found murdered in his tent about three miles from the post—he being the troop gardener. The third, First Sergeant Emanuel Stance, was the beau-ideal of the regiment, and one of the finest men in that fine cavalry regiment. He was murdered on Christmas day 1887, by the same character of ruffians who attempted to kill Diggs. These three murders occurred right under the noses of our officers, and no effort whatever was ever made to apprehend, or bring to justice the red-handed murderers. Had the officers of the 9th Cavalry pursued the murderers with one half the zeal they pursued me in an effort to convict me of that circular every murderer would have been found, tried and hung. The circular made its appearance on the 17th of March 1893. That night about retreat roll call Colonel Reuben F. Bernard, who had assumed command of the post in the absence of Col. Biddle, sent for me and accused me of writing, having printed and circulating the incendiary circular with a view to inciting the soldiers of Fort Robinson to acts of violence against the citizens of Crawford, Nebraska. I disavowed responsibility for, and disclaimed all knowledge of the offensive circular, and had up to that time made an honest effort to find out something of its origin—for I disapproved of it just as heartily as the Lieutenant Colonel did. But the Colonel wanted a victim and made me the scapegoat. He ordered me confined to the guard-house, in solitary confinement; to be seen by no one except in the presence of the officer of the day. I was kept in that status until the first day of June '93, when the Judge Advocate of a court-martial then sitting at the Fort sent for me and read—for the first time—the charges against me. I was confined on the 17th of March; I should have been released on the 25th of March, for the law plainly said then, and does now, "when an officer or soldier is to be tried by court-martial, a copy of the charges must be furnished him within eight days after such confinement, or he shall be released from arrest and restored to duty." So there has been no court-martial in the proper legal sense, and the action of the court is null and void. I am claiming now the right to an honorable discharge with all pay and allowances. I beg to apologize now for this digression. I would not have taken up so much time with this extraneous matter had not the honorable commissioner of pensions gone out of his way to drag it in. He didn't even take the trouble to quote the record correctly. He says, "Found guilty of bringing into his barracks an incendiary circular and saying this is my show and so forth." The record shows no such thing, and I insist that the board of appeals send for that record and see for itself just what the finding of that court-martial is. I was found guilty of "giving one circular to one man," and that is all. Just why the honorable commissioner saw fit to allude to this at all is mysterious. Why he misquotes the record is inexplicable. It is explainable on one theory and one only, viz., the determination to keep me out of a pension at the behest and request of some person or persons unknown to me. I am forced to this conclusion by two circumstances, namely, What was said to the late lamented honorable Cyrus A. Sulloway, who was told by some one at the pension bureau that "McKay is an impudent 'Nigger' whose services while in the army was not honest and faithful, and he ought not to receive any consideration." Mr. Sault, sec. to Sen. McLean, of Conn., was also told something similar. I shall not undertake it to quote him. I might not do it accurately. I hope to have a congressional investigation which will bring out the truth from Mr. Sault himself. The honorable secretary of the interior, and the members of the board of appeals will doubtless be approached by the same party who has made it his business to whisper poisonous words to members of Congress who have, from time to time, interested themselves in my behalf. If such should happen, I beg to ask the privilege of confronting my accuser—a right guaranteed to every American citizen, and one which ought never to be denied. I take my stand beneath the flag of my country. I rest my case on the law and the facts. I am a "liberty bond holder." A purchaser of "War Stamps." I have relatives by the score in the National Army ready and willing to shed their blood for the liberty of the world. I tendered my services to my country in 1898, and again in 1917. German brutality, duplicity, murder, rapine and cowardice are all obnoxious to me. I pray God their methods may never find imitators in this our beloved country. I have been mistreated by the Pension Bureau. I believe I was so treated because I am a colored man and belong to a poor despised, unfortunate much-abused race. I now appeal for justice, not because I am colored, but because I belong to a race who has never furnished a traitor and are now a unit in support of our common country.

Respectfully,
Barney McKay

Chapter Forty-Four

Recollections of a recruit

Eugene Frierson joined the 10th Cavalry as a "recruit from depot" in January 1893. By the time that he wrote this three-part article for the *Colored American Magazine*, he had twelve years of Army experience, a reputation as an excellent marksman, and the rank of squadron sergeant major. He was also sufficiently mature to laugh at his experiences and mistakes as a young soldier, which he presented in an articulate and lucid narrative.

When Frierson came into the 10th Cavalry, the years of hard campaigning were over. "Life in Montana and North Dakota was a great relaxation for our veterans after their strenuous work in Arizona," Major Edward Glass later wrote. "They enjoyed the hunting and change of scenery and became acquainted with the country, making long practice marches, sometimes in the dead of winter, through blizzards. . . ." The regiment's major operations involved strikes and civil disturbances in the summer of 1894 and returning the Crees, who had fled south from Canadian reservations, to their homes in the summer of 1897.[1]

Frierson's essay told the story of a long 1893 practice march. It showed the relations between privates and their sergeants, who included in this case old-timers such as Washington Brown, who had been cited for bravery against Geronimo, and William McBryar, who held a Medal of Honor for valor against Apaches in Arizona. Frierson described his training, told of encounters with wild creatures, and described the routines of camp life, and publication of his recollections once again showed the interest of the black community in the activities of African American soldiers.

Eugene P. Frierson, "An Adventure in the Big Horn Mountains, of, The Trials and Tribulations of a Recruit," Part I.[2]

Early in October 1893, a Squadron of the Tenth Cavalry, consisting of Troops B, E, G, and K, stationed at Fort Custer, Montana, proceeded on its annual practice march under command of Lieut. Col. D. Perry. "Practice March" is a march made by troops, foot and mounted, annually, for the purpose of giving "recruits" (young soldiers) an idea of field service, a knowledge essential to the duties of a soldier in time of actual warfare, and to give older soldiers more practice and experience in the duties and knowledge pertaining to the same.

Each troop, with but few exceptions, was filled with recruits who had never crossed the plains of that wild, historical country before. But all were filled with "field aspiration" and were as gleeful as their older comrades in taking the field. The course of march was to a point about 45 miles southwest of the fort leading along the Big Horn River in the Big Horn Mountains, thence by return through the Little Horn Valley, by the historical Custer Battle Field to post, traversing an entire distance of more than 120 miles. The period of the march was only ten short Montana days. The first day out from the fort found a great many of our "recruit aspirants" wishing that they were at home by their mother's side, or at least in post, for their seating capacity was very much worn from fare, [sic] wear and tear, occasioned by their inability to maintain a firm seat in the saddle during several miles of the regulation gait of eight miles an hour. One of the most effected aspirants, with much regret, was the writer of this story.

Nothing was very certain with the younger soldier until after "Mess Call" (supper), when all were soon stretched out upon their improvised beds, having unconditionally succumbed to the effects of his first day's experience, leaving the old soldier awake to participate in the usual camp fire yarns. However, the recruit was persistent in his determination to accomplish the journey without casting discredit upon his ability as a cavalryman, the next day having closed with him in a far better condition to endure a long, continuous journey.

All went very well with the boys for several days. About the fifth day out from post the command remained over in camp a day to allow the horses and men to recuperate and to give those who desired it, an opportunity to fish and hunt, and enjoy the full benefit of the field life. It was on this very day that Privates Collins, Walden, and I, all members of Troop K, obtained permission for an extensive hunt and general exploration of the Snow Capped Mountain that seemed only a few miles from camp. After the regular and customary duties were performed, armed each with a carbine and revolver, we proceeded on our journey. The first two or three miles were made without incident. Upon arriving at what first seemed like the foot of the great range of mountains, we were surprised to find ourselves confronted by a great canyon that seemed to be inhabited by nothing but game of the largest and most dangerous kind, such as bear, deer, wolves, coyotes, wild cats, and a number of other gentlemen and ladies of the animal species that would proudly welcome such adventurous young soldiers as we into their community. After a few minutes' pause of wonder we decided to descend into the great valley below that seemed, with the exception of a gentle breeze, as silent as death. Being armed with a .45-calibre carbine and revolver each, we thought we were as brave and defiant as a recruit could be under ordinary circumstances, each being extremely nervous and shaky under the weight born upon his legs.

At any rate, we proceeded (after drawing lots to see who should precede) by file down a narrow trail that wound its way into the great canyon below. I have always been unlucky since, but I was fortunate enough that day to draw the lot than entitled me to "bring up the rear." When about two-thirds of the way down the trail Walden, who preceded, came to a sudden stop and looked around with astounded countenance, as though the next step would have precipitated him into eternity. Collins, who stood at his back, was apparently in the same predicament. After carefully and cautiously scrutinizing the country in the immediate vicinity, I saw to my surprise a large "Grizzly" standing upon its hind legs bowing to each and every one of us as gracefully as if by pre-appointment. Taking the situation in at a glance, I brought my .45-calibre to my right shoulder and without sighting (being extremely nervous) pulled the trigger. This seemed to be great sport for Mr. "Grizzly," who shook his head as an indication of a miss. At this stage of affairs, Walden, who was by virtue of his lot, and owing to his inability to climb the cliffs on either side, still in front, fired the shot that caused our informal friend to drop to his all-fours and make a hasty retreat. Being inspired with what we thought was an accomplished feat we, or rather they,—for I remained a little in the rear to reload my rifle—proceeded to follow at a rapid pace. Collins being more inspired than either of us, succeeded by some way or another in getting in front of Walden, in order to claim the skin of the beautiful black bear.

After reloading my rifle I took to a fast gait, to at least be on hand at the "skinning," and had proceeded only a short distance when, to my surprise, I beheld Collins beating as hasty a retreat as circumstances would permit under emergency conditions, followed as closely as conditions would allow by Walton and our "friend," in the order named.

In some way Collins had succeeded in successfully giving Walden the "leap frog act" in his effort to reach the point of starting.

It wasn't long, however, before the situation was totally comprehended by me, and as the vote seemed unanimous, it fell to my lot to lead, and having, at the point of starting, at least twenty feet advantage, I soon succeeded in coming out No. 1 at the top of the hill. It was soon apparent to our "friend" that he was no match for this fleet-footed trio, for Collins was second to top of hill, followed closely by Walton by at least a neck. We soon saw that it was time to try some of our knowledge acquired during target season. Although recruits, we were marksmen, but needed only a little staying quality, which is very essential to a soldier. We succeeded by our combined efforts in sending our "friend" to the "happy hunting ground."

After having accomplished this, we decided to resume our journey and accomplish our desire to reach the great snow capped mountain that seemed as far now as before leaving camp. Returning along the trail we were more enthusiastic and adventurous than ever. After reaching the valley we were in the midst of one of the most beautiful scenes in Southwestern Montana, being surrounded with wild flowers of every variety and a beautiful brooklet running gently by. After spending a short time there we proceeded across the foot hills that seemed only an outpost to the great mountain beyond. We successfully reached the table land, and sat down to partake of a small lunch that we had thoughtfully prepared before leaving camp. Having rested about fifteen minutes, we continued our tramp. When within what seemed a few rods of the mountain, we were even more surprised to find that the greatest valley in Montana laid between us and the lone Snow-Capped Mountain, being more than seven miles wide. However, we were determined, and carefully groped our way far into its interior. The greatest problem now remained to be solved. How could we reach the lone mountain that held a commanding position overlooking the entire country for hundreds of miles around.

The day had begun to close, the sun having long before crossed the meridian, and night was near at hand; but we pressed bravely on. At last we came to the base of the great mountain, which was very steep and appeared to be seldom frequented. After a short pause we attempted to climb to its summit, but without avail. Night having silently crept upon us a speedy return was necessary in order to reach camp, which was more than ten miles away. We at once began the return trip, and succeeded in crossing the great valley before darkness fell with all her dismal.

We were still adventurous and full of glee, and our hope of reaching camp was as strong as that of reaching the mountain, which now was our only guide; for by keeping the mountain directly behind us we were sure of landing safely at camp. All trace of trail or road having been lost, we were at the mercy of the howling wolves and crying coyotes that seemed almost upon our very heels. Having reached an unsurpassable cliff, we were obliged to detour our line of march, and by so doing laid ourselves liable to spending a night among the wild creatures.

By mere chance we came to the very stream that passed through our camp, and by keeping in touch with it were able to reach camp at about 10 o'clock that night very much worn from our experience. We were aware of the calls that we had failed to respond to, and immediately proceeded to explain our absence to the 1st Sergeant, who was sitting in his tent smoking an old cob pipe. After listening attentively to our tale of woe he promptly took us over to explain the little incident to the Troop Commander, who immediately gave us orders for the next day, which meant to "take pains and walk."

Eugene P. Frierson, "An Adventure in the Big Horn Mountains, of, The Trials and Tribulations of a Recruit," Part II.3

After receiving our walking orders for the next day, and instructions to report before leaving camp for an idea only of about where the troop would camp, and to receive a compass to guide us, we returned to our tents to take a much needed rest. After laying aside our arms, we proceeded to look up the cook, who had by that time drawn his 240 pounds of avoirdupois into his bunk, but being a thoughtful old gentleman, had laid aside something that would at least maintain life until morning. After partaking of all that could be found, we returned to our tents and were soon in dreamland. The next morning we turned over our arms and equipment to the Quartermaster Sergeant, as previously directed, and proceeded to the Troop Commander's tent to receive the instructions pertaining to the itinerary of our march. After receiving instructions to the effect that the troops would march about thirty miles in a certain direction, armed with compass alone, we departed upon our journey.

We had not gone very far before the troops passed us at an eight mile gait. We received everything uncomplimentary from our comrades, and were soon left behind in a cloud of dust, with nothing in sight but a broad prairie, a compass and a number of cattle. We were as adventurous as the day before and kept up courage by relating our experience of the previous day with the "Grizzly."

But about thirty miles to walk seemed more than our contract with the government contemplated, and the first shade tree we came to we sat down to rest. While resting we decided we could "cut out" about ten miles by taking a more direct line, utilizing the compass for this purpose. Leaving the road entirely, we soon found ourselves in sight of the troops again but had not gone very far in this direction, however, before we had a very frightful experience with a herd of cattle. An old bull of many years' experience upon the plains decided that trespassing upon his premises, without permission, was a direct violation of the rules and regulations of this command, and immediately displayed his contemptibleness by making a few acrobatic stunts, charging the right wing of our advance. Being armed with nothing by a compass and there being no trees in sight, the reader can imagine our predicament. We were trained athletes and were soon off in a 100 yards free-for-all dash, and after a few tree frog vaults succeeded in gaining the other side of a gulf that prevented our antagonist from carrying off all honors. I wished very much for the rifle that I had so nervously fired the day before at the "Grizzly," but of course I had just as well wished for my horse, for each was well out of my reach. We sat down for a few minutes to regain some of the compressed air that had escaped our bellows during the dash, after which we proceeded on our journey and were soon far out upon the prairie.

We had a small lunch and partook of it on our way and had soon forgotten about the latest incident, when, to our utmost dissatisfaction and surprise, we were greeted by a big brown wolf standing about thirty feet to our right front. He seemed very much carried away over the appearance of such healthy and tender looking youngsters. What should we do: What could we do? We were unarmed, except for the compass, and it wasn't designed to accomplish a one desire [sic], that of having wings, so we moved on as though we had seen nothing, and soon our adversary advanced to extend formally his appreciation of our appearance at so opportune but unexpected time, but of course, we were not civil enough to adhere to such formal proposals as were now in progress by the gentleman. We detoured a little from our original plans—that of keeping on a bee-line—but the wolf gentleman seemed very determined in his desire to have us exchange a few friendly terms with him at a close range, and was willing, if we hadn't the time to stop, to accompany us a short distance to accomplish this one desire. Seeing that we could not shake him easily, we turned and greeted him with a few stones that we had fortunately come in possession of and soon induced the intruder to return to his place of peace. There was no time to lose at this stage of affairs, and we pushed on, and soon had covered about fifteen miles.

After resting awhile at a small spring we continued our journey until within sight of the troops that were now in the act of bivouacking for the night.

Seeing that the compass had served its purpose and had guided us almost on a direct line to the very sight of the camp, we decided to remain on watch, at a safe distance, until camp had been pitched, wood and water supplied and horses groomed, and descend upon camp at the sounding of mess call, "just in time," but being a little wearied from our two days' experience were soon asleep, and failed to respond to mess call, tattoo or call to quarters. Well, after waking up and seeing that darkness had long ago stretched her folds over the earth, and the old soldier had crept away from the fireside into his resting place beneath the willows that are so numerous along the Big Horn and Little Horn rivers, we proceeded cautiously to camp. When within the limits of camp, and a few yards of our destination, we were shocked almost into insensibility by a challenge from the sentinel on post: "Halt! Who comes there!" The same being repeated several times, with the remark, "If you don't halt I will shoot."

After recovering our wits we halted and gave a half way satisfactory answer and were admitted into camp, with orders to report to the First Sergeant at once. We reported to the First Sergeant as directed and were called upon to explain the cause of our late arrival in camp.

We tried to explain the uncertainty of the location of camp and our long journey over the "take pains and walk" route, but were greeted with a stern look from the upper corner of the left eye of the "old top," which was sign sufficient to us that our story was of little credit. After a slight pause the old gentleman asked if we hadn't arrived upon the hill overlooking camp at about the same time the command arrived in camp. Well, we couldn't face the old man and deny it, and admitted that little fact under conditional circumstances, but were again directed to report to the Troop Commander the next morning for the usual orders over the "take pains and walk" route.

Eugene P. Frierson, "An Adventure in the Big Horn Mountains, of, The Trials and Tribulations of a Recruit," Part III.[4]

The next morning we were up bright and early, and after breakfasting, reported for our usual walking orders and were soon off upon the prairie. We were veterans over the walking route, and proceeded at quite a rapid pace and soon were far out from our last camp. The morning was a beautiful one; the sky was cloudless, except for a few white specks here and there; the wind was calm and, with the exception of a few risings here and there, the prairie was almost as smooth as the sky above. Everything seemed in our favor to accomplish the journey to camp without incident.

Having reached a large tree, we stopped for a few minutes' rest and were soon well upon our way again. The day passed away without incident and the close of it brought us safely to camp. After visiting the mess tent we received our equipment, turned in prior to our "take pains and walk" journey, with instructions to mount with the command the following morning.

Our places were filled around the campfire that night and we held prominent, as well as worthy positions, among our older comrades in relating our three days' experience over the "take pains and walk" route. At 9 o'clock sharp tattoo was sounded, the fireside was vacated and our bones were soon resting in a small but comfortable improvised bunk. The next morning found us all in unusually good spirits. The day was an ideal one and three more days would find us back in old Fort Custer, so we were as prompt as possible and were soon mounted upon our steeds alongside the other Cavalrymen enroute to the next camping place.

The boys were all busily engaged in something or another; some were singing, some whistling and others thinking of the girl "I left behind me." The Captain rode at the head of the column and seemed as cheerful as the enlisted men in returning to their good old post that was yet two days away, but would, in due time, appear upon the horizon slightly to the northwest, just as it had disappeared some ten days previous. The command was halted, and the men and horses were given about fifteen minutes in which to rest. "Attention" was sounded and we were off again for the camp that was to mark our eighth day from post. Having been out of the saddle for three days we were inclined to shift from one side to the other in search of an easy place, thereby causing several little risings under the seat known as the horse's back, the same having been discovered upon our first halt by the Troop Commander, who had made an inspection just for such a thing. We were cautioned that if our horses' backs were not in a normal condition upon reaching camp, we could make up our minds to "hoof" it the remainder of the distance—about seventy miles—so were soon applying every known remedy to prevent any undue inflammation, and acting upon the advice received from an old soldier, I applied a remedy not known in veterinary science, and soon discovered, after making another halt, that in order to reach camp with a sound horse, it necessitated his being unsaddled and led. I looked around for an encouraging nod from some comrade, but was met on every side by a frown and an occasional burlesque from some more fortunate recruit, so I decided to make the best of it until I could communicate with my comrades, I would have been satisfied to finish the trip with them over the "take pains and walk" route. But the old "top" rode to the rear of the column and said: "'Cruit, fall out." I obeyed.

He very abruptly ordered: "Unsaddle that horse, put your saddle upon the wagon train, turn your horse over to the corporal here, and you can get to camp the best way you can. You 'cruits should be in a cotton field, for you are a menace to the government." Well, I was soon left far behind upon the prairie at the mercy of all the wild creatures of the country, as well as a tribe of Crow Indians, who were harmless, and whose only aim in life was eating dogs, running horse races and gambling; yet I was not discouraged and was determined to make the very best of it, and to accomplish the journey in the best way and to gain the respect and confidence of my superiors. I soon reached camp again. After my arrival in camp alone, I proceeded to look up my two comrades and enlist their sympathy to the extent of having two more companions for the next day; but they were more fortunate than I in the day's journey, having arrived in camp with sound horses.

Finding that I could not enlist my comrades' sympathy to the extent of being passengers over my route, I proceeded to my old friend, the cook, and was soon capable of taking things as they were presented. During the evening, the First Sergeant reported to the Troop Commander in regards to my (the writer's) journey over the usual route the next day. During this conversation I was called upon for some kind of explanation in regards to the physical condition of my beautiful steed, whose name was Keptomania [sic], and, of course, allowing me to be both counsel and jury, I soon had orders to mount the wagon next morning, which was to be the ninth day out from post. The tenth day was to find us back in the dear old fort.

I felt very much relieved and was soon telling my comrades about my latest success. After stables the regular meal was served, after which the troops attended retreat roll call, and were soon free until morning to stroll up and down the banks of the Little Big Horn River and toss pebbles into the deeps. Some were hunting, some fishing, some bathing in the beautiful stream, and others doing various kinds of other things essential to field life. "Tattoo" found us all lying in a well-deserved bunk dreaming of the various incidents of the day. The next morning we were in an unusually good humor, and by 7 o'clock were ready to mount and begin the beginning of the end. One day only was left for us to spend upon the prairie, so all were imbued with the spirit and principle essential to good soldiers in time of actual warfare—a spirit that each and every soldier in Uncle Sam's Army has in him when he is about to embark upon some perilous mission, a spirit that moves him, causes him to feel that danger is one of the working tools of his profession, thereby relieving his frame from all fear or danger.

A number of beautiful scenes were passed during the day, the close of which found us camped upon that famous Custer Battle Field where, on June 26, 1876 more than three hundred brave soldiers of the 7th U.S. Cavalry lost their lives making a last brave stand; headstones mark their last positions; some stood alone; some more fortunate ones sacrificed their lives together; headstones appear in the position of a squad or platoon, showing that they had congregated together there to die for their country. The next morning all were up and stirring before day. This was to be our last day upon the prairie. The post could be seen slightly above the horizon and a little to the northwest, so the reader can imagine how full of joy was each heart. At exactly 7 A.M. "Boots and Saddles" were sounded and the command was soon jolting along toward the post. We halted to rest for a few minutes, but the march was soon resumed and quickly we were in plain view of the post. Another half an hour found us in line at a halt and ready to dismount, unsaddle and repair to the barracks. After unsaddling we were marched to the barracks, dismounted, and then and there called from labor to refreshments, to enjoy the pleasures of a well earned garrison life. There are few pleasures to equal the experiences of a recruit.

Chapter Forty-Five

A 24th Infantry masquerade ball

The black press and the Buffalo Soldiers had a close connection with each other. Soldiers subscribed to the papers and reported on their activities at western posts. At least one first sergeant, Robert M. Johnson of the 10th Cavalry, went so far as to pay the postage on subscriptions taken out by his men.[1] The editors published their letters for their civilian readership, which eagerly awaited news of the soldiers.[2]

This report from Fort Bayard, near Silver City, New Mexico, describes a company soirée and concentrates on the costumes worn by the soldiers and their guests.3 Three soldiers attended dressed as some kind of Indian, and the appearances of two were referred to as "comical."

(Correspondence of the *Army and Navy Journal*)
Fort Bayard, N. M.

January 28, 1894

A masquerade ball was given by Co. F, 24th infantry, on the night of Jan. 25, and was made a complete success by the skillful management of Sergts. Rose, Abbot and Jackson. Before dancing commenced a quartette was sung by four of the leading singers of the fort. The costumes worn were as follows:

Mrs. Gussie Lee, as an English Princess, wore a Swiss dress covered with sunflowers; Miss Smith was dressed as an English Dude; Miss Maggie Lee, as a Japanese Princess, wore a deep red silk dress decorated with large white stars; Miss Annie Smith, as a Chinese Lady, wore a yellow creton; Mrs. Emma Gage, as a Bashful Young Lady, played her part to perfection; Miss Sallie Worlds, disguised as an Old Hag, was superb. Other ladies of the garrison appeared unmasked.

Of the gentlemen the first to appear was Mr. Dickerson, from Central City; he was dressed as a large, gawky old lady looking for a husband, but his appearance as a lady failed to attract attention as he was not "in it." J. W. Hold was dressed as an old Indian squaw and, as usual, was comical. Comba, who is naturally comical, was dressed as an Indian chief, and did his share of entertaining the spectators; Morton played his part very nicely as Chinese dwarf; Barquette, dressed as a Prussian Officer, acted as peacemaker; Sergt. Hall

Men of F Company, 24th Infantry, at Fort Bayard, New Mexico, in 1892 wearing an experimental blanket roll. Some of these men may have attended the Company F masquerade ball described in Chapter 45 (Courtesy National Archives and Records Service)

was dressed as a wealthy southern gentleman; Shaw, dressed as a Policeman, acted his part to perfection by swinging his club and clearing a space for the invited guests to enter the hall; Sergt. Wilcox played the English Lord perfectly; Sergt. Buford, who is known to be a dude at all times, could not resist the temptation of playing the same part on this occasion. But of all, Robinson, of Co. D, was most admired by the spectators as an Idiotic Indian Squaw. Dancing was kept up until morning, when the participants retired to their respective quarters. The music rendered by Fitch, Lee, Loving and Alexander was excellent.

Observer.

Chapter Forty-Six

The death of Lieutenant John Hanks Alexander

John Hanks Alexander, class of 1887, was the second African American to graduate from the United States Military Academy at West Point. He served with the 9th Cavalry for seven years before he died after an apoplectic seizure in 1894, leaving Charles Young the only black officer in the Army. W. E. Annin, who knew Alexander from Annin's tenure as post trade at Fort Robinson, wrote this appreciation and obituary, which was first published in a Lincoln, Nebraska, newspaper, and then reprinted in a Crawford, Nebraska, paper.[1]

Captain A. W. Corliss of the Eighth Infantry, who was secretary of the officers' club at Fort Robinson, had this article clipped and put in his scrapbook. He may well be the captain mentioned on the article.

The publication of a regimental order lamenting Lieutenant Alexander's passing followed the standard procedure in noting the death of officers.[2]

Lieut. Alexander

Of late years there have been only two colored officers in the United States army. Both were of course graduates of West Point. Both were second lieutenants in the same regiment, the Ninth cavalry, whose headquarters is at Fort Robinson, Neb. The war department has been notified this week of the death of the oldest of the two, Second Lieutenant John H. Alexander, who died while on college detail at Wilberforce academy in Ohio. I knew Lieutenant Alexander quite well. He was a bright, well set up, handsome mulatto, whose soldierly qualities and ability as a man his brother officers fully recognized. His colonel, one of the best in the service, when I saw him last at Fort Robinson, told me that Alexander was one of the very best of his duty officers. "He can always be depended on to perform his duty," said Colonel Biddle, "and to carry out orders given him. He is modest and unobtrusive. He carries himself admirably in a very difficult position."

Lieutenant Alexander was educated first at Oberlin college and received his appointment to West Point from an Ohio district. He graduated with good standing in the class of 1887, and was assigned as a second lieutenant to the Ninth cavalry, which, as is known, is a colored regiment commanded by white officers.

It can readily be imagined that his career, both in the academy and in the army, was more or less a stormy one. Officially he was the equal of every cadet and officer with whom he was thrown in contact, distinctions of rank excepted. Socially he was a negro. He had and could have no social intimates whether at West Point or in the garrison. His commission gave him a life-time position as an officer and his shoulder straps and uniform delegated to him authority equal to that of any other officer of his rank. But outside of that the poorest white laborer was more to be envied in some respects than the brainy, soldierly-looking mulatto who drew sabre in drill and parade with L Troop of his regiment.

There was no open ostracism, no expression of antagonism, no insults or studied cuts. But the line was everywhere drawn at official intercourse. He made no calls upon the families of brother officers. He was not expected at receptions and balls. If he came and stayed for a moment, as a matter of form, he always quietly withdrew. He messed by himself, although most of the remaining unmarried officers used the officers' mess and enjoyed the comradeship which it brought. He lived more or less alone. Official etiquette would not permit him to mingle with the enlisted men of his own color. His color debarred him from association with his official equals. I always felt sorry for Lieutenant Alexander until I talked with him last summer upon this very subject. He was then acting as commissary and canteen officer, and he took great pride in showing me how he conducted the affairs of the two offices. Then I asked him whether his position in the regiment was a pleasant one. He promptly answered that it was.

"I have no fault to find," he said. "I am treated with all the consideration I deserve, from the colonel down." He said the same thing to Senator Manderson, who was present. In talking over the question of colored officers in the army, Lieutenant Alexander was inclined to doubt the advisability of such appointments to the academy. "The natural prejudice against the negro," he said, "cannot be eliminated by army order. I do not believe that he can be forced into social equality. My own experience has taught me what a man is in the army, and I have no possible cause of complaint of any official treatment which I have received. I have tried to do my duty, and I think it has been appreciated in the regiment. No man can force himself into society anywhere. I have not attempted it here. I think I have gained the respect of my associate officers by keeping in the back-ground and not intruding myself where possibly I might not be wanted. I have often declined invitations of a social or semi-social nature, so as to give no offense to anyone. I am in no sense a martyr, nor am

I ostracized by the garrison. I simply keep within my own lines. In that way I am never snubbed, because I don't give anyone an occasion to snub me. Officially I stand on the same level as anyone of my rank, and am treated with every consideration. I feel sure that I have gained the respect of the command. That is all I have a right to ask." That day, while in company with Lieutenant Alexander, I was asked to dine at the officers' mess. The colored lieutenant was also invited. He promptly declined. The captain who gave the invitation refused the declination. "We really want you," he said. "You must come." We dined together, the colored lieutenant occupying a seat at the end of the table.

When dinner was over, he told me that it was the first time he had ever taken a meal at the officers' mess and he doubted whether he was wise in doing so at that time. "Captain——," he said, "was very kind to ask me, and he meant what he said; but I have been consistent in drawing the line as closely as those around me might wish it drawn, and I don't want to injure my present pleasant relations with the garrison by giving ground for criticism which may make matters unpleasant in the future."

That was last July. I never saw the young colored soldier afterwards, but am told that up to the time of his departure for college duty in Ohio he fully maintained the good opinion which he had won for himself in the regiment. If Lieutenant Alexander had been white he would have everywhere recognized in this country as a courteous gentleman. If he had lived in France he would have been so recognized despite his color. Here he was simply a gentlemanly mulatto. With the "Chasseurs d'Afrique" of the French army he would have been, socially as well as officially, the equal of his brother officers. Here he was tolerated on the unique basis of official recognition and semi-covenantry in army social life. He was wise in recognizing the social limitations which confined him, and still wiser in not attempting by painful and fruitless endeavor to batter them down. His modesty, courtesy and ability commanded respect, and he received it because he deserved it. He will be spoken of with kindness in the regiment where he served in a very difficult and thankless position. He will be recalled as the last but one of two colored officers—a man who did not disgrace his position; who never whined for sympathy or posed as a martyr; who did his duty cheerfully; and who, by his manners and self-control made his holding of a commission easier for himself and those with whom he was thrown into daily contact.

Fort Robinson, Nebraska

March 30, 1894

Orders No. 20
Headquarters, 9th Cavalry

It is with sincere sorrow that the colonel commanding announces to the regiment the death of Second Lieutenant John H. Alexander, which occurred suddenly at Springfield, Ohio, on the 26th instant.

Lieutenant Alexander was born at Helena, Ark., on June 6, 1864. He was appointed a cadet at the United States military academy in 1883; graduated from that institution June 12, 1887, and was thereupon appointed a second lieutenant in this regiment. He had recently been assigned to duty as professor of military science and tactics at Wilberforce University, Wilberforce, O., and had scarcely entered upon his duties there at the time of his death.

Devoting ability and energy to the zealous performance of every duty, appreciating the delicate distinctions of social intercourse which the peculiar and oft-times trying position of his office thrust upon him, Lieutenant Alexander succeeded in winning the respect and admiration of his brother officers, obtaining from all an acknowledgement of his capacity and worth.

He was manly, courteous and honorable; always a gentleman, with a high sense of the duties and obligations of an officer.

As a mark of respect to the memory of Lieutenant Alexander, the officers of the regiment will wear the usual badge of mourning for thirty days.

Lieutenant Grote Hutchinson
Adjutant
9th Cavalry

Chapter Forty-Seven

A MATTER OF COMPLEXION

Corporal William Staff of Company C, 24th Infantry, successfully petitioned the War Department to have official records of his complexion changed from "Negro" to "mulatto." Staff's request went up the chain of command, with seven forwarding endorsements, to the Office of the Adjutant General.[1] After his request was approved, a clerk revised the Enlistment Register for 1892 by lining through the word "negro" and writing "light mulatto" across the top.[2]

Fort Huachuca A.T.
September 13th, 1895

To The
Adjutant General
United States Army

Sir:

I have the honor to respectfully state that my complexion as shown by the records of this company, are "Negro." While I feel sure that my Company Commander can state hereon that it should be "mulatto." I respectfully request that should it be consistent with Law, that authority may be granted the Commanding officer of this Company to erase from the records the word negro and insert, in its stead the word mulatto. I would also state that I was enlisted by Lieut. Abbott, Jr., 12th Infantry, at Fort Leavenworth Kansas, June 30th, 1892.

Very respectfully
Your obedient servant,
William Staff
Corporal, Co. "C," 24th Infantry

War Department
Adjutant General's Office
Washington October 17, 1895

The Commanding Officer
Co. "C," 24th U. S. Infantry
Fort Huachuca, A. T.

Sir:

In the case of Corporal William Staff, of your company, I have the honor to inform you that the records on file in this office have been corrected to show that his complexion is *light mulatto*, instead of "negro," and the Assistant Secretary of War directs that the retained records be corrected accordingly.

Very respectfully,
Your obedient servant,

Assistant Adjutant General

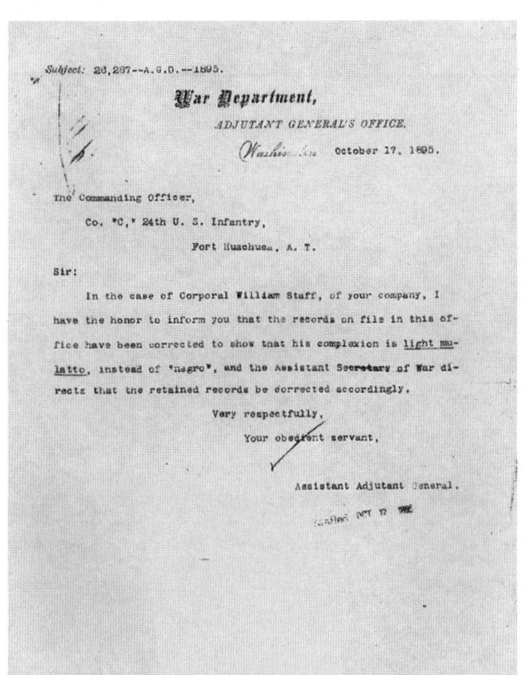

Subject: 26,287--A.G.O.--1895.

War Department,
ADJUTANT GENERAL'S OFFICE.
Washington October 17, 1895.

The Commanding Officer,
Co. "C," 24th U. S. Infantry,
Fort Huachuca, A. T.

Sir:

In the case of Corporal William Staff, of your company, I have the honor to inform you that the records on file in this office have been corrected to show that his complexion is light mulatto, instead of "negro", and the Assistant Secretary of War directs that the retained records be corrected accordingly.

Very respectfully,
Your obedient servant,

Assistant Adjutant General.

Mailed OCT 17 1895

Approval of Corporal William Staff's request (Courtesy National Archives and Records Service)

Chapter Forty-Eight

Chaplain Allen Allensworth and the Post School

As historian Robert Jefferson observed, black chaplains toiled for "God, Race, and Nation."[1] This was certainly true of Chaplain Allen Allensworth (1842–1914) who served from 1886 to 1906 and retired as a lieutenant colonel, the first African American officer to reach that rank. He was known and respected throughout the Army for his work in education.[2]

He and his fellow regimental clergymen conducted religious services, but they also operated the schools for soldiers that were required by law for the black regiments. These schools served the soldiers by teaching them skills they could use in and out of the Army. They also served the Army by improving the soldiers' abilities to perform as clerks and telegraph operators. This article reports both the secular and the sacred sides of the chaplain's work; it also shows the enlisted men resorting to their own initiative and resources to fill a need unmet by the Army.[3]

Fort Douglas, Utah

. . . The post school here, under the direction of Chaplain Allen Allensworth, is in a flourishing condition. It has a membership of 120 students. The course of instruction, besides having the regular primary classes and classes in grammar, arithmetic, history, etc., has also classes in printing, telegraphy, clerkship (such as making out company and regimental papers), signaling, etc. The interest taken in the school by the enlisted men is gratifying in the extreme to the chaplain, who takes great interest in this part of his work. The graduates in the course in clerkship are generally detailed as company clerks, or as clerks in the Adjutant's office, Commissary or Quartermaster's Department, and are always efficient in that kind of work. There are few schools in the Army that are run on the plan of the one at Fort Douglas, at least if there are they are very seldom heard of. A school of this kind is very useful, and should be encouraged in every post in the United States.

The religious services conducted by Chaplain Allensworth are also well attended. At every meeting the chapel is filled by the enlisted men, who take a hearty part in the services. The regiment has a very fine organ, which has just arrived. Until lately the chapel has been so poorly lighted that it was almost impossible to read by it [sic] at evening services. The enlisted men, finding that the Quartermaster's Department would not furnish them with the necessary lamps, settled the matter by buying several large lamps from their own pockets.

Chapter Forty-Nine

A "GLORIOUS CALLING"

Sergeant Major Edward L. Baker, Jr., may well have been the most distinguished African American soldier of his generation. He was highly literate, served as the senior sergeant in the 10th Cavalry, received a Medal of Honor for saving a comrade's life under fire in Cuba in 1898, and commanded a volunteer infantry company in the Philippines. Unable to attain what he most wanted out of his professional life, a Regular Army commission, Baker symbolized both the opportunity available to the black soldier and the limits on his prospects.[1] When this article was published, he had seventeen years of service. The essay concentrated on the positive aspects of a military career.

"The Environments of the Enlisted Man of the United States of To-Day"[2]

The Great Napoleon is credited with the following assertion: That there were only two professions open to a gentleman, Statecraft and the profession of Arms, in other words, the grandest known to the world was the profession of Arms.

Taking this as our text, we claim that the profession of Arms, is the most glorious calling within the reach of man, and different from Statecraft in this, that it is open to all from the highest to the most humble. While all may not expect to reach the highest pinnacle of fame still the humblest enlisted man may enjoy and partake of the glory which the profession of arms sheds upon all its followers and he may always feel that while he may not be at the top, he at least is one of the most important parts of the establishment and that the glory of the whole is a part of his heritage. In no other profession in the world will he find himself in so enviable a position.

As a rule, the enlisted man of today, comes from laboring classes, original enlistments being restricted by law, to those who are physically competent, less than thirty years of age, unmarried, of good character and habits, and who are able to speak, read and write the English language. When he satisfies the recruiting officer of his ability to enter the service, he is given a chance to convince himself, by six days probation, as to whether or not, he desires to accept the profession. If he agrees, he does so voluntarily, and the suggestion is ventured he will find himself more comfortably fixed in it, than in any other position in civil life, open to the class from whence he came. His future however, is in a great measure, what he makes it. As no one who is indifferent to obligations as a man and his duties as a soldier, can hope even to receive a favorable consideration towards securing the great rewards held out for those who serve honestly and faithfully any more so than he can hope to secure the superintendency of the establishment, in civil life, in which he worked for years as an idle and indifferent clerk. It is therefore of the utmost importance that he keeps clearly in view of the soldier's motto: "Be honest and upright, accept cheerfully, execute literally and absolutely all orders received, no matter how unimportant in character or trivial in detail they may seem." No army could exist without its discipline, nor business corporation survive without its rules. The reputation and prosperity of all civil concerns depends upon the celerity with which its business is conducted and manner in which its patrons are treated by its employees. It is therefore seen that disciplined or trained hands are required in all walks of life.

The demands upon the intelligence, zeal and activity of the enlisted man of to-day are by far greater than ever before, consequently in his profession, he must be educated in many things aside from his duties as a combatant in the Drill Regulation.

The drills of to-day are so varied in character and employment that that sameness which existed in the old tactics which would otherwise prove monotonous has been to a marked degree eliminated, if not entirely removed. Too much attention cannot be given to the individual instruction of the soldier in order to obtain collective results, and the first essential in enabling him to meet the requirements are physical development and endurance, which training has of recent years, been and is being more and more systematized; to encourage and stimulate the soldier, is the best method by which to bring about the desired results, so one day in each month at many posts, during the warm season, is announced as field day, on which all military duties are laid aside, and all sort of manly sports, such as running, jumping, base ball, etc., are indulged in, prizes and passes being awarded to winners.

All enlisted men, in addition to their pay, receive rations, clothing, bedding, medicines and medical attention free of charge.

His salary only represents one-third and in most cases one-fourth of his pay and emoluments. His wages are increased with his usefulness and further increased for length of service.

He has no essential expenses except laundry bill.

He can deposit his saving with the government, and will be paid interest at the rate of four per centum and at the same time not be induced to remain away from the reading room for fear of picking up the morning paper only to see that the bank has closed its doors, or else the departure of head officials for some of the Latin American Republics or across the International boundary.

His rations are plain and simple, but wholesome in quality and sufficient in quantity. His mess compares more than favorably with many of the concerns conducting that line of business on the outside.

His bedding here is all that can be desired. Each individual is provided a good set of woven wire springs, mattress and pillow with the necessary changes of linen.

His clothing is almost unlimited in variety and is suited to all climates. It is of excellent quality and the allowance is liberal from which with frugality he can save quite a sum payable on discharge. No one on the outside receiving the same amount of money required to present a tidy appearance could begin to clothe themselves. The soldier secures his clothing at less than cost. The government stands the transportation and the individual does not.

Another inestimable advantage is, that his health is far better in service than out, in consequence of regular habits, and exercise, a pure atmosphere and comfortable surroundings. The medicines are of the modern character and medical attendance comprises the very best surgical skill. You may say that you have never been sick, but know not when you will be.

Innumerable inducements are offered to all for their moral and social welfare and intellectual improvement. Very few of the larger posts are without church facilities. The services are ably conducted by an efficient corps of clergymen known as Chaplains, who also deliver many interesting lectures on topics well worthy of note. You are welcome to attend and be free of all cares as the contribution basket is unknown.

He has free access to the library and reading rooms, where he may spend much of his time, with profit to himself and benefit to the service looking over the excellent assortment of books, periodicals and newspapers which contain many refined and instructive pictures.

Schools are in operation at all posts and those who desire may acquire a good English education free and the time spent there not necessarily be after the 6 P.M. signal has been announced from the factory or foundry.

There are numerous other facilities designed for his recreation and comfort, among them the gymnasium, ten pins and bowling alleys and the Post Exchange (a co-operative store,) where he may obtain such articles as he desires at reasonable prices. Proper rooms are also set apart there, provided with billiard and pool tables. In addition to these, many of the companies have their own libraries and most all of them amusement rooms, provided with billiard and pool tables, where the men can assemble and indulge in proper and manly sports, such as sparring, dumb-bells, foils, chess, dominoes, etc.

Passes are granted to visit neighboring towns; permits are given to hunt and fish; furloughs can be obtained to visit friends and relatives afar, in all cases your pay and allowances go on and strange as it seems, you are even paid for not eating your rations during such absence. Your mind is free to wander to all the entertainments offered by professional or home talent, all fears being dispelled that another man has your job.

Spacious and well equipped amusement halls are provided where he is at perfect liberty to dance or otherwise enjoy himself, to his heart's delight. He may also appear at the same place and witness many interesting musicales rendered by efficient Army bands.

When employed outside the company at laboring work, he receives 35c. and as a mechanic 50c. per diem extra and is relieved from ordinary military duties. This may seem small wages and especially so for the skilled artisan, but when it is considered that on the outside, he is laid off one half the time for one cause or another, possibly on account of the works closing down or the whim of a walking delegate.

By moving around to meet the vicissitudes of service, chances are afforded him for a better knowledge of the country, its resources, inhabitants, etc., than are to others in the pursuits of civil life.

Those discharged for wounds received, or sickness incident to the service, are entitled to a pension, as are also their widows and children, in case of death.

A comfortable home is maintained for those who become infirm, by a small taxation at the seat of the government.

When honorably discharged, he is never left stranded, his travel pay and allowances are always ample to reach home.

After thirty years of service, he is eligible for retirement from active service upon three fourths of his pay and allowances which is equivalent to being worth $10,000 or $12,000 (just reckon at 4 per cent.) His pay is regular and he is perfectly free to follow whatever he chooses, for a further livelihood.

The road is open to all for higher enlisted grades which carry separate quarters

Wilberforce, Ohio
August 25, 98

To the Adjutant General
Washington DC

Sir:-
I have the honor to most heartily recommend for appointment as Captains in the Colored Regiments Sergt-Major E. L. Baker of the 10th Cavalry and Sergt Wm McBryer of the 25th Infantry. These men were both First Lieutenants in the immunes, are old soldiers, highly intelligent and gallant. I recommend them from personal knowledge.

Very respectfully
Your obedient servant
T. G. Steward
Chaplain 25th Infantry

Chaplain T. G. Steward's letter recommending a Regular Army commission for Edward Baker (Courtesy National Archives and Records Service) and allowances suitable for a family, pay ranging from 23 to 69 dollars.

Certificates of merit, for distinguished service; Medals of Honor for distinguished gallantry in action and prizes for excellence in any target practice are enviable acquisitions, but are in the reach of us all.

All have access to the commissary, where a choice lot of excellent staple and fancy groceries can be had at prices that are certainly envied by the citizens in this locality if not throughout the country, as is the army itself, wherever serving. This department is very obliging, they will also order any special articles of groceries desired, or in fact anything from a pair of boxing gloves to a sewing machine and deliver them at cost price, exclusive of transportation, one condition however in the latter instance, being that you must accept what you order. So you are again relieved from paying exorbitant prices for the comforts of life. In fact a comfortable home is provided. The barracks are comfortable, well lighted, heated, with bathing facilities and other conveniences, many of them are modern in appointment. Though the enlisted man is expected to endure hardships in time of trouble, his welfare is not neglected in times of peace.

There are numerous avenues open whereby the enlisted man may better fit himself to cope with the masses should he desire to return to civil life. The following are some of the useful arts and crafts open which he may be able to gain a fair knowledge of or a thorough insight into, clerks, telegraph operator, musician, cook, apothecaries, saddlers, blacksmith and mechanics of various grades.

And above all he returns disciplined thereby enabling him to continue serving his country as a good peaceable and law abiding citizen. In the army he learns to submit to things that which of necessity must be submitted to and not simply as a matter of submission. Those who may question the value of discipline, I can only quote the following from the well known author Saxe: "Should anyone from ignorance not perceive the immense advantage that arises from a good discipline, it will be sufficient to observe the alterations that have happened in Europe since the year 1700."

The name army is loathsome. If it were more closely studied many of the better class would seek its ranks and rejoice to have found at last a haven where there are no "rainy days."

The life of a soldier is one full of desire and bright hopes for the future, although he is looked upon as an incumberance and tax in time of peace. If active service never comes, which alone brings about that respect and admiration to which he is justly and rightfully entitled, he can nevertheless claim an honorable life and is sure to receive a decent burial.

Chapter Fifty

Chaplain George Prioleau on a segregated railroad car through Texas

George Prioleau was an educated, articulate, and successful man. As a graduate of Wilberforce University, a minister in the African Methodist Episcopal Church, and an Army chaplain, he was living proof of the success that a son of slave parents could attain, even in the context of the rise of Jim Crow. Before accepting the chaplaincy of the 9th Cavalry, he served a number of Ohio congregations, and the Cleveland *Gazette*, Ohio's leading black weekly always showed an interest in his activities. Prioleau occasionally provided the *Gazette* with reports of his activities, such as this 1899 trip across the Southwest by rail.[1]

Prioleau

The Ninth Cavalry's Chaplain, an Ohian, has Lively "Jim Crow" Car Experience.

His Experience with Railroad Officials and Five Mexican and Poor White Toughs—A Pointer for Afro-Americans Traveling in Texas.

Special to *The Gazette*.

New Orleans, La.—I left Ft. Grant, A. T., on leave of absence on July 2d, traveled in a mixed coach until I arrived at El Paso, Tex. I knew that my passage was at an end with my white and Mexican cousins, even the Indians. So, with a mind made up to submit to the inevitable, I entered the coach set aside for Negroes, but it was full of greasy and dirty Mexicans. I deliberately wended my way to the coach for white people, took seat and settled myself, but my seat was hardly warmed before the porter informed me that I could not ride in that car, that I must go forward. I refused; he called the conductor and I still refused,

Chaplain George Prioleau with his wife and daughter, around 1903 (Courtesy Anthony Powell)

creating quite an indignation among the passengers. I said to the conductor so that everyone could hear, that I ride only with the two leading races of this country through Texas—the white man and the Negro. I do not ride with greasy Mexicans. The state of Texas has reserved them for the whites, put them out of the Negro coach and I will go out of here; if not you will have to leave me at El Paso, or carry me along with these, my cousins—the whites. Well, a "Jim Crow" coach was put on to the rear, they hustled me out of my coach and I entered and had it all to myself. The "Jim Crow" coach of the Southern Pacific differs from all I have ever ridden in. It is exactly like the other coaches, with all conveniences for the traveler. From El Paso to Houston I kept out of my coach every white and Mexican traveler except two distinguished white men who wanted to talk with me. From them I learned that the Negroes of Texas are not without friends of the dominant race; that they prefer the Negroes as laborers and citizens to the Mexicans and Italians.

On the night of the 3d I objected to a lot of Mexicans and poor whites riding in my car. They were sent out, but while the conductor and porter were busy in another section, five toughs came into my coach, surrounded me and began to abuse and threaten me. I asked them very coolly what did they want, why molest me, etc. etc. I said, "gentlemen," reaching up, and getting my coat, which was my fatigue or undressed blouse, putting it on. I replied, "now, then, sirs, take and do what you wish and it will be hotter for you than the lower regions." Well, sir, it was amusing to see that the two little letters, U. S., a cross, and two shoulder straps could frighten five bullies. One said, "Come, boys, let that 'nigger' alone." There were at least twenty-five who came to the door and looked in to see what "it" was. I had peace from that point until I reached my destination. The conductor said to me that "colored women always object to the whites and Mexicans riding with them, but colored men never do." If "colored" men and women traveling in Texas make objections to them, the white man will soon get tired and the law would be wiped out prohibiting the Negroes riding with them. If the law must exist, there ought to be a first-class and a second-class for Negroes as there is for whites.

I have noted the difference between the Afro-American republican north and that of the south. The advantage of those north over the south is only in their franchise. Those north may vote and occasionally hold a public position, and while the Afro-Americans south are deprived of this blessing largely: they come in for a larger portion of the spoils from a national republican victory. This is doubtless due to their preponderance in numbers. This is seen here, at Jacksonville, Charleston and Savannah, in the custom house. Upon my arrival in this city the Daily "Picayune" gave me an interview of over a column. More anon. Geo. W. Prioleau.

Chapter Fifty-One

Benjamin O. Davis qualifies for a commission in the Army

At the start of the twentieth century, Captain Charles Young of the 9th Cavalry was the only African American officer in the Regular Army. The campaign in Cuba had recently ended, and the fighting in the Philippines created the ongoing need for a larger force. As part of this expansion, the Army appointed more than 1,400 new officers from the enlisted ranks, from civilian life, and from the volunteer units organized for the war against Spain and for service in the Philippines. Although there were many qualified black applicants, John E. Green of the 24th Infantry and Davis were the only two who received appointments.[1] So it was big news when they both passed examinations that made them eligible for promotion to the rank of lieutenant. Black newspapers all over the United States picked up and gave prominence to the story.

The two articles reproduced here represented two ends of the spectrum of reporting. The *Richmond Planet*'s front-page article was straightforward, concentrating on the essential details of Davis's success on the examination and giving a few biographical details. The piece from the *Colored American Magazine* (Washington, DC), written by Thomas H. R. Clarke, a black former volunteer officer who had served with Davis in the Eighth U.S. Volunteer Infantry shortly after the Cuban campaign, was considerably longer and contained much more detail. It also showed the important role of Captain Young in mentoring Davis, while the latter was an enlisted man at Fort Duchesne, Utah. Clarke's article ended with the extraordinary suggestion that Davis might someday become a general in the Army, a rank that Davis did in fact achieve thirty-nine years later.

"Colored Boy's Rise From the Ranks"[2]

Benjamin O. Davis, of the District of Columbia, has passed the examination open to enlisted men of the regular army for appointment as a second lieutenant.

He is the first colored man to pass.

The tests were held recently at Fort Leavenworth, Kan., and the results have just reached the War Department. Of the eighteen enlisted men who entered,

Davis, who is a sergeant major of the Ninth Cavalry (colored), passed third in order of merit. Under the law the successful candidates will be appointed to vacancies as they occur.

Davis will be the first Negro soldier to rise from the ranks to a commission in the regular army. He is the son of Messenger Davis, of the office of the Secretary of the Interior, was educated here, and was Major of the Colored High School Cadet Corps. At the outbreak of the Spanish war he volunteered and was appointed a lieutenant in the Eighth Regiment of Immunes.

After the mustering out he tried for a commission in the regular service.

The only way open was through the ranks. He enlisted as a private in the Ninth Cavalry, was advanced to sergeant major of a squadron, and had served in that capacity for about one year when he entered for the examination.

There is but one colored officer in the army at present, Captain Charles Young of the Ninth Cavalry, a graduate of West Point, now at Wilberforce College, Ohio.

"Up From The Ranks"[3]

The time has passed so rapidly since the event of which I am about to write occurred, that it seems to have been only several months instead of years ago.

It was on a spring day toward the closing of the school year that I dropped into Mott School to see Dr. W. B. Evans, the principal. A lesson in numbers was in progress. A young brown boy of sixteen years was working out an Algebraic problem on the black board. I watched him until he stopped with the conclusion. It was correct. Another problem was given him in equations. Again his answer was correct. I marked the swiftness of his work and his unhesitating manner.

"Who is the boy, Doctor?"

"Ollie Davis, the brightest pupil in the room."

Two years later I met Captain Benjamin O. Davis of the High School Cadet Corps, drilling his company in front of the High School. His military bearing and superb self-confidence could escape the attention of no one. On his face were lines of more than youthful determination—something exactingly severe as he "dressed" his company. I concluded that I had picked out the winner of the medal at the rapidly approaching competitive drill. I was wrong. The volley fire from both kneeling and lying positions were "good"—another company attained excellence therein.

The war with Spain had come. I was commissioned Second Lieutenant

9th Cavalry officers at Fort D. A. Russell, Wyoming, sometime between 1909 and 1912. Captain Benjamin O. Davis is in the second row, and Chaplain George Prioleau is in the front row (Courtesy U.S. Army Military History Institute)

in the 8th U.S. Volunteer Infantry. Three weeks after my company had rendezvoused at Fort Thomas, Ky., First Lieutenant Benjamin O. Davis came down with company "G" and proceeded at once to place it in the very highest state of efficiency in the drill and manual of arms. He was soon selected by Lieutenant Colonel Hughes as his battalion Adjutant, which position he continued to hold until the muster out on March 6th of the following year. His work in the 8th was characterized by intelligence and tireless energy. The amour propre of successful and inexperienced youth, never, however, ran him "up against it."

One bright moonlight night at Chickamauga Park, just after "taps" had sounded, we were sitting around a Sibley stove in which pine knots were sizzling and burning, and filling the tent with health-giving aroma; a bottle of "Deep

Rock" on the table and having a quiet smoke, Frank Steward, Proctor, Purnell, Davis and myself, discussing every imaginable topic, but more particularly the possibilities of getting off to Cuba, Davis suddenly arose and said, "If ever we are mustered out, and there seems to be some talk about it, Mr. Davis will be found in the ranks of the regular army." He and Proctor entered the 9th Cavalry together. Proctor became 1st Sergeant, his old place, and afterward Captain in the 49th U.S. Volunteer Infantry; Ollie became post sergeant-major, the highest non-commissioned rank.

At Fort DuChesne, Utah, where the 3rd Squadron of the 9th Cavalry was stationed was Lieutenant Chas. Young, at that time the only colored officer in the regular establishment. He became very much interested in Sergeant-Major Davis and encouraged him to study and take the examination for a Second Lieutenancy. Even the white officers encouraged him to do so and offered him every necessary aid and instruction. Under Lieutenant Young he plied himself at his severe task for nearly two years. History, Geography, International law, Mathematics, Surveying, Drill regulations—each in turn was taken up and mastered so completely that when he penned the last syllable of his answers at Fort Leavenworth, Kansas an average of ninety-one per cent had been made, and the news was flashed across the country that a colored soldier had broken into the military "holy of holies." Brains and determination had conquered every obstacle that had stood between him and the attainments of his dreams.

Lieutenant Davis is in the possession of a fine physique, broad shoulders and tapering waist. Lithe and muscular, a rough rider by nature. His countenance is pleasing. He is in every respect a splendid representative of the race. Two years of service in the regular army have greatly broadened his mental vision. He is just twenty-two years of age, and is in the contemplation of a future, brilliant and dazzling. It may be brilliant with the stars—not the heavens—but of a brigadier. Quien Sabe?

Chapter Fifty-Two

DIFFERING VIEWS OF GARRISON LIFE AT THE TURN OF THE CENTURY

A private soldier still received $13 a month at the turn of the century, the same pay he earned during the Civil War. Nevertheless, as the editorial from the Indianapolis *Freeman*[1] made plain, the life of a soldier had considerable appeal in the black community. There were two reasons for the attraction. In the 1890s, with the end of the Indian wars, military life became routine and less dangerous for all soldiers. Moreover, opportunity for blacks, always meager, became even more constricted as the era of institutionalized segregation known as Jim Crow emerged. The Army still offered respectable employment, a regular wage, and an opportunity to rear a family in a supportive community setting.

Corporal Stephen Barrow, in his article, "Christmas in the Tenth Cavalry," reinforced the impression given in the editorial. Barrow portrayed Army life at Fort Robinson, Nebraska, as a model of middle-class virtue and comfort, with soldiers surrounded by family and friends, in an atmosphere of religiosity, respectability, and abundance. Chaplain William Anderson, who feared the harmful consequences of drugs, alcohol, and the presence on post of "town women of bad repute," would have disagreed with such an idyllic view. Although loathing the effect of pernicious substances, Anderson was realist enough to long for the time when post exchanges could sell beer and fewer men went to town, where far greater dangers awaited them.

Both Anderson and Barrow continued to call the Army home. Anderson stayed until 1910, when he retired with a disability caused by a fever that he contracted in Cuba. Barrow served nearly thirty years, as an officer during World War I and as a warrant officer in the 1920s, before retiring just before 1930.[2]

Editorial, Indianapolis *Freeman*

The U.S. Army is making an effort to obtain a better class of colored men than heretofore. With the termination of the Indian wars, and the concentration of regiments near the large cities, the soldier's life in garrison is one of comfort and leisure. Many of our ambitious young men, especially clerks, tradesmen, etc., could not do better than enter the service.

"Christmas in the Tenth Cavalry"[3]

To go into details of the pleasures and enjoyments consistent with the environment of the soldier of to-day would be merely a monotonous recital to the masses on the outside, for two reasons: In the first place public sentiment is better educated to things military than it was a decade ago; and secondly, the avenues of comfort and happiness are being opened more and more to the soldiers every year. Once upon a time, when the Red Skin was a dangerous foe here in the West, we had but little time to contribute to the thoughts of the Fourth of July, Thanksgiving Day, or the Christmas holidays, but now since our aborigine antagonists have been subdued and pacified, we find more opportunity to enjoy the diversions of life with our civil-life brother than before.

We have kept the public informed on previous occasions as to how the summers and winters, inclusive of their respective holidays, are spent by the colored boys in blue, and it will no doubt afford our mothers, sweethearts, and friends some little pleasure to know how we enjoyed the past Christmas holidays. The writer is a member of Troop "K" of the Tenth Cavalry, having been in the troop with the regiment from the time we were in Cuba in the late war, until now. My impressions are naturally gathered principally from what came under my observation in this troop, although one troop is, as a rule, typical of the other.

On Christmas Eve it will be noticed that the Christmas tree idea is by no means obsolete in the Army. Quite a number of the men, as well as the greater part of the officers, assembled at the Post Chapel on the evening before Christmas to assist in the distribution of presents to the children of the garrison. One of the officers donned the role of Santa Claus and "issued" from the Christmas tree much to the delight of the little people.

As it is customary with all Americans to rise early Christmas morning, it was regularly complied with here on December 25th. The weather was fine and the day in itself was ideal for Christmas—with a slight remnant of snow from the preceding week, it was typical of the season in the West. The sun rose slowly from its Eastern horizon to begin its Christmas journey across a cloudless sky, the heat of its rays being slightly effected by the counteraction of a sparsely scattered snow and a seven-mile wind from the North. Some of the boys had scarcely retired from the festivities of the precious evening when things began to get lively. The forenoon of the day was taken up by the men of the garrison paying each other visits, and looking over their comrades' Christmas presents, and presenting congratulations for "A merry Christmas." The Regimental Band serenaded the troops shortly after breakfast,—if one could call it breakfast, as we are as a rule so filled with Christmas, few, if any, partake of the mess provided on such occasions—taking each of the troops in succession, which added immensely to the day's program.

The forenoon gradually parted, and the nearer it came to one o'clock the nearer it drew to the climax of the Christmas day festivities—dinner, and the more we began to feel like partaking of the repast which we all knew was being prepared for us. Then it was that we began to indulge in reminiscences of home, comparing it to our present Army home. The "K" Troop dining room was exquisitely decorated for the occasion by some of the boys of the troop earlier under the direction of Private Williams and the writer, who having acquired some knowledge of table arrangement in civil life, made an elegant display of the culinary department of the troop. The dining room of the troop appeared quite artistic with its cedar draperies. Nothing was spared to make the dinner complete, neither time nor money, and I feel safe in saying that the "K" Troop Christmas dinner of 1904 eclipsed all previous feasts. The Christmas performances were crowded into the background, when the curtains were drawn back for the reception of the troop and its guests at 1:30 P. M. The troop orchestra composed of Messrs. Williams, S. Morgan, Stewart, Hubbret, and Green, furnished music especially prepared for the occasion. Among the most notable of the guests present were Chaplain William T. Anderson, Captain and Mrs. Harry La T. Cavanaugh, 1st Lieutenant Augustus C. Hart, 2nd Lieutenant Henry R. Adair, Squadron Sergeant Major and Mrs. Eugene Frierson (ex-trooper), Squadron Sergeant Major and Mrs. L. L. Vaughn (ex-trooper), Sergeant Winger, Hospital Corps, and Miss Fannie J. Anderson.

The First Sergeant of the Troop, Robert Johnson, delivered the address of welcome, and upon the insistence of the troop an impromptu speech was delivered by the troop Commander, Captain Harry La T. Cavanaugh, whose words expressed a delight equal to those of the enlisted men of the troop. He seemed well pleased with the troop of which he has been commander for a number of years. By request, the blessings were invoked by Chaplain Anderson—and dinner was served. It consisted of Egg Nogg, Celery, Oyster Soup, Olives; Turkey, Cranberry Sauce, Mutton, Veal, Giblet Gravy, Pork, Brown

Gravy; Green Peas, Sugar Corn, Baked Stuffed Potatoes, Tomatoes; Shrimp and Potato Salads; Orange Ice; Strawberry Ice Cream, Apple Pie, Angel Food, Pumpkin Pie, Lady Fingers, Plum Pudding, Macaroons, Rice Custard, Assorted Nuts, Fruit, Raisins, Coffee and Cigars.

So a very pleasant Christmas repast was enjoyed by Troop "K." The remainder of the afternoon being spent with our friends around the garrison.

In the evening quite a number of the church going soldiers gathered at the Chapel to hear the Chaplain's discourse on the origin of Christmas, while a number of the others closed the day as they deemed best. The Christmas week was carried out on the same scale; and New Year's Day was not without many features.

The chaplain's reports[4]

December 1902:
. . . The Chaplain discovered that a number of the men of the garrison had begun to use cocaine and opium, as there is no law to prevent the Druggist from selling these drugs to any person, we were compelled to use moral suasion. The Druggist of Crawford and the citizens have promised to prevent the sale of these drugs to soldiers. We have lectured the soldiers and endeavored to show them the great dangers of these drugs. We believe that this is but one of the evils that comes to soldiers as a result of the present canteen law. We hope for the restoration of the Exchange as it existed prior to the passage of the act of Feb. 2nd 1901. . ."

March 1903:
. . . We continue the effort to stop the Druggist from selling cocaine and morphine to the soldiers. I insist that unless some radical measures are taken to prevent the sale of these drugs to our soldiers, terrible will be the result. . .

August 1904:
. . . We have been trying to keep the town women of bad repute out of this garrison, as much trouble is occasioned by their presence. We have had several servants put out of the garrison and forbade them returning, but it seems a hard matter to keep these people out. The wife of Sergt. Wm. Bell was among the number ordered out of this garrison, but she frequently returned and especially to attend balls and entertainments.

On Monday night July 25/04 she attended a Ball given by one of the organizations and afterwards before leaving the garrison entered into a quarrel with Sergt. Bell and shot him. He died the next day from the effects of his wound. Sergt. Bell was a good soldier and much loved by all who knew him.

Another soldier came near meeting with similar results not long since. The presence of these women in the garrison has a demoralizing effect upon the good. At times these bad women are employed as servants and they take this opportunity to do all the mischief possible. . . .

Chapter Fifty-Three

The names of a soldier

As the statements of George Washington and Lucinda Carter to Pension Bureau Special Examiner Henry Tracy showed, soldiers and their partners could have complicated lives.[1] In the case of the soldier, the complexities could include even his name. This trooper, an original member of the 10th Cavalry who enlisted in 1867, had three. In these depositions, Washington explained his names and discussed his family tree, ailments, personal relationships, and travels. Carter added her perspectives on life with soldiers on the frontier. Both signed their statements with "X"'s.

Washington had intimate relationships with two Native American women, Lucinda Marshall Carter, who was Creek, and Clara Mountain, who was probably Cheyenne or Arapaho.[2] So one was from the five civilized tribes that had been moved west into what became eastern Oklahoma, and the other was from one of "the relocated Plains tribes," forced onto reservations in the western part of the state. These two groups were very different from each other. The five civilized tribes were town dwellers and farmers who were frequently literate and had owned black slaves before emancipation. The "relocated Plains tribes"—Kiowa, Comanche, Cheyenne, and Arapaho, among them—were semi-nomadic warrior-hunters. These disparate groups only discovered their commonality and the lure of "a pan-Indian culture" under the pressure of white expansion and discrimination. Lucinda Carter came from the Creek nation, which along with the Seminoles, was the most tolerant and inclusive of the five tribes—members of all of which had owned black slaves—in attitudes toward blacks. The Chickasaws were the least open, excluding their freedmen from the franchise and tribal schools and prohibiting marriage between African Americans and Creek Indians.[3]

Washington's multiple names and his domestic arrangements may have complicated the special examiner's efforts to validate the pension claim. Nevertheless, despite that fact that very small amounts of money were involved and certainly no crime was alleged, claims agents' detailed and penetrating inquiries seem to show a reluctance to accept the story of Washington's life at face value. There has been no study of racial considerations in the application of the Indian War pension system, but an analysis of the Civil War system indicates that in fact it was more difficult for black applicants to obtain pensions and that claims agents applied more rigorous standards of proof in cases concerning African American veterans.[4] The Washington case suggests that the same disparity might have existed in Indian War pension applications.

Deposition of George Washington, age 63, occupation livery business, Colony, Washita County, Oklahoma Territory, September 5, 1905.

I have had two terms of service in the regular army. I first enlisted in Co. C, 10th U.S. Cav., in 1867 and was discharged at Fort Supply in 1872. Do not remember the exact dates of my enlistment and discharge. Went in again in Co. A, 10th U.S. Cav. in the latter part of 1872, I think it was, and was discharged at Ft. Concho, Tex., I think in 1875. I was discharged on account of disability—the asthma. That is all my service.

I am a married man. Have been married only once. I married an Indian woman named Clara Mountain. I took her in the Indian way at first 21 years ago. We were lawfully married after that but do not remember the year. We were married at the Darlington Agency near Ft. Reno, O. T., by a commissioner named Sampson. There is a record of our marriage in the office there at Darlington. My wife was never married before. She was a young girl when I married her. We have always lived together as husband and wife, and she is still living with me.

I have just one child under 16 years of age. His name is Cloud Chief Washington. He was seven years old last spring. I have another boy Washeen who will be 16 sometime this fall. No, he will be 17 sometime this fall.

I am not drawing any pension, but am an applicant on account of the asthma. I guess it is under the old law. Some call my trouble bronchitis. No, I guess I never applied for pension but once. The reason I waited so long after my discharge before applying for pension was because I didn't know much about it, and then I kept getting along. When I was right bad I would think I would apply and then when I got better I didn't apply, as I thought I would get along. No sir, I have no other disability that I got in the service but the asthma or bronchitis. Of late years the rheumatism is getting so it bothers me a good deal. No sir, I have nothing else but the asthma or bronchitis and the rheumatism. No sir, I have no heart trouble; just the choking up from the asthma.

I was born in Mexico but can't tell you just when. I am about 63 years old. I am about half colored and half Mexican. I have lived always amongst the

Mexicans and Indians. Before I went into service I lived in Mexico, Texas, and up on the plains of Colorado. My occupation was working around cattle and horses and sometimes nothing. My health was good, was excellent before I went into the army.

The first five years service I was in excellent health. But soon after I went back in the second time I began to fail and kept getting worse until they finally discharged me. My time wasn't quite up and I didn't want to go, but they discharged me. My asthma was caused by exposure while out on the Staked Plains. I do not know just what year it was in, but I think it must have been sometime in 1874. We were up on the Staked Plain when it came on me. Then when I got back to Ft. Griffin, Tex., it got worse. I didn't go to hospital there but stayed in quarters 3 or 4 days. When I got to Ft. Concho, Tex., I was put in the hospital. I was in the hospital off and on until finally got so bad I couldn't get out and was discharged. I was around there in a little town called Angelo for perhaps two or three months. While I was there I was treated for the asthma by the same doctor who had treated me before I was discharged. I think his name was Brown, but I am not sure.

From Ft. Concho, Tex., I came to Ft. Sill, O.T. I must have been there about 2 years I guess. I knocked about there doing first one thing and then another. Was about Neal W. Evans store there some. He is in Elreno, O.T. Then I took care of Capt. Baldwin's horse some and also Lieut. Lebo's horse. Don't know where these men now are. Amongst those who knew me while I was at Ft. Sill are Neal W. Evans, Elreno, O.T., and colored [man] named Henry Wooden, who I think is still at the trader's store there at Ft. Sill. A white man named Conover knew me at Ft. Sill. He is now running a store at Anadarko. A white man named Clark who has an Indian wife knew me at Ft. Sill. I used to work for him some. He is about Anadarko some place. Jim Pete knew me there too. He is in the same store with Conover. There was a doctor there at Ft. Sill who treated me once, but I forget his name. I got patent medicine mostly. I used Green Mountain and have used it right straight ahead ever since. From Ft. Sill I worked for the agent at Anadarko probably 3 or 4 months. His name was Hunt. From Anadarko I went to Darlington, O.T. It has been all of 20 or 25 years since I first went to Darlington.

From there I came down here about 12 or 13 years ago. I came down here with John Seeger when he came down here and first started this place. I have been right here ever since. While I lived at Darlington, I used to go down into the Chickasaw country once in a while but not to do anything and not to stay long. Since my discharge I have lived practically all the time at Ft. Sill, Darlington, and here. The other places where I have been were only for short periods.

At Darlington for six years I didn't do any work at all. I just rode a horse and managed the teams—showed others how to do it—hauling wood for the Indian Schools. I worked in a laundry when I first went to Darlington from September until the following spring. But I had to quit it on account of my asthma. Couldn't stay in the house. I didn't do any other work. Part of the time I didn't do anything, wasn't able. I could do a little driving or riding. I couldn't load or unload wagons or chop wood. Dr. Westfall, Darlington, O.T., treated me for asthma while I was at Darlington. Other doctors who treated me there are Dr. Gray, a government doctor—Dr. O'Bray is another—there were two others but I can't call their names. Do not know where they are. Those who know I had the asthma at Ft. Darlington are Dr. Westfall, Phil Putts, Darlington, O. T.; Jesse Bent, Darlington, O.T.; Robert Burns, Darlington, O.T.

Since coming here I haven't been able to do much on account of my asthma. I tried to farm on my wife's farm, but I had to give it up. I didn't do anything but look after the stable and some little driving...

Additional Deposition of George Washington, October 18, 1905.

(Ques.) What is your full and correct name? (Ans.) My full and correct name is George Washington. (Ques.) Are you known by any other name? (Ans.) Yes sir, I am known here the last few years as Wash Robinson. (Ques.) Explain how you happen to be known as Wash Robinson and state when you took that name. (Ans.) I do not know just what time it was. I think though it was sometime in the seventies. It was since I came out of the army. A good many years after I came out of the army. I enlisted under the name of George Washington. I served under that name, was discharged under that name, and was known by that name only, for a long time after my discharge. After I came out of the army an uncle of mine by the name of Riley Garrison came to Darlington, O.T., hunting me up. He is the only one of my folks that I can ever remember of seeing. When he came to Darlington and saw me he told me I ought to take my father's name of Robinson. My uncle told me that by taking my father's name I might some day run on to some of the rest of my folks, but I never did. So I took the name of Wash Robinson. I took part of my father's name and part of my own. This uncle afterward died in New Mexico.

I do know but seems to me he said my father's name was Bill Robinson. My father was a Missouri darkey, so my uncle said, and in the early days was stolen by the Mexicans and carried to Mexico. There my father took a Mexican woman. There were three of us children by this Mexican woman but the others are dead. My mother and father are both dead. I have no relatives living. No sir, none of my brothers, sisters, aunts, uncles, cousins are living.

(Ques.) How did your uncle Riley Garrison find out that you were at Darlington? (Ans.) He didn't know it at all until he came up there with cattle from Texas. I met him when he came there and told him where I was born and about my life. He said he knew me, and then he told me about my father. Uncle Riley Garrison was my mother's brother. He was half Mexican and half negro. (Ques.) Is there anyone who will know about your uncle Riley Garrison visiting you at Darlington and telling you that your father's name was Robinson? (Ans.) No sir, he was at Darlington but a short time.

(Ques.) How did people know to call you Wash Robinson when they had known you by the name of George Washington? (Ans.) After my uncle told me I told them my father's name was Robinson and then they wondered why my name wasn't Robinson. When I went to work for John H. Seeger when I first went up to Darlington I told him my name was George Washington. When Neal Evans first knew me he knew me as George Washington. He knew me at Ft. Sill when I was soldiering. Henry Wooden was in the same regiment. He was in Troop L. John Moon knew me when I was in the army. So did Ike Hughes and Henry Hawkins. Hughes and Hawkins both live northeast of Geary. Before I ever went into the army at all my name was Rafel Hannõn. That was my Mexican name. Sometimes they called me George. No sir, I never was known by the name of George Washington before I went into the army.

(Ques.) How did they happen to give you the name George Washington when you enlisted? (Ans.) They just did it. (Ques.) Who did it? (Ans.) The Sergt., I guess. When I went to enlist I told them my name was Rafel Hannõn. The man said he didn't know how to spell it. I told him then he could call me George. Then when they came to call the roll they had my name down as George Washington. (Ques.) Was there any of your troop who knew what your Mexican name was but that your name was placed on the rolls as George Washington instead of Rafel Hannõn? (Ans.) I do not know whether they did or not. I never told them anything about it. They called me George Washington and they didn't know me by any other name. Then I wasn't able to talk much English. I talked Mexican and I didn't talk much to any of my comrades.

I hadn't any particular bunk mates. Slept just with one and then another. Ike Hughes knew me well during my first enlistment. Then there were some Johnsons.

I can't think of any others in my Company. Henry Hawkins of Co. C knew me. (names read from list.) I knew Tom Ford well. I don't remember Buckner. I remember Chandler well. I remember all of them but Buckner. These boys were all in C Troop. None of these belonged in A Troop. William Francisco was from Canada.

None of these knew me before I went into service. I was living down in Texas on the range herding cattle and breaking horses before I enlisted. I went to Galveston from there to New Orleans and then to St. Louis where I enlisted.

(Ques.) Give me the names of people who knew you before you enlisted and also their last known post office addresses. (Ans.) Nobody that I can remember. I just worked amongst cowboys—white men and Mexicans. Another cowboy, a white man, and I took a notion we would enlist so we went up to St. Louis, where I enlisted. I do not know what did become of him. I can't think of his name.

I worked for several men in Texas. I worked for a man by the name of Millett. I never saw him but once and don't know where he is. His ranch was from the Red River to the Rio Grande. I ranged everywhere. No sir, I can't give you the name of anyone who knew me before I enlisted. I was born in Mexico.

(Ques.) In one of the papers in your case you are represented as saying that you were born in Mo., in Johnson Co. Is that true? (Ans.) No, who filled that out made a mistake. I was born in Mexico. I was in Missouri in Johnson Co. I don't know when that was. I expect I was about 13 or 15 or 16 years old. I was in Johnson Co. at different times, sometimes was there a month. I stayed some with an old colored man named Hunns. He is dead. I do not know of anyone in Missouri who knew me. I have no picture of myself. Did have some but they were burned up. I had a negative taken a few days ago. The picture is to be finished sometime today. Have understood your questions, have heard this read, and my answers are set down correctly.

Additional Deposition of George Washington, December 18, 1905.

(Ques.) In the last statement you made to me, did you give me the true reason for your changing your name from George Washington to Wash Robinson? (Ans.) Yes sir. (Ques.) What was the reason? (Ans.) Because I was told that my father's name was Robinson, and that if I took that name I might find some of my people.

(Ques.) Why did you leave San Angelo, Tex., after your last discharge and come up into Oklahoma? (Ans.) Well, I just left down there. Wasn't feeling very good down there, and I had soldiered up here and so I came back up here.

(Ques.) Didn't you have some other reason for leaving San Angelo? (Ans.) Yes. I had other reasons. (Ques.) What were they? (Ans.) Well, about a woman. I had a woman, wasn't married to her, just kept her. She got to getting drunk and running with other men at night. She and I lived together while I was in the army and I knew she was doing that way before I was discharged. After I was discharged she kept on getting drunk and running with other men, and as I hadn't any right to fuss with her about it for we were not married, I just left her down there. That is the reason why I left there and came up into Oklahoma.

(Ques.) Didn't you have another reason for leaving San Angelo when you did? (Ans.) No sir. (Ques.) Did leaving that woman have anything to do with you changing your name? (Ans.) No sir, not a thing on earth. Her name was Lucinda Marshall from the Creek Nation. She was half negro and half Indian. I didn't change my name for her. I didn't marry her and didn't have to change my name on account of her. I first met her at Ft. Arbuckle, Ind. Ter. She had had another man but he run off and left her. She had one child by him. I took up with her at Ft. Arbuckle after I had gone into the army. I had two children by her, or she said they were mine, I don't know. These two children were named Mallia Ann Washington, a girl, and George Washington, a boy. I do not know where they are now. I believe the boy was born in 1871 and the girl sometime in 1873. While this woman and I lived together she was known as Lucinda Washington.

(Ques.) Isn't it a fact that you and this woman Lucinda were married by a colored preacher at Ft. Arbuckle? (Ans.) No sir. I just simply asked the captain if I could bring her to the company as a laundress. Our captain's name was Burns, Edward Burns [Byrne], I think. I do not know where he is. (Ques.) Isaac Hughes says that you and this woman Lucinda were married at Ft. Arbuckle by a colored preacher. (Ans.) He don't know nothing about it, for he was at Ft. Supply at the time. (Ques.) What became of Lucinda Washington? (Ans.) I left her at Ft. Concho, Tex., and I heard afterward she went to Ft. Elliott, Tex., with a man, but forget his name. No sir, his name was not Carter. He belonged to L Troop of the 10th Cav., but I can't think of his name. If she ever married, I never heard of it. Cheyenne Fanny, a Cheyenne Indian woman, told me that she saw this woman Lucinda in the Panhandle of Texas.

(Ques.) Did you work for anyone while you lived at San Angelo, Tex., after your discharge? (Ans.) No one, except George Goldsby, don't know where he is, and I hauled some wood with a bull train.

(Ques.) Did you know a Mexican at San Angelo by the name of Antoine or similar name? (Ans.) No sir, I never knew a Mexican there by that name or any name like that. (Ques.) Didn't you go to work for a Mexican just before you left San Angelo or just after you left there? (Ans.) No. (Ques.) Isn't it a fact that just before you left San Angelo you went to work for some man, that you had some trouble with him, and left there on that account? (Ans.) No man I had trouble with cause me to leave there. The reason I left there was as I have told you on account of the actions of that woman Lucinda. (Ques.) Didn't you take some horses belonging to another man when you left that section of country? (Ans.) No sir, I didn't leave with any horses. (Deposition of Lucinda Carter read to claimant.) I just came up from down there with a man who had some cattle. I can't tell you the man's name. Her statement that I stole two horses down about San Angelo is not true.

(Ques.) How was your health during your service in Co. C, 10th U.S. Cav, your first service? (Ans.) While in Co. C my health was good. I never felt anything. I did get hurt by a horse jumping on [my] left foot at Ft. Riley. I was in the hospital maybe 8 or 10 days. Then I came out all right. I had some little sicknesses in C Company but not to amount to anything. My health was excellent in C Company and was all right for about two years in "A" Company. I began to smother on account of the asthma. They called it bronchitis then. I have been bothered with it ever since.

(Ques.) What was the nature of those little sicknesses you say you had while in C Company, your first service? (Ans.) Why just pains in the breast, pains in the side, and headaches. (Ques.) What was the cause of the pains in your breast? (Ans.) Why, I didn't know unless it came from breaking pitching horses. Lots of the soldiers were green with horses. The government furnished a good many wild horses, and I had to break them to ride for the boys. I do not know what else caused these pains in my breast and side but riding these pitching horses. (Ques.) Did your lungs trouble you any while in your first service? (Ans.) Yes sir, they would kind of wheeze and sting a little.

(Ques.) What did you call this wheezing and stinging in your lungs that you say you had while in your first service? (Ans.) Why, I just thought it was colds. I had awful colds every once in a while and would cough like everything every once in a while. (Ques.) When you had this wheezing and stinging in your lungs during your first service, did you call it phthisic? (Ans.) Yes sir, some of them said it was a kind of a phthisic. Some of the soldiers called it that. But I would get over that in a short time. I only had two little spells of the phthisic while I was in my first service. But I didn't go to the hospital on account of it. I had one little spell while I was up on the plains.

(Ques.) When did you notice the first symptoms of the phthisic? (Ans.) I think it was in 1871. (Ques.) Had you ever noticed any symptoms of the phthisic before 1871? (Ans.) No sir. (Ques.) Did you have any phthisic before you ever went into the service? (Ans.) No sir. (Ques.) Did you ever have any wheezing or stinging in your lungs at anytime before your enlistment in 1867? (Ans.) No sir, I never did. No sir, my lungs never hurt me and never bothered me in any way prior to my enlistment. They were sound as a die. I never had any sickness or any kind before my first enlistment. I never felt the phthisic until I think it was in 1871 when we were going to Santa Fe, N. Mex., on a surveying party. I was up on the staked plains at the time.

(Ques.) Are you positive that you never had phthisic or asthma or any symptoms of either trouble until in 1871 while on this surveying party? (Ans.) I am certain I never did. None that I can remember at all. They say the first spell came on me was I got up one morning feeling pretty full. I told some of the soldiers I was all stuffed up. They said I had a touch of the phthisic. But by ten o'clock I was all over it. It didn't bother me any more while in that Company.

(Ques.) Who were with you when you first had the phthisic up on the plains in 1871? (Ans.) Why, just some of the soldiers. None of them around here was along. Sixty-five or seventy soldiers were along on that scout. About half of our Company were left back and were not on this scout, but it has been so long ago, I can't remember who were along. (Ques.) Can't you give me the names of any who were on this scout? (Ans.) No sir, to tell you the truth, I can't think of their names.

(Ques.) Give me the names and addresses of some of your Co. C, 10th U.S. Cav. (Ans.) I do not know that I can give you their addresses. Isaac Hughes was in the same Company but wasn't on these scouts. William Turner was a Co. C man, but I do not know where he is. Thomas Ford but don't know where he is. Willis Bailey; Green Johnson, but he is dead; Shelvin Shropshire, George Garrett, William Marlowe, Nathan Smith. I generally slept with William Turner before I got my woman. Henry Kidd was another soldier. I can't tell you where any one of these comrades is. In answer to your question, I will say that I can't remember a single person who knew me before I ever went into the army. Because they were all down in Mexico, and I didn't know anybody but Mexicans. I've heard all the testimony read that you have taken. I am satisfied. Have understood your questions. Have heard this read. Am correctly recorded.

Deposition of Lucinda Carter, age unknown, occupation doing washings, Clarendon, Donley County, Texas, December 13, 1905.

(Photograph of claimant shown deponent without giving her any clue to the identity of the original.) That looks some like my husband Henry Carter. I have been married only twice. My first husband's name was George Washington. (Ques.) Does this photograph look anything like your first husband George Washington? (Ans.) This don't look anything like George Washington to me. I married George Washington a good while ago at Ft. Arbuckle, Ind. Ter. He was a soldier when I married him. He was in D Company 10th U.S. Cav. I was acquainted with George Washington quite a while before I married him. He was a soldier when I got acquainted with him there at Ft. Arbuckle. He was in Co. D, 10th U.S. Cav. I can't say how long I had known him when I got married. We married by an old colored preacher. I forget his name, but he is dead now. Some soldiers and some women saw us married but I forget who they were it has been so long ago. I want to tell you the truth. I have made untruthful statements to you about being married to George Washington. I was frightened when you first came, and told you that George Washington and I were married. We were not married but lived together without marrying. Yes sir, that is right.

(Ques.) Are you certain that you were never married to George Washington? (Ans.) Yes sir, I am certain I was never married to George Washington. (Ques.) Did you ever know Isaac or Ike Hughes? (Ans.) No sir. (Ques.) Isaac Hughes was in the same company that George Washington was in, and he (Isaac Hughes) says that you and George Washington were married at Ft. Arbuckle, Ind. Ter., by a colored preacher. Now, as a matter of fact Mrs. Carter, weren't you and George Washington married at Ft. Arbuckle as you first stated to me? (Ans.) I was frightened when you first asked me, but I can say as before God that I never was married to George Washington. I was married to Henry Carter at Mobeetie, Texas. I know it is a disgrace to live with a man without marrying him. But there were others who were laundresses the same as I was who lived with soldiers without marrying them. I had two boys and one girl by George Washington. The oldest boy is named George Washington after his father. I do not know how old he is. He lives in Mobeetie, Tex. The other boy is Joe Washington, who is about 21 years old or over. The girls name is Mallia. She has been married and has children. I can't tell you how old her oldest child is. He is a boy but isn't more than half grown. Joe Washington is my youngest child by George Washington.

(Ques.) What year did you marry George Washington? (Ans.) As I told you I never married George Washington. I do not know what year I began living with him as his wife. I was just a young woman when I began living with him, but I can't tell you how old it was. I can't tell you how long we lived together but it was a long while. Long enough for him to be discharged. He was sickly and was discharged on account of disability. He had a kind of asthma, and he wasn't fit for a soldier and they discharged him. We lived together at Ft. Concho, Tex., for two or three months after his discharge. He didn't do anything, just laid around and finally left. I haven't seen him since. I had heard that he was dead but paid no attention to him. No sir, I never tried to find him at all after he left me. I wasn't married to him, and I didn't care anything about him. We went from Ft. Arbuckle to Ft. Concho and there is where he left me. I never lived with him any place else.

(Ques.) Did you and he live together at Ft. Supply. (Ans.) Yes sir, I forgot that. We did live together at Ft. Supply. (Ques.) Did you and he live together at Ft. Sill? (Ans.) Yes sir, we lived there at Ft. Sill, but I can't say for how long. (Ques.) How long was George Washington in the army after you and he began living together? (Ans.) I couldn't tell you that either. (Ques.) Did he serve out one term of enlistment and then re-enlist while you and he were living together? (Ans.) Yes sir. He was in the army twice while we lived together.

(Ques.) Where did you and he live between his two services? (Ans.) When he was discharged the first time at Ft. Supply he came down to Ft. Sill where we lived until he enlisted again. He didn't finish out his second term of enlistment. He was sick all the time and was discharged before his time was up. He claimed to have the asthma, and I don't know that he had any other sickness while in the army. (Ques.) When did he first say that he had the asthma? (Ans.) I couldn't tell you that. He was sick all the time, was in the hospital, and the doctor said he had asthma. I can't tell you the doctor's name who said this. (Ques.) Did you notice that the asthma bothered him any? (Ans.) Yes sir. Just in his wheezing. I can't tell you when I first noticed that wheezing. (Ques.) Did he first complain of the asthma while he was in the first service or was it while he was in the second service? (Ans.) I couldn't tell you that either. (Ques.) Did he have any asthma while in his first service? (Ans.) I couldn't tell you that. I didn't notice it. He looked like a healthy man after I got acquainted with him. (Ques.) Did you notice any wheezing or any symptoms of throat or lung trouble from the time you first got acquainted with him up until he was discharged at Ft. Supply? (Ans.) No.

(Ques.) What kind of a looking man was he? (Ans.) He was a kind of brown skinned man. He was tall and slender. (Ques.) What did they generally call him in the army? (Ans.) George Washington. (Ques.) Did they ever call him Big Wash? (Ans.) I don't know. I never heard him called anything but George Washington. (Ques.) Was he ever known as Wash Robinson? (Ans.) Not as I know of. He never told me anything about his past life. He never told me where he was born or raised or where he had lived. He never told me what he had done for a living.

(Ques.) Did he have any brothers or sisters? (Ans.) Not as I know of. He never told me anything about his people. I do not know whether he had ever been married before I knew him or not. I do not know where he went after he left me at Ft. Concho, Tex., and I do not know anything about where he has lived since he left me. I've never heard anything of him at all. I have really been married but the one time and that was to Henry Carter. He was a soldier in the 24th Inf I think. In F Co., I think. He left me in Mobeetie, Tex. He was to come back, and I've never heard from him. I suppose it has been over seven years since he left me. I never applied for a pension on account of Carter. I couldn't apply for a pension, when I didn't know whether he was dead or not. He told me when he left that he would either come back or send for me, but he never did either. I did hear once that he was coming, but as he didn't come, and I never heard from him, and I just thought he was dead. I am not related to George Washington, and don't think I have any interest in his pension claim. I think I have understood your questions. I have looked again at the photograph you have, but I can't say that it looks to me any like the George Washington I lived with.

(Ques.) Why did George Washington leave you? (Ans.) He left me at Ft. Concho, Tex., or just beyond there at a little place called San Angelo. He wasn't mad or anything and didn't say he was going to quit me. He told me he was going to work. He went to work for a Mexican fellow named Antoine. Antoine came back and told me George Washington stole a couple of horses from him and run off, and I haven't seen Washington since. I believe that Mexican Antoine is dead. I can't name anybody who knew about Washington taking those horses. I can't name any of the men who were in the army with George Washington. I didn't get much acquainted with them. I never knew Henry Wooden or Henry Hawkins, or Isaac Hughes. If I ever knew them I've forgotten. I have heard this statement read, and my answers are recorded correctly.

Chapter Fifty-Four

Mary Church Terrell, "A Sketch of Mingo Saunders"

In August 1906, a midnight shooting affray in which one person was killed took place in Brownsville, Texas. Up to that time, tensions had been high between the black soldiers of the 25th Infantry who were stationed at Fort Brown on the edge of town, and the white and Hispanic townspeople. The soldiers denied any involvement in the shooting, and none was ever proved. Despite the lack of proof, President Theodore Roosevelt asserted the existence of a conspiracy of silence among the 160 men of the battalion and dismissed them all from the service. Mingo Sanders, a veteran soldier with a fine record and wartime experience in Cuba and the Philippines, was the senior man among those discharged. He became the symbol of the injustice perpetrated by the president.[1]

Mary Church Terrell (1863–1954) was a distinguished teacher, writer, and civil rights leader whose life spanned the entire period from emancipation to the Supreme Court decision to desegregate the schools of Topeka, Kansas (Brown v. Board of Education). She was active in the struggles for desegregation and women's suffrage, and was instrumental in the desegregation of Washington, D.C., restaurants after World War II.[2]

"A Sketch of Mingo Saunders"[3]

To look at Mingo Saunders, late 1st Sergeant Co. B of the Twenty-fifth Infantry, nobody would believe that he had just been dismissed from the Army without honor, after serving continuously and faithfully for twenty-six years. His countenance is as unruffled and as free from any trace of melancholy as is one of Raphael's angels, and in general demeanor he is as cool as the proverbial cucumber. To be sure I had 'phoned Sergeant Saunders to come to see me just as soon as I learned his Washington address through the courtesy of the War Department. But when I realized all at once that this man, who, I fancied, must be the picture of despair from the very nature of the case must even then be on his way to my residence, I was suddenly seized with a dread of meeting him and wondered why on earth I had asked him to call. But when I actually saw Sergeant Saunders in the flesh, as serene and mild as a May morning, at evident peace with himself and all the world, I was provoked that he could be so calm.

If the consciousness of innocence leads to the countenance [of] contentment and peace, then there is no doubt whatsoever that Mingo Saunders is free from guilt. Almost any jury would acquit him of the charge of participating in the Brownsville disturbance on his face. Even in a man who has enjoyed superior educational advantages and training, the philosophical manner with which Sergeant Saunders bears his dismissal without honor from the Army, in spite of his long and faithful service would be rare, but in a man who has had almost no education at all, it is very remarkable indeed. And his sweetness of spirit is by no means the result of indifference to his fate or the inability to realize the terrible misfortune that has overtaken him, but it is because he feels he has done his very best to discharge all the obligations resting upon a soldier from the day he enlisted till he became the victim of circumstances over which he had absolutely no control and is manly enough to accept what a cruel fate has sent without a whine. When the man, who but a few weeks ago was 1st Sergeant in Co. B of the Twenty-fifth Infantry was a boy, schools for the youth of his race in Marion Co., S. C., where he was born, were very rare indeed. Even where there were schools and the desire to learn, the poverty of a child's parents frequently made it impossible for him to avail himself of the educational advantages offered and to gratify his thirst for knowledge. This was the case with Mingo Saunders. After attending school just long enough to learn to read and write a bit, his parents were obliged to put him to work. From his earliest recollection, he says, he wanted to be a soldier. "Once I saw a military company parading in Charleston, S. C.," he said, "and I thought it was the prettiest sight I had ever seen. I made up my mind right then and there that I would be a soldier some day, if I lived. Picking up a newspaper one day I read that there was a recruiting station in Charleston. Just as soon as I could get there, I went and enlisted in the Army on the 10th day of May, 1881."

It is amusing to hear Sergeant Saunders describe the sensation of disappointment—an experience through which probably nine out of ten recruits pass, when he discovered that the life of a soldier was by no means one of idleness and ease. "Before I entered the Army," said he, "I thought that all a soldier had to do was put on a pretty uniform and parade every now and then," with a hearty laugh at his own ignorance, "but I soon learned better than that." "Please tell me about the battles in which you have actually engaged," I said. "I want to know something about the service you have seen." In complying with this request Sergeant Saunders displayed the most remarkable memory possessed by any human being with whom I am personally acquainted. Place after place in this country and abroad and date after date on which engagements occurred in which he participated are reeled off apparently without the slightest effort. Fortunately for me, however, he had in his pocket an official record of his service in the Army which had been given him by the War Department. From these official documents I learned that Mingo Saunders was with the 5th Army Corps in the campaign against Santiago, Cuba, June, July, and August, 1898. On July 15 [sic] he was at El Caney and in front of Santiago July 2nd, 3rd, and again on the 10th and 11th. With his pliers together with the other soldiers in his company he helped cut the wires in sight of El Caney, while the bullets were cutting the rest. It is thrilling to hear Saunders tell the story of the battle of El Caney. "The bullets rained down on us," said he, "like hail out of the sky, but we kept on moving forward, advancing alternate[ly] by rushes. One of the men killed in this battle stood right by my side."

While Saunders' company was held in reserve, so that it might re-enforce the 10th Cavalry, another Colored Regiment at San Juan, and they were all peacefully sleeping one night, they were suddenly awakened by a shower of bullets in their camp. The soldiers were completely demoralized for a time, of course. But as soon as Saunders awoke and realized what had happened he formed Company B and reported to his Captain. It was during the campaign in Cuba that Sergeant Saunders had the opportunity and the pleasure of giving Lieut. Col. Roosevelt and his Rough Riders some food, after they had lost all their rations in an engagement with the enemy. "Boys," called Col. Roosevelt coming into our camp one day, "can you give us some rations? And I can see Col. Roosevelt now," remarked Saunders in relating this story, "just as plain as I saw him that day in Cuba. Our men had just received a fresh supply, so we all gladly divided our hard tack and bacon with the lieutenant-colonel of the Rough Riders, now president of the United States." With the Eighth Army Corps Saunders also served in the Philippine War during the insurrection from 1899–1901. He was at La Loma, October 9th, 1899, and at O'Donnell, November 18, the same year. In 1900 he was at Commizi, January 5; at Subig, January 29, February 9–10, and September 21 and 23. The most thrilling experience which Saunders had during his service in the army, perhaps, was when he, as leader, with two other men, carried a telegram through the enemy's country from Bam Bam to O'Donnell, November 28, 1899. The message had to be taken by Sergeant Saunders at night over a road which he had traveled but once before and which was alive with hostile Filipinos, each one carrying a rifle. The message contained important orders from General Burt to

Major Johnson of the 9th Infantry, who was also in command of the 25th. "We men traveled fifty yards apart," said Saunders, "so that if one were captured, the others might have a chance to escape. Being in the lead I crossed the streams first and examined the ground thoroughly to see if there were any insurgents around. As soon as I crossed, I whistled, the man behind me did the same and the third man whistled twice as a signal that we had landed safe on the other side. As we slipped along, dodging first one danger and then another, we often came so near outposts of Filipinos that we could hear them talk. At four o'clock in the morning, we reached O'Donnell and went into the midst of our camp without being known. I was certain it was best to conduct the men through our own outposts without giving a signal or being seen, and I did so."

Returning the next day, Saunders had proceeded two-thirds of the distance to his own camp, when he came upon Company C of the 9th Infantry, which was engaged in a battle with the insurgents. The captain of this company was so sure Saunders and his two companions would be murdered, if they went further without protection that he detained them till he could send the 22nd Infantry to guard the brave, black soldiers to their own camp. Saunders was also with the first party of Americans whoever ascended Mt. Ararat, and under Lieut. Martin (who has since become a captain) helped to locate a camp containing 2,000 insurgents. Among the many deeds of valor which may be placed to the colored soldier's credit is the rescue of four white men who belonged to the 9th and 12th Infantry, and who had been held as prisoners by the Filipinos for six weeks. "The faces and heads of the men were terribly gashed with bolos," said Sergeant Saunders, in relating the story. "Two of the men had been shot, one of whom survived the wound and the other was killed instantly." Among the services rendered by this brave black soldier which contributed no little to the victory of his country's arms may be mentioned the capture of insurgents on several occasions, with their rifles, bolos, sabres and the destruction of a certain distillery with all the enemy's supplies.

Sergeant Saunders also knows a bit about Indians, since he was in the Dakotas for a considerable time. As a sharpshooter he has medals which show the accuracy of his aim. Ever since February 3, 1900, Saunders has been first sergeant of his company and there is no doubt that if he had been an educated man, he would be very little, if any, below the rank of captain. Although Saunders has enlisted nine times, he has been injured but once in all those twenty-six years, having been struck in the eye by a soda bottle which exploded and which made him one-quarter blind, as his enlistment paper states.

Although Sergeant Saunders is by no means an old man (he is not much more than fifty years old), he has been a veritable father to the young men of his race, who have enlisted in the army. Just as soon as he had the opportunity, he would take them aside and advise them as to the best course to pursue, if they wished to succeed and be promoted.

Nothing illustrates Sergeant Saunders' breadth and generosity more than the following incident:

A certain young colored man who had graduated from one of the best schools in the East, enlisted in the Army and was in Company B in the Philippines. He was detailed to act as Sergeant Saunders' clerk. Feeling that he was superior to the First Sergeant from an educational point of view the clerk was rather slow about performing the duties assigned him. But Saunders bore with him patiently and made no complaint. Finally, however, the clerk entered a protest of some kind to the commanding officer, who asked Saunders for an explanation. Disgusted at the young clerk's behavior, Captain Martin read him a lecture which he will probably never forget. But—and this is the point—Sergeant Saunders was asked shortly after this occurrence to recommend one of his men for the position of clerk at headquarters. Saunders knew that if the man appointed to that place gave satisfaction, he would probably be promoted in a few months to the position of Color Sergeant, a rank higher than his own, for which the fortunate man would receive more pay than himself. Feeling that his young refractory clerk was the man best qualified from an educational point of view to fill the position he immediately recommended him to General Burt, who appointed him. When I expressed surprise that he could so far forget the misbehavior of his former clerk as to use his influence to advance him in the service, Sergeant Saunders declared that he could never understand how anybody who called himself a man could stand in the way of a fellow's promotion simply because he himself did not like him, or because the two had had a scrap, when there was no other reason to oppose him.

By nature Mingo Saunders is a philosopher, which accounts, of course, for his remarkable poise and peace. When I asked him how he could bear his terrible misfortune so calmly, he replied that everybody in this world must have a certain amount of trouble. "If it is not one thing, it is sure to be another. I have always been very lucky," said he. "I have had plenty to eat and enough to wear. I have been in the army twenty-six years, as you know, without receiving so much as a scratch. That little wound in the eye isn't worth talking about. I am a heap sight better off than those fellows who have come home from their service in the

Philippines and Cuba crazy or in poor health. And I am better off than the fellows who got killed, some [of] them shot right by my side. And so to tell the truth, I sometimes think this discharge was due me. Besides I know I am innocent and I am sure the other fellows are just as innocent as I am, and I tell you, that helps me a heap." Nothing illustrates the high estimate placed upon the character of Saunders by his officers more than the statement of Sergeant [sic] Penrose: "When I asked Saunders if he knew anything about the Brownsville trouble and he told me he didn't, I knew he was telling the truth."

"Mingo Saunders is the best non-commissioned officer I have ever known," said Brigadier-General A. S. Burt, during a conversation I had with him not long ago. "And I have been in the Army forty years," he continued.

The 25th Infantry has always been the joy and pride of General Burt's heart. It is delightful to hear him discourse upon their many virtues. "They are the best soldiers in the world," he said with emphasis and fire in his eyes, which is a challenge for anybody to dispute him. Unless my memory has played me a trick, General Burt told me that the 25th Infantry was the first body of soldiers out both in the Spanish-American and the Philippine wars. While General Burt was taking his colored soldiers to Cuba, he was frequently asked during their stops at southern stations whether he thought the Negroes would fight. "'Will your Colored men fight, General?' I was asked over and over again," said General Burt, firing with indignation at the very idea that anybody could even ask such a question. "Will they fight?" I replied, "Why they would charge into hell, fight their way out and drag the devil out by the tail."

Chapter Fifty-Five

The racial climate in Brownsville, Texas, after the shooting incident

Vance H. Marchbanks's career extended from 1895 right up to the start of World War II in 1939. He served a total of forty-three years and nine months as a sergeant, officer, and warrant officer.[1] When he wrote this letter, he had more than ten years under his belt.[2] For black soldiers, little had changed since the days of Emanuel Stance. Texas was still a hostile and dangerous environment.[3]

"A Soldier's Opinion of the Recent Excitement at Brownsville, Tex."[4]

Mr. Editor:

One full-grown wolf will stampede 10,000 sheep, while if the same herd should have come in contact with the wolf while it was in its infancy they would have disdainfully trampled it under their feet.

Such seems to have been the situation at Brownsville, Texas, during the recent excitement, which resulted in the killing of one white man, and the wounding of another which was supposed to have been done by some unknown member of the 25th Infantry, stationed at Fort Brown, Texas.

I have before me clippings of the *San Antonio Daily Express*, from the 15th to the 20th of August, inclusive, all of which contain appeals from the citizens of Brownsville, to everybody, from the president of the United States to the town "cop," saying: "Our women and children are terrorized, and our men in constant alarm and fearfulness; please remove Negro troops and replace them with white troops; send state troops; do something right away, for we are scared to death," or words to that effect.

Now, Mr. Editor, no one not a true hearted American colored soldier can realize the situation of affairs at Brownsville. The writer was stationed down there about ten months in 1899, and is well acquainted with the sentiment of its people.

The majority of the inhabitants of that section are a class that think a colored man is not good enough to wear the uniform of a United States soldier—yea not good enough even to wear the skin of a dog.

Vance Marchbanks wearing the chevrons of a first sergeant, sometime after 1902 (Courtesy Huachuca Army Museum)

They sneer at a colored soldier on the sidewalk and bar him from their saloons, resorts, and places of amusement.

Why, when I was down there, one Sunday I thought I would go down to Point Isabella, on the Bay to spend the day. So in company with a young lady I went down to the depot and purchased two tickets (taking advantage of the excursion rate then offered), boarded the train (which was only a little better than walking), went into the car and took a seat. When the train started, one of the so-called "Texas Rangers" came up to me and told me I was in the wrong place. I said, "No, I guess not; I just read your law, and it says the Negro and white passengers will not ride in the same coach except on excursions." He replied, "Don't make any difference, you get out of here; you are too smart anyway; I will break this gun over your head if you say much," the meantime menacing me with a six-shooter, of the most improved villainous pattern and caliber. Well I obeyed his orders because I was alone and could not help myself. I knew that I was being treated wrong, but he held a "Royal Flush," and I had only a "four-card bob," and I knew I could not "bluff" him.

A colored man who has the disposition of a toad frog (I mean one who can stand to be beaten on the back and puff up and take it), is all right; he can stay in that country. But those who feel hot blood running through their veins, and who are proudly and creditably wearing the uniform of a United States soldier; standing ready to protect and defend the American flag against any enemy whomsoever, to obey the orders of the president of the United States and the orders of the officer appointed over them (which they have always done with pride and honor), cannot stay down there in peace with honor. The people do not want them either because they will probably not be able to carry out their favorite sport, hanging a colored man to a limb, or tarring and feathering him and burning him at the stake without trial, while the colored soldiers are stationed there. The majority of the old settlers in southwest Texas are bandits, original members of the Ku-Klux-Klan, murderers and thieves who have sneaked down in that almost uncivilized part of the United States in the early days and mixed up with the Mexicans in order to escape the eagle talons of a pursuing and outraged justice.

Very respectfully,
Vance H. Marchbanks
Squadron Sergeant Major 10th Cavalry
Fort Washakie, Wyoming

Chapter Fifty-Six

Charles Young and African American heritage

Charles Young (1864–1922) was the third black graduate of the United States Military Academy, after Henry Flipper and John Alexander. For all of his remarkable personal achievement as the first black officer to reach the rank of colonel, he had a broad sense of responsibility to his community. As seen in chapter 54, he made important contributions to the success of Benjamin O. Davis, who ultimately achieved a rank higher than that reached by Young.[1] As this letter shows, he also took seriously the need to celebrate important cultural figures.[2] Young himself finally got his own monument, in Cleveland, Ohio, at the end of the twentieth century.[3]

Dunbar Memorial Fund
Wilberforce, O. June 29, 1907

Editor, Gazette—Dear Sir: Dr. Davis W. Clark, 222 W. 4th Street, Cincinnati, is treasurer of the monument fund for marking the grave of the poet, Paul L. Dunbar, at Dayton. About $500 has been contributed, mostly by whites, but it is believed that our people desire to aid in this movement. All contributions are to be sent to Dr. Clark, on or about Emancipation day. Every penny contributed from school children will greatly help. Will you not aid in the work of honoring our dead poet?

Very sincerely,
Chas. Young
Capt. U.S. Army

Chapter Fifty-Seven

Violet Cragg's pension request

The life of a soldier's wife was as grueling and tumultuous as that of any soldier. Violet Williams Cragg, like many of the soldiers themselves, had been born into slavery, separated from her family, and sold to a new master. Also like many of the troopers, she served in the Civil War, but as a nurse rather than as a soldier. It was on the basis of this service that she applied for a pension.

Her life in the Army as the wife of Sergeant Allen Cragg of the 9th Cavalry was also hardly tranquil. She worked extremely hard, first as a servant for officers' families at numerous posts in Texas, New Mexico, and Indian Territory, and later as a laundress for her husband's unit. She also endured an assault by Private Jerome Patton of the 9th Cavalry at Fort Robinson, Nebraska. Patton bashed her head and fled to the nearby town of Crawford, with Sergeant Cragg in pursuit. Shots were fired at least twice in the course of the chase, before the sheriff intervened, trapped Patton in a stable, and arrested him.[1]

Deposition of Violet Cragg, 309 Galisteo Street, Santa Fe, New Mexico, September 26, 1908:[2]

My home is in Los Angeles, Calif. I am visiting my daughter, Mrs. Ella Taylor, wife of Stephen Taylor. She is 42 years old, but I was not married to her father. I am the widow of Allen Cragg, Co. G 117th U. S. C. Vol. Inf., and Sergeant retired Troops F, M and E 9th U.S. Cav, who died in Los Angeles, Calif., on Oct. 23, 1907. I was married to him at Junction City, Kans., on June 1, 1885, by the probate judge of Davis County, Kans., J. F. Ayars. I had never been previously married. I never had a husband in slavery although I was a slave up to the time of the Emancipation Proclamation. The father of my daughter, Mrs. Ella Taylor, was Howard Whitney, a white man. I was never supported by him and was never known as his wife and never lived with him as his wife. We were not recognized as husband and wife. My daughter was born in St. Louis, Mo., and I lived there about two years before her birth. I remained in St. Louis until she was two years and a half old. I then came to Fort Union, N. M., with Captain Bloodkit and his wife, and worked for them there and at Fort Selden, N. M., also at Fort Duncan,

Texas, where he was cashiered from the army.[3] I was with them three or four years. I was born at Jefferson City, Mo. I was born a slave and belonged to Jim Evans. When I was 11 or 12 years old I was taken away from my mother and sold to a Dr. Abbey at Fort Gibson, Miss. I was taken on a boat from Caledonia, Mo., where I had been sold to a slave trader, to Fort Gibson, Miss., with a lot of other colored people like cattle and Dr. Abbey bought me at the market. I was really taken on the boat to Grand Gulf, Miss., and Dr. Abbey bought me at Grand Gulf and took me to Fort Gibson where he lived. I was a servant in his house until I went to St. Louis about 1863. The Yankees came thru there and told us colored people to leave and I walked eight miles with some other colored people to Grand Gulf, where General Grant had his headquarters, and there were some white ladies there. I hired out to a Mrs. Coutts and went with her on a boat called the City of Alton and went with her to Peoria, Ill. I stayed with her at Peoria, Ill., about two months and I then went to St. Louis and got work. I nursed in the Contraband Hospital in St. Louis for three months. I then worked about two years or longer at the Orphan Asylum for colored children from the South. I worked there for a Mrs. Weed after my child was born and before she was born I stayed at the contraband rendezvous and waited on table. My daughter is 43 years old instead of 42 and was born in March 1865, a month before President Lincoln was assassinated. No, I did not have any husband either white or colored. I was 18 years old when my daughter was born and I was only about 16 when I came to St. Louis, Mo. The City of Alton was a hospital boat and there were twelve doctors on it. Dr. Edenton of Peoria, Ill., was one of the doctors on the boat and I knew him at Peoria, Ill. Dr. Abbey had two sons, Sidney and George. George was a captain in the Confederate army. Dr. Abbey's wife was living. I was known by the name Violet Evans when I was bought by Dr. Abbey and afterwards I was known as Violet Abbey. My father was Jefferson Williams and I took the name Williams after I was free. He died in Sacramento, Calif. My mother is dead too. I went to Sacramento to visit him once. That was about 1894. I never saw my mother after I was sold away from her. I have a sister two years and a half younger than I am, Mrs. Sarah Dorsey, who lives in Sacramento, I don't know her husband's first name. I never saw her from the time I was sold "down the river" until I saw her in 1894. My father said it was 37 years since he had seen me. I have no other brothers or sisters living. After I was at Fort Duncan, Texas, I worked for different families at Matamoras, Brownsville, and Ringgold Barracks, Texas, Camp Supply, Ind. Terr., and Dodge City, Kans. I went from Dodge City to Junction City, Kans., and was married to soldier at the latter place.

Much of the time I worked as a laundress, doing the washing of a great many different people, and it is impossible for me to name persons with whom I was acquainted in all the different places I lived before my marriage. My memory is very poor since I became paralyzed on my left side seven years ago and I have a nervous trouble and my heart is weak. This high altitude affects my heart. I was never married, however, until I married the soldier. My daughter lived with me or near me until my marriage to soldier and her husband was a soldier in the same regiment as Allen Cragg. He is now retired and living in Santa Fe. He and my daughter can testify that soldier and I were not divorced. Jeremiah Brabham knew me at Dodge City, Kans., and he and Israel Murphy knew me at Junction City, Kans. They also knew us for seven or eight years in Los Angeles and Israel Murphy served with my husband in the 9th Cavalry. I had lovers and sweethearts during the period before I married Cragg, plenty of them, but I never had but one lawful husband. I never had a license to marry but one man and I was never married to but one man and that was Allen Cragg. I never knew nor heard nor had reason to believe that my husband was married before his marriage to me. He always claimed that he had never been married before and he enlisted as a single man in 1880 and in 1885 and his last discharge showed that he was a married man while the others did not show it. He was born in Kentucky and went into the army as a drummer boy during the war. I don't know where he grew up. He had a brother Clay who died, but I don't know of his having any brothers or sisters living. Israel Murphy served with him in the volunteer service and knew him long before his marriage and they served in the same troop in the 9th Cav. I worked for the U. S. Consul at Matamoras whose name was Wilson. I worked for a Mrs. Tuttle at Fort Duncan, Texas. I washed for a lot of soldiers and officers at Brownsville and Ringgold Barracks. I cannot give names. I worked for an old lady in Dodge City, Kans., who kept a restaurant, but I do not remember her name. I became acquainted with soldier only a short time before I married him. I am utterly unable to furnish any further data as to non-prior [sic] marriage of either myself or my husband, Allan Cragg. I have no photograph of soldier taken during the war or very soon after, but will furnish one taken with me after our marriage, or can furnish one taken in his soldier's uniform about 1889. The latter is the better likeness and I should like to have it returned to me after it has served its purpose. I have understood and thoroughly comprehended the questions asked and my answers are correctly recorded in this deposition which I have heard read. Soldier had a scar on his leg, but don't remember which leg from a gunshot wound received during his volunteer service. The wound was in the calf of the leg. There were no other marks or scars on his body as far as I know. I cannot write. I applied for a pension as an army nurse several years ago in Los Angeles and my claim was rejected because I did not serve six months. The contraband hospital was in ward 6 at Benton Barracks. I have no papers in my possession referring to said claim and I have forgotten the name of the attorney who filed the claim for me. He was an old soldier in Los Angeles and a regular pension attorney. I have heard the foregoing read, have understood the same, and am correctly recorded herein.

her
Violet "X" Cragg
mark

Chapter Fifty-Eight

Enduring patriotism

Black soldiers knew that the Army did not treat them fairly. They were vulnerable to civilian racism, denied advancement to commissioned officer status except in rare cases, and even their government could deny them due process, as President Theordore Roosevelt had done in dismissing an entire battalion after Brownsville. Yet they persisted in their faith in the United States and in their willingness to serve. In times of national emergency, veterans were quick to offer their services to the Army. Horace Bivins (retired 1913), Augustus Walley (retired 1907), and even seventy-year-old George W. Ford volunteered for service for the war in Europe in 1917. Even Barney McKay, who had been sent to prison for possessing a leaflet in 1893 (see chapter 43), offered to enlist for World War I. William McBryar, a Medal of Honor hero who along with Edward Baker was one of the finest black soldiers of his time and who also failed in his quest for a Regular Army commission, also volunteered, first for duty on the Mexican border in 1914 and then again in 1916 as tensions increased in Europe. The first time, he did so by the letter, which is transcribed here. The second time, with the number of potential volunteers growing rapidly, he used the Adjutant General's Office's Form No. 88–4.

Bee, McNeil Island, Wash.
June 10, 1914
The Adjutant General, U.S.A.
War Department
Washington, D. C.

Sir:

I take pleasure in offering my services to the U.S. Government if needed in connection with our present entanglement with the Mexican Republic.

I first enlisted in the regular Army in Jan'y 1887, and was assigned to the Tenth U.S. Cavalry, Troop K.

Was appointed a Lieutenant fro the 25th U.S. Infantry, to the 8th and the 49th U.S. Vol. Infantries during the Spanish American War and the Philippine Rebellion and served in each regiment until mustered and served fifteen years altogether in the regular and volunteer forces of the United States.

Very respectfully,
Wm McBryar

N. B.—This form must be filled up entirely in the handwriting of the applicant.

Lock Box 209
Steilacoom Wash
February 1916.

THE ADJUTANT GENERAL,
UNITED STATES ARMY,
WASHINGTON, D. C.

Sir:

I hereby make application for appointment as Major of Infantry in the United States Volunteers, and in connection with that application I respectfully submit the following answers to the questions printed hereon and the names of five persons who have known me for several years and can testify to my general character and standing in the community in which I live. I also inclose herewith three letters of recommendation as to my antecedents, character, business or professional qualifications, educational qualifications, and military qualifications and experience.

1. In what town, county, and State (or foreign country) were you born? Elizabethtown Bladen County North Carolina
2. On what date were you born? February 14, 1861
3. Are you a citizen of the United States? If so, state whether by birth or naturalization. Yes; am a citizen by birth
4. Are you married? Yes If married, state number of children, if any No children
5. What service have you rendered to the Government of the United States? (a) In the Regular or Volunteer Army. Give dates Regulars Jan 3 1887 to Sept 14 1898. Volunteers Sept 7 1898 to Mch 1899. Again in Regulars Mch 1899 to Sept 20 1899. Again in Volunteers Oct 1899 to June 30 1901. Again in Regulars [illegible] 1901

(b) At the United States Military Academy. Give dates —

(c) In the Navy. Give dates —

(d) In the Marine Corps. Give dates —

(e) At the United States Naval Academy. Give dates —

(f) In the Revenue Cutter Service. Give dates —

(g) Under any other Department of the Government. Give dates Have been in the Federal penitentiary service [illegible]

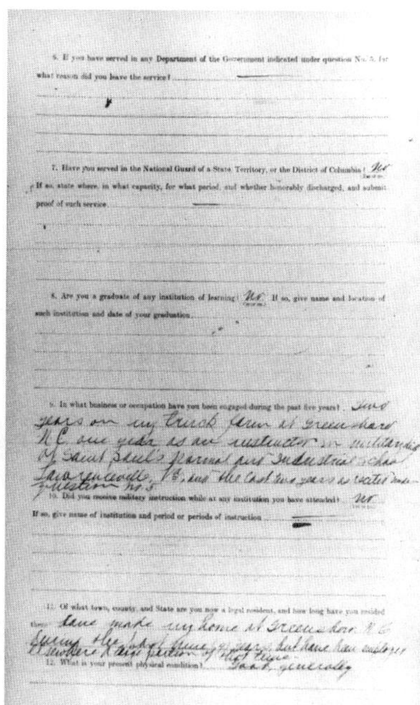

6. If you have served in any Department of the Government indicated under question No. 5 (g), for what reason did you leave the service? —

7. Have you served in the National Guard of a State, Territory, or the District of Columbia? No If so, state where, in what capacity, for what period, and whether honorably discharged, and submit proof of such service. —

8. Are you a graduate of any institution of learning? No If so, give name and location of such institution and date of your graduation.

9. In what business or occupation have you been engaged during the past five years? Two years on my truck farm at Greensboro N.C. one year as an instructor in military of Saint Paul's normal and industrial school Lawrenceville, Va. and the last two years as stated in question No. 5

10. Did you receive military instruction while at any institution you have attended? No If so, give name of institution and period or periods of instruction. —

11. Of what town, county, and State are you now a legal resident, and how long have you resided there? Have made my home at Greensboro N.C. during [illegible] but have been employed elsewhere [illegible]

12. What is your present physical condition? Good, generally

13. If you desire appointment in the mounted service or as a field officer what are your qualifications as to horsemanship? Have had nine years in the U.S. Cavalry.

14. What is your full name? Give correct spelling of each given name, as well as surname. William McBryar

The names, occupations, and addresses of the five persons to whom reference is made in the first sentence of this application are—

NAME	PROFESSION OR BUSINESS	ADDRESS
1. Jas. B. Dudley	Presdt A & T College	Greensboro N.C.
2. [illegible] Palmer	[illegible]	[illegible] Greensboro N.C.
3. H. B. Delany	[illegible] Bishop	Raleigh N.C.
4. [illegible]	[illegible] A & T College	Greensboro N.C.
5. O. P. Halligan	[illegible]	McNeil [illegible]

I certify on honor that the foregoing answers are in my own handwriting and that they are true and correct to the best of my knowledge and belief.

Very respectfully,
Wm McBryar

(Permanent P.O. address) Route 4, Box 190
Greensboro N.C.

Adjutant General's Office Form 88–4, with William McBryar's application to rejoin the service (Courtesy National Archives and Records Service)

William McBryar at the turn of the century, in the uniform of a volunteer officer (Courtesy National Archives and Records Service)

Chapter Fifty-Nine

An Army widow's lot

Mrs. Mary Smith of Indianapolis, Indiana, the widow of 10th Cavalry soldier John Smith, described her difficulty in making ends meet and need for a pension.

"Widow of the 10th U.S. Cavalry"[1]

Mr. Geo. W. Webb

Dear Sir:

I am a subscriber for the *Winners of the West*, and am a widow of an Indian War Veteran. My husband, John Smith, was a private in troop A, 10th U. S. cavalry, and was in the campaign against the Cheyenne and Kiowa Indians. Since my husband's death, 24 years ago, I have had a mighty hard time making a living, and to think how hard it was for 15 years working, and toiling, to get what money was due an Indian War widow, and finally after 15 years of trying and red tape, I received $12 per month. I am almost as bad off as before I got it, because that won't even pay my rent. I am 70 years old, and am hardly able to do anything towards making a living for myself, and that little money is all I have to depend on. Therefore I am putting myself on record as in favor of the U.S. Congress taking action on any bill that is just and helpful to the Indian War Veterans and widows.

Very truly yours,
Mrs. Mary Smith
Indianapolis, Ind.

Chapter Sixty

From Buffalo Soldiers to clergymen

Not all old soldiers just faded away. Some of them went on to noteworthy careers in a variety of endeavors. George W. Ford, an original member of the 10th Cavalry, served as a major in a volunteer unit during the Spanish-American War period and became superintendent of the Springfield, Illinois, national cemetery.[1] Rienzi Lemus, at one time a soldier in the 25th Infantry, became the long-time president of the Brotherhood of Dining Car Employees, and George Washington Williams, a Civil War and frontier veteran, later made a distinguished career as a historian.[2] The two veterans of the 10th Cavalry noted here both served in the regiment at around the turn of the twentieth century.

Walter Chenault[3]

Chenault, Rev. Walter, born, Lexington, Ky., May 6, 1883; son of parents whom he never knew; attended Russell Grade School of Lexington, Ky., and also high school; Butler University of Indianapolis, Ind., 1905–07; received B.S. degree from Normal College, 1911; was converted at the age of 9. Enlisted in the 10th Cavalry for the service in the Spanish-American War in 1898; re-enlisted in 1899 and served in same regiment, doing garrison duty Cuba from 1899 to 1902. Held the local church offices of a steward, local preacher, Bethel AME Church, Marion, Indiana; licensed to preach at Bethel Church by Rev. J. P. Q. Wallace, June 1919; admitted to Indiana Conference at Indianapolis in 1919 by Bishop Levi J. Coppin. Ordained Deacon at Indianapolis in 1919 by Bishop Levi J. Coppin; taught in the grade schools in several Indiana counties. Ordained Elder at Kokomo, Indiana in 1922 by Bishop Levi J. Coppin. Also taught in the Correctional School at Plainfield, Indiana, 1912–1913; clerk in the Indianapolis Post Office from 1914–1917; pastored Hill's Chapel AME Church, 1919–1920; Lost Creek Circuit, 1920–22; Princeton, Indiana, 1922–24; New Albany, 1924–25; Vincennes, 1925–26; Franklin, 1926–27; Saint Paul, Indianapolis, 1927–29; Frankfort-Lebanon Circuit, 1928–30; Bethel AME Church, Bloomington, Indiana, 1930–32; Princeton, Indiana (2nd time), 1936–37; Bethel AME Church, French Lick, Indiana, 1937–41; New Castle, Ind., 1941–43. Completed Bethel

AME Church, Princeton, Indiana, in 1923; made extensive repairs on churches at St. Paul, Indianapolis; Franklin, Ind.; published articles in Indianapolis dailies, Indianapolis Recorder, Christian Recorder, Southern Christian Recorder. An independent in politics; Asst. Secretary of Indiana Annual Conference 1937–1943; Chief Secretary of same conference, 1943. Married to Estella Harris, Marion, Indiana in 1911. Children: Wilbur, Wade, Charles, Melvin (boys), Harriet, Juanita, Evelyn (girls). Member of NAACP; pastor of Shaffer Chapel, AME Church, Muncie, Indiana, since October, 1943.

Thomas Clement[4]

Clement, Rev. Thomas Jefferson, pastor of Wesley Chapel AME Church, Houston, Texas; a native of Texas, the only child of a minister and school teacher, natives of Virginia who having graduated from Hampton Institute came to Texas to make their careers. Thomas Jefferson Clement was a coal miner, hotel and railroad man, soldier (Sgt. Troop K, 10th Cavalry), musician etc., before he felt a definite call to the ministry. He was converted (he calls it received his B.A., "Born Again") at the age of fourteen in Mount Lebanon AME Church, in Franklin County, Virginia. All except the first two years of his ministry have been spent in his native state of Texas. His success as a preacher and a pastor is well known in the African Methodist connection. He is serving in his 9th year as minister to the largest congregation of Negro Methodists in Texas—Wesley Chapel AME Church, Houston, Texas.

Notes

Introduction

1. The number of battles and skirmishes, and the number in which black units participated, was derived by collating three separate lists: Adjutant General's Office, *Chronological List of Actions, &c., With Indians, From January 1, 1866, to January, 1891*; Francis E. Heitman, *Historical Register and Dictionary of the United States Army, from its Organization, September 29, 1789, to March 2,* 1903, vol. 2 (Washington, DC: Government Printing Office, 1903), 426–49; George W. Webb, *Chronological List of Engagements Between the Regular Army of the United States and Various Tribes of Hostile Indians Which Occurred During the Years 1790 to 1898, Inclusive* (St. Joseph, MO: National Indian War Veterans, 1939).

2. For a nearly comprehensive listing of this literature—a total of 334 citations—through 1997, see Bruce A. Glasrud and William H. Leckie, "Buffalo Soldiers," in Glasrud, comp., *African Americans in the West: A Bibliography of Secondary Sources* (Alpine, TX: Center for Big Bend Studies, 1998), 32–54.

3. This book reproduces documents from four National Archives and Records Service (hereafter cited as NARA) record groups: Record Group (hereafter cited as RG) 94, the records of the Adjutant General's Office, the Army's administrative office; RG 153, records of the Judge Advocate General's Office, which administered the system of military justice; RG 391, Records of United States Regular Army Mobile Units, which include records of the various regiments; and RG 393, the records of United States Army Continental Commands, which include the records of individual posts and the various layers of command, including military districts, departments, and divisions.

4. *Great Plains Quarterly* 17 (Winter 1997): 4, 15. Some of the best writing on this matter, emphasizing the cultural chasm that separated black soldiers from their native adversaries, was done in the mid-twentieth century by Kenneth W. Porter. See his "Negroes and Indians on the Texas Frontier, 1831–1876: A Study in Race and Culture," *The Journal of Negro History* 41 (July 1956): 185–214, and (October 1956): 285–310; and "Negroes and Indians on the Texas Frontier, 1833–1874," *Southwestern Historical Quarterly* 53 (1949): 1512–63.

5. For an insightful theoretical discussion of the perceptual basis for this cultural gap and its relationship to racism, see Joel Kovel, *White Racism, A Psychohistory* (New York: Pantheon Books, 1970), especially chapter 8.

Chapter 1

1. While crediting black soldiers for a significant role in the Union victory, William H. Freehling noted that he knew "of only one battle, at Milliken's Bend, where black combat troops exerted a make-or-break impact on a critical Union victory." Freehling, "Sure Black Troops Helped the Union Win the Civil War, But How???" (paper presented at the Southern Historical Association meeting, Louisville, KY, November 2000).

2. There are many valuable studies on black soldiers in the Civil War. Some of the best general histories are Dudley Taylor Cornish, *The Sable Arm: Black Troops in the Union Army, 1861–1865* (Lawrence: University Press of Kansas, 1956); Joseph T. Glaathar, *Forged in Battle: The Civil War Alliance of Black Soldiers and White Officers* (New York: The Free Press, 1990); Noah Andre Trudeau, *Like Men of War: Black Troops in the Civil War, 1862–1865* (Boston: Little, Brown, and Company, 1998).

3. For excerpts of the Congressional debate and documents relating to the law and the earliest efforts to recruit soldiers for the new black regiments, see Morris J. MacGregor and Bernard C. Nalty, eds., *Freedom and Jim Crow, 1865–1917*, vol. 3, *Blacks in the United States Armed Forces: Basic Documents* (Wilmington, DE: Scholarly Resources, Inc., 1977), 16–96.

Chapter 2

1. Special Orders, Fort Harker, RG 393, NARA; Muster Roll, K/38th Infantry, April 30 to June 30, 1867, Fort Harker, KS, RG 94, NARA.

2. Letters Received, Department of the Missouri, 1867, RG 393, NARA.

3. Ibid.

4. Ibid.

Chapter 3

1. The reports are in Letters Received, Department of the Missouri, 1867, RG 393, NARA, and in George A. Armes, *Ups and Downs of an Army Officer* (Washington, DC, 1900).

Chapter 4

1. See David W. Blight, *Race and Reunion: The Civil War in American Memory* (Cambridge, MA: The Belknap Press of Harvard University Press, 2001), 221–32, 286–87.

2. Robert Ewell Greene, *Who Were the Real Buffalo Soldiers? Black Defenders of America* (Fort Washington, MD: R. E. Greene, 1994), 369.

3. Quoted in Peggy Samuels and Harold Samuels, eds., *The Collected Writings of Frederic Remington* (Garden City, NY: Doubleday and Company, 1979), 250.

Chapter 5

1. George Bird Grinnell, *The Fighting Cheyennes* (Norman: University of Oklahoma Press, 1955), 281.

2. *Winners of the West* 1 (July 1924): 1; 1 (October 1924): 3; 5 (August 1928): 2; 6 (May 1929): 2.

3. *Journal of the Military Service Institution* 13 (March 1892): 215–24.

4. *The Beecher Island Annual: Ninety-Third Anniversary of the Battle of Beecher Island, September 17, 18, 1868* (Beecher Island, CO: The Beecher Island Battle Memorial Association, 1960), 86–89.

Chapter 6

1. See Byron Price, "Mutiny at San Pedro Springs," *By Valor & Arms: The Journal of American Military History* 1 (Spring 1975): 31–34; Frank N. Schubert, *Black Valor: Buffalo Soldiers and the Medal of Honor, 1870–1898* (Wilmington, DE: SR Books, 1997), 13–15.

2. On the issue of mutiny and the response of black soldiers to punishments that seemed reminiscent of treatment under slavery, see Ira Berlin, ed., *The Black Military Experience*, series 2 of *Freedom: A Documentary History of Emancipation 1861–1867* (Cambridge, MA: Cambridge University Press, 1982), 438–40; B. Kevin Bennett, "The Jacksonville Mutiny," *Military Law Review* 134 (1991): 158–72.

3. Quoted in Robert Wooster, *Soldiers, Sutlers, and Settlers: Garrison Life on the Texas Frontier* (College Station: Texas A & M University Press, 1987), 176.

4. *Daily Herald* (San Antonio, TX), April 10, 1867.

Chapter 7

1. Certificate of Disability for Discharge, October 14, 1868, Pension File SO 1032593, Cathay Williams, NARA.

2. See DeAnne Blanton, "Cathay Williams Black Woman Soldier 1866–1868," *Minerva* 10 (Fall/Winter, 1992): 1–12.

3. Surgeon's Certificate in Case of Cathay Williams *alias* William Cathay, September 9, 1891, and Original Invalid Claim, Cathay Williams *alias* William Cathay, February 19, 1892, Pension File SO 1032593, Cathay Williams, NARA.

4. William Jennings, "Female Buffalo Solider," bi-fold advertising brochure, Frank Schubert private collection, Alexandria, VA.

Chapter 8

1. On Stance's career, see Schubert, "The Violent World of Emanuel Stance, Fort Robinson, 1887," *Nebraska History* 55 (Summer 1974): 203–19; Schubert, *Black Valor*, 9–26.

Chapter 9

1. Schubert, *Black Valor*, 10; Margaret Lewis, "A Soldier's Story" (Frank Schubert private collection, photocopy); Mary L. Williams, Fort Davis National Historic Site, to Margaret Lewis, San Diego, California, March 27, 1996, Frank Schubert private collection; Monthly Return, 9th Cavalry, April 1871 (NARA, RG 94, microfilm M-744, reel 87).

2. *Frontier Times* 4 (April 1927): 9–11.

Chapter 10

1. William H. Leckie, *The Buffalo Soldiers: A Narrative of the Negro Cavalry in the West* (Norman: University of Oklahoma Press, 1967), 26. In asserting that the term reflected respect on the part of the Indians, Leckie followed Major Edward L. N. Glass, *The History of the Tenth Cavalry, 1866–1921* (1921; Fort Collins, CO: Old Army Press, 1972), 18, and H. B. Wharfield, *10th Cavalry & Border Fights* (El Cajon, CA: Author, 1965), 55–56.

2. See, for example, Monroe L. Billington, *New Mexico's Buffalo Soldiers, 1866–1900* (Niwot, CO: University of Colorado Press, 1991), xi; Garna L. Christian, *Black Soldiers in Jim Crow Texas 1899–1917* (College Station: Texas A & M University Press, 1995), xiii. Also see Louise Barnett, *Ungentlemanly Acts: The Army's Notorious Incest Trial* (New York: Hill and Wang, 2000), 59. Barnett added a wrinkle to the usual story, asserting that the men of the 10th were so taken with the name that they "promptly enshrined the image of the buffalo on the regimental crest." The regimental crest was adopted in 1911. See General Orders No. 1, Headquarters 10th Cavalry, February 11, 1911, Miscellaneous Records, 10th Cavalry, RG 391, NARA.

3. One of the popular names for the soldiers among whites was "brunettes." See, for example, Robert G. Carter, *On the Border with Mackenzie or Winning West Texas from the Comanches* (1935; New York: Antiquarian Press, Ltd., 1961), 86, 87; De B. Randolph Keim, *Sheridan's Troopers on the Borders: A Winter Campaign on the Plains* (1870; Williamstown, MA: Corner House Publishers, 1973), 46. For usage of "Buffalo Soldiers," see *Sidney (Nebraska) Telegraph*, September 21, 1878, and *Army and Navy Journal* 16 (April 3, 1880): 704. Perhaps the most intriguing name for the soldiers, used by an anonymous correspondent for *Harper's Weekly* magazine in 1898, was "black war cloud." *Harper's Weekly*, May 14, 1898, 475, 478.

4. Frederic Remington, "A Scout with the Buffalo Soldiers," *Century*, April 1889. The

article is reprinted in Samuels and Samuels, *The Collected Writings of Frederic Remington*, 30, and in a pamphlet published in Palmer Lake, Colorado, by The Filter Press in 1974, No. 27, in a series called "Wild and Woolly West Books." Also see *Army and Navy Journal* 31 (August 25, 1894): 906 and 32 (June 8, 1895): 672; *Laramie (Wyoming) Boomerang*, July 22, 1892.

5. Frances M. A. Roe, *Army Letters from an Officer's Wife, 1871–1888* (New York: D. Appleton, 1909), 55, 65, 77–78, 103–4.

6. John Gregory Bourke was an Army officer, ethnologist, and writer, who served as General George Crook's aide-de-camp during the 1870s. He wrote several books about the Indians and about campaigning in the West. *On the Border with Crook* (New York: C. Scribner's Sons), first published in 1891, is probably his best-known work.

7. "The Comanches and the Peace Policy," *The Nation* 17, no. 245 (October 30, 1873): 286–287, reprinted in *Army and Navy Journal* 11 (November 8, 1873): 197.

8. *Army and Navy Journal*, 11 (December 20, 1873): 292.

Chapter 11

1. Frank Schubert, *On the Trail of the Buffalo Soldier: Biographies of African Americans in the U.S. Army, 1866–1917* (Wilmington, DE: Scholarly Resources, 1995), 50–51.

2. On the mutually supportive and interdependent community of old Buffalo Soldiers, see Frank Schubert, *Buffalo Soldiers, Braves and the Brass: The Story of Fort Robinson, Nebraska* (Shippensburg, PA: White Mane Publishing Co., 1993), 150–57.

3. See William A. Dobak, "Black Regulars Speak," *Panhandle Plains Historical Review* 47 (1974): 19–27.

4. George P. Rawick, general editor, *The American Slave: A Composite Autobiography*, vol. 4, Texas Narratives, parts 1 and 2 (1941; Westport, CT: Greenwood Publishing Company, n.d.), 143–46.

5. Rawick, *The American Slave*, vol. 5, Texas Narratives, parts 3 and 4, 141–43.

Chapter 12

1. J. Lee Humfreville, *Twenty Years Among Our Hostile Indians* (New York: Hunter & Co., 1899).

Chapter 13

1. *Army and Navy Journal* 11 (April 25, 1874), 580.

Chapter 14

1. On efforts to provoke decisive military confrontations with indigenous opposition by both British and American forces, see James O. Gump, *The Dust Rose Like Smoke: The Subjugation of the Zulu and the Sioux* (Lincoln: University of Nebraska Press, 1994), 86.

2. "The Years of Exciting Experiences and Hard Service in the 10th U. S. Cavalry," *Winners of the West* 2 (March 1925): 2–3.

3. Twenty-three years later, George Berry, then a sergeant in G Troop, carried the flags of the black 10th Cavalry and the white 3d Cavalry up San Juan Hill, Cuba.

Chapter 15

1. On the Seminole Negroes, see Kevin Mulroy, *Freedom on the Border: The Seminole Maroons in Florida, the Indian Territory, Coahuila, and Texas* (Lubbock: Texas Tech University Press, 1993); Kenneth W. Porter, *The Black Seminoles: History of a Freedom-Seeking People*, edited by Alcione M. Amos and Thomas P. Senter (Gainesville: University Press of Florida, 1996).

2. For more on Bullis and the scouts, including the fight near Eagle's Nest Crossing of the Pecos, see Schubert, *Black Valor*, 27–40. For a copy of the order, see microfilm M-929, roll 2, NARA.

Chapter 16

1. File 2794 , Adjutant General's Office (hereafter cited as AGO) 1875, RG 94, NARA.

Chapter 17

1. British colonial troops also used this approach with devastating effect. See Charles E. Callwell, *Small Wars, Their Principles and Practice*, 3d ed. (Lincoln: University of Nebraska Press, 1996), 40–41. First published in the 1890s, Callwell's treatise was virtually a textbook on British small wars in many colonial locations.

2. William H. Leckie, *The Military Conquest of the Southern Plains* (Norman: University of Oklahoma Press, 1963), 220–24.

3. File 4348 AGO 1875, RG 94, NARA. For an example of the use of this tactic by Captain Louis Carpenter and H Troop of the 10th Cavalry, see Allen L. Hamilton, *Sentinel of the Southern Plains: Fort Richardson and the Northwest Texas Frontier, 1866–1878* (Fort Worth: Texas Christian University Press, 1988), 154–55.

Chapter 18

1. File 1073 AGO 1875, RG 94, NARA.

Chapter 19

1. Oscar J. Martinez, *Troublesome Border* (Tucson: University of Arizona Press, 1988), 60–62.

2. File 100, AGO 1876, RG 94, NARA.

3. Colonel Joaquin Terrazas.

4. File 2005, AGO 1876, RG 94, NARA.

Chapter 20

1. "The Morals of the Colored Troops," *Army and Navy Journal* 14 (January 27, 1877): 395.

Chapter 21

1. See Theodore D. Harris, comp. and ed., *Black Frontiersman: The Memoirs of Henry O. Flipper* (Fort Worth: Texas Christian University Press, 1997).

2. File 2199, AGO 1880, RG 94, NARA.

3. *Army and Navy Journal* 17 (October 11, 1879): 176.

Chapter 22

1. *Army and Navy Journal* 17 (August 30, 1879): 64.

Chapter 23

1. George F. Hamilton, "History of the Ninth Regiment U.S. Cavalry, 1866–1906," typescript (U.S. Military Academy Library, West Point, NY, c. 1909).

Chapter 24

1. Adjutant General (hereafter cited as AG) Document File 41940, RG 94, NARA.

Chapter 25

1. John Bigelow, "Tenth Regiment of Cavalry," *Journal of the Military Service Institution* 13 (March 1892): 215–24.

Chapter 26

1. This complaint could just as easily have been made by the commanders of all frontier regiments, white or black. Moreover, it reflected a use of frontier troops in all kinds of construction work that dates back to the days of the Imperial Roman Army, nearly two thousand years earlier. See Michael L. Tate, *The Frontier Army and the Settlement of the West* (Norman: University of Oklahoma Press, 1999). On the Roman frontier army,

see Yann Le Bohec, *The Imperial Roman Army* (London: Routledge, 1994); Derek Williams, *The Reach of Rome: A History of the Roman Imperial Frontier 1st–5th Centuries AD* (New York: St. Martin's Press, 1997); Steven K. Drummond, "The Roman Army as a Frontier Institution in the First and Second Centuries A.D." (Ph.D. diss., University of Kansas, 1981); Alan K. Bowman, *Life and Letters on the Roman Frontier: Vindolanda and Its People* (London: British Museum Press, 1998).

2. See Barnett, *Ungentlemanly Acts.*

3. File 2169, AGO 1880, RG 94, NARA.

4. John H. Nankivell, *History of the 25th Infantry* (1927; Fort Collins, CO: Old Army Press, 1972), 36.

Chapter 28

1. Leckie, *Buffalo Soldiers,* 164.

2. Quoted in Samuels and Samuels, *The Collected Writings of Frederic Remington,* 432–435.

3. William Loren Katz, *The Black West: A Documentary and Pictorial History of the African American Role in the Westward Expansion of the Nation* (New York: Touchstone Books, 1996), 152–54.

4. Schubert, *On the Trail of the Buffalo Soldier,* 167.

5. Telegrams Sent, Fort Concho, Texas, RG 393, NARA.

Chapter 29

1. From the private collection of Ms. Susan K. Lemke, Washington, DC. Used with permission.

Chapter 30

1. Veterans Administration (hereafter cited as VA) Pension File XC 896871, John C. Howerton, NARA.

Chapter 31

1. General Court Martial Order No. 71, Headquarters, Department of the Missouri, 10 Oct 1883, RG 153, NARA.

Chapter 32

1. Record of Court-Martial of Edward Hamilton, C/9th Cavalry, August 1884, General Court Martial Case Files, RG 153, NARA.

2. See Schubert, *Buffalo Soldiers, Braves and the Brass,* 83–88.

Chapter 33

1. Powhattan H. Clarke, letters to his parents, Clarke papers, Missouri Historical Society, St. Louis, MO.

2. Scott had served with D Troop of the 9th Cavalry during the Milk River fight against the Utes in October 1879. Mark E. Miller, *Hollow Victory: The White River Expedition and the Battle of Milk Creek* (Niwot, CO: University Press of Colorado, 1997), 167.

Chapter 34

1. Leckie, *Buffalo Soldiers*, 245; Bigelow, "The Tenth Regiment of Cavalry," 223; Glass, *History of the Tenth Cavalry*, 24.

2. VA Pension File SC 138442, John F. Casey, NARA.

Chapter 35

1. *Army and Navy Journal* 24 (December 25, 1886): 431.

2. *Army and Navy Journal* 24 (January 15, 1887): 497.

3. *Army and Navy Journal* 24 (March 26, 1887): 695.

Chapter 36

1. Charles Creek was also a soldier in the 9th Cavalry who had been interviewed by Don Rickey.

2. This was Emanuel Stance. See Schubert, *Black Valor*, 24–26.

3. George Webb was editor of *Winners of the West* and a driving force behind the National Indian War Veterans, an organization that lobbied for pensions.

4. Colonel Guy V. Henry, a longtime officer in the 9th Cavalry, commanded a battalion of the regiment during the Pine Ridge campaign of 1890–1891.

Chapter 37

1. Schubert, *Black Valor*, 91–100. Also see Larry D. Ball, *The Wham Paymaster Robbery of 1889: A Story of Politics, Religion, Race, and Banditry in Arizona Territory* (Tucson: Arizona Historical Society, 2000).

2. AGO, General Correspondence File, 1890–1917, RG 94, NARA (M-929, roll 2).

Chapter 38

1. See Robert M. Utley, *The Last Days of the Sioux Nation* (New Haven, CT: Yale University Press, 1963); Richard E. Jensen, R. Eli Paul, and John E. Carter, *Eyewitness at Wounded Knee* (Lincoln: University of Nebraska Press, 1991).

2. Schubert, *Black Valor*, 130.

3. NARA, M-929, roll 2.

4. Proceedings of a General Court Martial which convened at Fort Robinson, Nebr., pursuant to Special Orders No. 21, Headquarters, Department of the Platte, Omaha, Nebr., February 23, 1891, Court Martial Case Files, 1809–1894, RG 153, NARA, reproduced in M-929, roll 2.

5. NARA, M-929, roll 2.

6. Ibid.

Chapter 39

1. The best single book on the events described by Prather is still Robert M. Utley, *The Last Days of the Sioux Nation* (New Haven, CT: Yale University Press, 1963).

2. *Army and Navy Journal* 28 (March 7, 1891), 483.

3. Reproduced from James Mooney, *The Ghost Dance Religion and the Sioux Outbreak of 1890*, 14th Annual Report of the Bureau of Ethnology to the Secretary of the Smithsonian Institution, 1892–1893 (Washington, DC: Government Printing Office, 1896), 883.

Chapter 40

1. Schubert, *On the Trail of the Buffalo Soldier*, 404–407; Frank Schubert, "Theophilus Gould Steward," in *Dictionary of American Negro Biography*, edited by Rayford W. Logan and Michael R. Winston (New York: W. W. Norton & Company, 1982), 570–71. Also see William Seraile, *Voice of Dissent: Theophilus Gould Steward (1843–1924) and Black America* (Brooklyn, NY: Carlson Publishing, 1991).

2. AGO, File 4634, Appointments, Commissions, Personal 91, Theophilus G. Steward, RG 94, NARA.

Chapter 41

1. Schubert, "The Suggs Affray: The Black Cavalry in the Johnson County War," *Western Historical Quarterly* 4 (January 1973): 57–68.

2. RG 94, NARA.

Chapter 42

1. Frank Schubert, "Henry Vinton Plummer," *Dictionary of American Negro Biography*, 498–499; Earl H. Stover, *Up from Handymen: The United States Army Chaplaincy 1865–1920* (Washington, DC: Office of the Chief of Chaplains, United States Army, 1977), 88–90; Stover, "Chaplain Henry V. Plummer, His Ministry, and His Court-Martial," *Nebraska History* 56 (Spring 1975), 20–50.

2. On the group of Buffalo Soldier chaplains, see Stover, *Up from Handymen*, chapter

three, and Alan K. Lamm, *Five Black Preachers in Army Blue, 1884–1901* (Lewiston, NY: Edwin Mellen Press, 1998).

3. Letter to editor, *U.S. Army Visitor* 6 (April 1893): 3.

Chapter 43

1. See Schubert, *Buffalo Soldiers, Braves and the Brass*, 89–92.

2. RG 153, NARA. The sheet was also published in full inside an article, "Threatened by Soldiers," *Omaha Bee*, May 4, 1893, with a dateline of Chadron, Nebraska, May 3, 1893.

3. VA Pension File 2648848, Barney McKay, NARA. For more details on his life, see Schubert, *On the Trail of the Buffalo Soldier*, 281–82.

Chapter 44

1. Glass, *The History of the Tenth Cavalry*, 29–30.

2. *Colored American Magazine* 8 (April 1905): 196–99.

3. *Colored American Magazine* 8 (May 1905): 277–79.

4. *Colored American Magazine* 8 (June 1905): 338–40.

Chapter 45

1. Corporal Joseph W. Wheelock, "Our Own Editors and Publishers," *Colored American Magazine* (January 1905), reprinted in Schubert, "The Fort Robinson Y.M.C.A.: A Social Organization in a Black Regiment," *Nebraska History* 55 (Summer 1974): 177–78.

2. Black soldiers were not unique in this regard. Irish soldiers subscribed to the *Irish World*, which was published in New York City, and responded to the paper's appeals for charitable remittances to Ireland. Jack D. Foner, "The Socializing Role of the Military," in *The American Military on the Frontier*, edited by James P. Tate (Washington, DC: Office of Air Force History, Headquarters, USAF, and United States Air Force Academy, 1978), 98.

3. *Army and Navy Journal* 31 (February 10, 1894): 407.

Chapter 46

1. *Crawford (Nebraska) Tribune*, April 6, 1894.

2. Orders, 9th Cavalry, 1875–1891, RG 391, NARA.

Chapter 47

1. Document File 26287, Records of the AGO, RG 94, NARA.

2. Register of Enlistments, 1892, RG 94, NARA (microfilm M-233, roll 46).

Chapter 48

1. Robert F. Jefferson, "Vestments of God, Race, and Nation: Black Chaplains and the Development of Theo-Political Identities During the U.S. Ninety-third Infantry Division's Stateside Training, 1942–1944" (paper presented at the Society for Military History Annual Meeting, Montgomery, AL, April 1997).

2. Frank Schubert, "Allen Allensworth," *Dictionary of American Negro Biography*, edited by Rayford W. Logan and Michael R. Winston (New York: W. W. Norton & Company, 1982), 13–14; Charles Alexander, *Battles and Victories of Allen Allensworth* (Boston: Sherman, French & Company, 1914).

3. *Army and Navy Journal* 34 (February 6, 1897): 407.

Chapter 49

1. Schubert, *Black Valor*, 145–61.

2. *Georgia Baptist* 19 (April 13, 1899): 1.

Chapter 50

1. *The [Cleveland] Gazette*, August 19, 1899, p. 1.

Chapter 51

1. Schubert, *Black Valor*, 158.

2. *Richmond Planet*, March 30, 1901, p. 1.

3. *Colored American Magazine* (Washington, DC), May 18, 1901, p. 10.

Chapter 52

1. November 13, 1897, 4.

2. Schubert, *On the Trail of the Buffalo* Soldier, 28–29; Schubert and Frank R. Levstik, "William T. Anderson," *Dictionary of American Negro Biography*, 15–16.

3. *Colored American Magazine* 8 (February 1905): 95–97.

4. Document File 53910, Records of the AGO, RG 94, NARA.

Chapter 53

1. VA Pension File SO 1157895, George Washington, NARA.

2. Washington's marriage to Clara Mountain took place at the Darlington Agency in western Oklahoma near Fort Reno on the North Canadian River. Darlington was the headquarters of a Cheyenne and Arapaho agency.

3. Murray R. Wickett, *Contested Territory: Whites, Native Americans and African Americans in Oklahoma, 1865–1907* (Baton Rouge: Louisiana State University Press, 2000), 27, 35–36, 79, 81–83, 172–74, 205.

4. Donald R. Shaffer, "'I do not suppose that Uncle Sam looks at the skin': African Americans and the Civil War Pension System, 1865–1934," *Civil War History* 46 (June 2000): 132–47.

Chapter 54

1. On the Brownsville affray, see John D. Weaver, *The Brownsville Raid* (New York: W. W. Norton, 1970); Ann J. Lane, *The Brownsville Affair: National Crisis and Black Reaction* (Port Washington, NY: Kennikat Press, 1971); Garna L. Christian, *Black Soldiers in Jim Crow Texas 1899–1917* (College Station, TX: Texas A & M University Press, 1995). For more biographical details on Sanders, see Schubert, *On the Trail of the Buffalo Soldier*, 369–70.

2. Evelyn Brooks Barnett, "Mary Church Terrell," in *Dictionary of American Negro Biography*, edited by Rayford W. Logan and Michael R. Winston (New York: W. W. Norton & Company, 1982), 583–85.

3. *The Voice of the Negro* 4 (March 1907): 128–31. Terrell consistently spelled his name "Saunders" throughout her article, but his name is always spelled "Sanders" in military records.

Chapter 55

1. James P. Finley, "1SG Vance Marchbanks: A Buffalo Soldier NCO," *The NCO Journal* 5 (Summer 1995): 19. His unpublished memoir, "Forty Years in the Army," is archived in the collection of the Fort Huachuca, Arizona, museum.

2. Schubert, *On the Trail of the Buffalo* Soldier, 286.

3. See Christian, *Black Soldiers in Jim Crow Texas.*

4. *The Voice of the Negro* 3 (December 1906): 549.

Chapter 56

1. Concerning Young's influence on Davis, see Marvin E. Fletcher, *America's First Black General: Benjamin O. Davis, Sr., 1880–1970* (Lawrence: University Press of Kansas, 1989), 22–25. Also see Fletcher, *The Black Soldier and Officer in the United States Army, 1891–1917* (Columbia: University of Missouri Press, 1974), 73–74.

2. *The [Cleveland] Gazette*, August 3, 1907, p. 2.

3. *Plain Dealer* (Cleveland), November 12, 2000.

Chapter 57

1. Schubert, *Buffalo Soldiers, Braves and the Brass*, 59.

2. VA Pension File WO 881404, Violet Cragg, NARA.

3. Cragg referred to Captain Edward Bloodgood of the 24th Infantry, who was later restored to duty and allowed to muster out honorably.

Chapter 59

1. *Winners of the West* 1 (November 1924): 2, 5.

Chapter 60

1. Schubert, "George W. Ford," in *Dictionary of American Negro Biography*, edited by Rayford W. Logan and Michael R. Winston (New York: W. W. Norton & Company, 1982), 230–31.

2. On Lemus, see Schubert, "Rienzi Brock Lemus," in *Dictionary of American Negro Biography*, edited by Rayford W. Logan and Michael R. Winston (New York: W. W. Norton & Company, 1982), 393. On Williams, see John Hope Franklin, "George Washington Williams, in *Dictionary of American Negro Biography*, 657–59. Also see Franklin, *George Washington Williams, A Biography* (Chicago: University of Chicago Press, 1985).

3. Richard R. Wright, Jr., comp., *The Encyclopedia of the African Methodist Episcopal Church*, 2d ed. (Philadelphia: A.M.E. Book Concern, 1947), 64–65.

4. Ibid., 67.

Index